BELONGING

A GUIDE TO
OVERCOMING LONELINESS

WILLIAM R. BRASSELL, PH.D.
EDITED BY LESLIE TILLEY

NEW HARBINGER PUBLICATIONS, INC.

Copyright © 1994 William R. Brassell
New Harbinger Publications, Inc.
5674 Shattuck Avenue
Oakland, CA 94609

Cover design and Digistration™ by SHELBY DESIGNS & ILLUSTRATES
Cover photo by Metin Noyan

Distributed in the U.S.A. primarily by Publisher Group West; in Canada by Raincoast Books; in Great Britain by Airlift Book Company, Ltd.; in South Africa by Real Books, Ltd.; in Australia by Boobook; and in New Zealand by Tandem Press.

Library of Congress Catalog Number: 94-067042

ISBN 1-879237-76-8 Paperback
ISBN 1-879237-77-6 Hardcover

1st printing 1994, 7,000 copies

The best elixir is a friend.

—William Summerville

The only way to have a friend is to be a friend.

—Ralph Waldo Emerson

With love to Esther, Emily, and Claire, who took up the slack while I was writing this book.

Contents

Introduction   ix

Part I Obstacles to Belonging

1   **Pinpointing Your Fears**   3
    Analyzing Your Fears ➤ You've Made a Start

2   **Changing the Way You Think**   15
    Thoughts—Seeds of Behavior ➤ Automatic
    Thoughts ➤ Thoughts That Lead to Loneliness
    ➤ Mistaken Beliefs—The Source of Illogical
    Thinking ➤ Be Patient, Be Persistent

3   **Overcoming Shame**   57
    The Effects of Shame ➤ The Origins of Shame
    ➤ Antidotes to Shame ➤ It Takes Time

4   Recognizing What Doesn't Work   **91**
The Pitfalls of Passivity ➤ Aggression—
A Caricature of Assertion ➤ False Assertiveness—
Alcohol, Drugs, and Casual Sex ➤ It Takes
Determination

Part II   Skills for Belonging

5   Practicing Relaxation   **111**
Progressive Deep Relaxation ➤ Autogenic
Training ➤ Fitting Relaxation into Your Daily Life
➤ An Essential Part of Your Toolkit

6   Using Self-Hypnosis   **131**
Understanding Hypnosis ➤ Inducing an Altered
State ➤ Practicing with Your Tape ➤ Principles
of Hypnotic Suggestion ➤ It's Planting Time

7   Neutralizing Your Fears   **159**
Breaking Fears into Manageable Pieces ➤
Constructing Fear Staircases ➤ The Neutralization
Process ➤ It Gets Faster from Here On

8   Learning Social Skills   **175**
First Impressions ➤ Listening to What Your Body
Is Saying ➤ Introductions ➤ The Gentle Art of
Conversation ➤ Opening the Conversation
➤ Forays into the Real World ➤ Opportunities
Abound

9   Becoming Assertive   **195**
Recognizing Your Rights ➤ The Role of
Emotions ➤ Lights, Camera, Action!

10   Taking Risks   **221**
Handling Difficult Situations ➤ Managing
Troublesome People ➤ Accepting Rejection
➤ Being a Friend ➤ Taking the Plunge

11   Looking Back, Looking Ahead   **249**
Taking Stock of Your Progress ➤ Setting and
Pursuing Goals ➤ When to See a Professional
➤ Now for the Fun Part

References   **257**

Introduction

Being alone can be restorative—time to create, produce, or relax and recharge mental and emotional batteries. Being lonely, however, is never productive or healing, and chronic loneliness is devastating.

I imagine that loneliness would have seemed a strange subject for a book a couple of generations ago. Friendships formed naturally and easily when people lived out their lives in the same communities, surrounded by people they had known since birth. Extended families lived just a few farms or streets apart.

Back then, a lack of connectedness with others was fairly rare; people virtually had to choose to distance themselves. We are not so lucky today. In our extraordinarily mobile society, extended families are scattered over many states and thousands of miles. With planning, family members may see each other once a year, perhaps less.

My family is a fairly typical example. We live seven hours' drive from my parents and eight hours' from my wife's—in opposite directions. We have to drive through three states to reach our closest siblings, and I can't begin to remember where all the cousins live.

After living in several large cities, my wife and I decided we'd like our children to grow up in a small community, and chose an azalea-bedecked town within sight of the Blue Ridge mountains. We've lived on the same street there for years, but the small towns of today aren't the same as those our grandparents lived in. We've seen friends and companions come and go, and we have been as touched by the constant national migration as if we had stayed on the move ourselves.

Other factors also promote isolation. Television, the demise of the front porch, even air conditioning—all work to keep us apart from neighbors. The modern work schedule of long hours and long commutes occupies time that was once available for social and leisure activities. When both adults in a family work outside the home, household tasks must be taken care of during evening or weekend hours. There is simply less time available for cultivating and nurturing social relationships.

Crime also plays a part. Media horror stories and crime statistics make us wary of strangers. People who have been victims or who have known victims of violent crimes have even more reason to be fearful. When simply leaving the home can seem risky, it takes a good deal of courage to reach out to new people.

Nonetheless, we humans are social creatures with a need to connect with our kind. When we can't, there is a vacuum that can suck all the joy and pleasure from our lives, leaving us in despair. Distractions, such as work, alcohol, shopping, and food, can keep loneliness at bay—for a while. But friends and companions are the only real remedy.

In my work as a psychologist and psychotherapist I frequently encounter people who have spiraled down into depression. When long-term loneliness is a factor in their despair, I introduce them to the procedures in this book. It's a joy to see them regain hope as they learn, little by little, that *they* determine whether they will remain lonely. *They* have the power to overcome loneliness.

You have the same opportunity to choose. It takes courage to reach out to others; it also takes effort and a committment to change. You will need to recognize the personal deficits that get in the way of your meeting people and to learn new ways of interacting that foster connection and friendship. *Belonging* is designed to help you in these tasks.

The Book's Focus

Although I hope you will enjoy this book and even find it inspirational, it was not written to provide enjoyment or inspiration. This is not a book for the nightstand; it is not to be read, enjoyed, and put aside. Instead, *Belonging* was written to provide you with tools for overcoming your loneliness. It will help you identify the obstacles that come between you and others. And it will help you learn to approach and interact effectively with strangers.

Because groups—parties, professional organizations, classes, hobby clubs, civic hearings—provide many opportunities for meeting people, and because group situations are commonly difficult for people, *Belonging* focuses on interactions in group settings. However, the information this book provides can be applied to any type of encounter: social or professional, one-on-one or one-to-many. It will help you develop the skills and confidence to fit into any group you wish, large or small.

How to Use This Book

Like any truly worthwhile goal, overcoming loneliness requires work. For the next several months, *Belonging* should be a part of your life. That may seem a long time to be involved with a book, but consideraing how long loneliness can last, it isn't long at all.

I suggest that you skim through the book before you launch into it seriously. See first how all the ingredients in this recipe for overcoming loneliness fit together. While all of the ingredients are necessary, you may have already acquired some of them. For example, part I deals with the obstacles that often keep people apart from others: fears, beliefs and ways of thinking that don't work, low self-esteem, and lack of assertiveness. Not all of these will necessarily be a problem for you, so you will want to concentrate on those that are and give the others less attention.

Similarly, it may not be necessary for you to work through every exercise in the book. But don't skip an exercise just because it seems tedious; skip it only if you have already reached its objective. It's like a ladder: You need to be standing solidly on one rung before you can go on to the next.

Part II consists of skill-building chapters, beginnning with deep relaxation and self-hypnosis. I urge you to follow this material carefully. Much of the work in later chapters builds on those techniques, so if you haven't acquired some proficiency with them, your progress may be limited. Furthermore, the skills of relaxation and hypnosis prove to be useful tools in many other aspects of life. By learning them you will give yourself a lasting gift.

Belonging is designed to stand alone; it includes all the information you will need in learning to reach out to people. If you want to pursue some topics further, the References section at the end of the book lists titles that may be of interest.

It's a Journey

Think of yourself now as beginning a quest that can quite literally change your life. Each chapter you absorb, each exercise you complete, moves you further along in your pursuit of belonging. Step by step, you will move along a path toward the life you've wanted.

When you end your quest, you will find that you not only belong, but you are also a more confident person. You will have gained the assurance that you control your destiny. You can go where you want to go, one step at a time.

Part I

Obstacles
to Belonging

1

Pinpointing Your Fears

Over the last few years, Hal had found his world growing smaller and smaller, his social choices gradually shrinking as his social fears grew. In his job as line supervisor in a furniture factory, Hal was respected and well liked, but he felt that people were beginning to find him standoffish. Some coworkers teased him about being too good to socialize with them.

Embarrassed, even humiliated, by the thought that someone would discover his "secret," Hal was reluctant to enter the shop canteen at breaks. He avoided coming to work early because he might have to talk casually with his peers. Although he could deal with them on business matters, he couldn't join in the banter that seemed so easy and enjoyable to everyone else. Despite desperately wanting to be belong, Hal was out in the cold.

Elaine, a busy 45-year-old woman with three adult children, had always been comfortable relating to friends. It was a different story, though, when Elaine had to deal with strangers, especially groups of strangers. She felt panicky going into any large group alone, and habitually avoided large social gatherings unless she had a good friend or two to go with her. Once there, she would stick with her friends even at times when it was obvious they would prefer to circulate without a tagalong. Nor could Elaine count on her husband, a gregarious fellow, to serve as her social crutch. As often as not, he'd strike out on his own, leaving her uncomfortably alone in his wake.

Though unhappy that parties were ordeals for her instead of pleasurable events, Elaine accepted the situation—until she began to plan her eldest daughter's wedding. It occurred to her then that she had three children and so probably two more weddings to go through over the next few years. It seemed she had the choice of either becoming overwhelmed with dread at the thought of meeting and greeting people in large groups or trying to overcome her social fears.

Phillip's motivation for overcoming social fears was even stronger than Elaine's. An ambitious and hardworking college professor, Phillip performed well and comfortably before any group when he lectured in his field. But he turned to jelly when he had to make small talk. Naturally, he dreaded most social occasions. He was at ease only if he had a colleague to talk shop with or his wife at his side holding up their end of the conversation.

When Phillip became academic dean of his liberal arts college, he was determined to carry out all of his obligations, even the social ones. Yet determination alone was not enough; he still had as much trouble as ever at faculty teas and retirement parties.

Sarah had never been someone who made friends quickly. She stayed quietly on the edge of groups and waited, nervously, for people to approach her. Or she avoided large gatherings altogether. She depended on close family ties and one good friend, who had recently married, for social contact.

When the company Sarah worked for as a public relations writer relocated to a different state, a thousand miles away, she was torn over whether to go along. Although she knew she wouldn't be able to find as good a job, nor one she loved as much, in her old town, the idea of leaving her family and friend was more than painful—it scared her. Sarah didn't think she would be able to make new friends. She worried that she would seem odd to people who didn't know her, or cold and stuck up. The thought of the loneliness she might have to endure terrified her.

Although he was an officer in his fraternity, Scott, a 21-year-old college senior, never felt that he really belonged. He lived in the fraternity house, but rarely hung out there because he couldn't cope with the kidding and conviviality of his fraternity brothers—not that he didn't like them and want to fit in. He spent a lot of energy avoiding people and covering up because his greatest fear was that others might find out that he was afraid.

Lora, a successful real estate broker, was also bothered by a dread that others would see how nervous she was in social gatherings. She equated social anxiety with weakness and lack of control. Although she felt isolated and knew she was missing out on an important part of life, she avoided going to her country club. Lora excused herself by thinking it was because, as a single woman, she didn't like to go without an escort. She had more trouble justifying her absence from the health club she had joined.

Anxiety About Anxiety

Although very different in many respects, Hal, Elaine, Phillip, Sarah, Scott, and Lora all wanted to belong. Each of them was as likable and intelligent as his or her peers, yet each felt unable to socialize and be a part of things. What did they fear? What kept them from joining in when they really wanted nothing more? Why did they hold back when they had as much to offer as anyone else?

To one extent or another, all six felt ashamed of their anxieties. They were afraid of people discovering how anxious they were. They were afraid of being considered incompetent or weak. Not only did fear affect the quality of their lives, it also compromised the way these competent and aspiring people felt about themselves.

In differing degrees, each of the six feared that others would recognize the signs of anxiety. Hal, the factory supervisor, worried about perspiring profusely, which he invariably did when he was nervous. Phillip, the college dean, was most concerned about a quaver in his voice; Scott, the student, about a tremor in his fingers.

The mother of the bride, Elaine, feared that her nervous giggle and tense body language would give her away. Sarah, the writer, worried about the dry mouth and cough that appeared in social gatherings. And the realtor, Lora, was mortified to think that a pronounced tic under her left eye might reveal her anxiety.

All of these people dreaded entering a room of strangers or casual acquaintances. When they could not avoid doing so, most of them felt more comfortable arriving early, before the room filled with people. Three of them felt the least comfortable when they had to enter a party or large gathering alone and circulate among the crowd. The other three were the most anxious when they were seated at a dinner or banquet so that they had no easy escape. All six of them dreaded meeting strangers, and their fears were magnified when they encountered strangers in groups.

These well-informed individuals felt at a loss to initiate or carry on social conversations. They worried that long silences would make them look like fools or oddballs. And they were concerned that when they did talk, their comments would seem inane and dull.

Hal and Scott agonized about not being quick or witty enough in their responses to teasing. Elaine, Scott, and Sarah fretted that people thought them cold, insensitive, and unsociable. Phillip and Lora felt that they came across as either vacuous and boring when they failed to say much or, worse, as hostile and belligerent when they forced themselves to join in debates. Both of them, as well as Hal, worried that their social ineptitude was damaging to their careers. Sarah was on the brink of sacrificing her career to her fears. Hal, Lora, and Scott sometimes felt terribly lonely and isolated. Philip, Sarah, and Elaine worried about being overly dependent on family and friends in social situations. None of them felt that the social part of their lives was satisfactory, yet they felt powerless to change it.

Analyzing Your Fears

People often express social fears in ways similar to the following:

- I'll say the wrong thing.
- I won't know how to dress.

- People will think I'm stupid.
- I'm so clumsy; I'll break something.
- I'll get sick if someone I don't know speaks to me.
- I'm not attractive enough—no one will talk to me.
- I won't be able to think of anything to say.
- I'll laugh too much because I'm nervous.
- They'll think I'm weird.
- I can't dance.
- I'll start shaking.
- I'm boring—they won't like me.

Although there are many variations on the theme of social fears, they all seem to fall into a few categories:

- Being judged and found lacking
- Losing control
- Being ignored or rejected
- Appearing foolish, stupid, or inept
- Being watched
- Revealing anxieties and weaknesses
- Coming off as tiresome or boring

Notice that there is overlap between fears on this second list. A fear of losing control, for instance, might be manifested by a fear of vomiting in public or of crying uncontrollably. Both of these fears could also be considered fear of revealing anxieties and weaknesses. Likewise, a fear of seeming stupid or boring may also include a fear of being judged.

Neither of these lists is exhaustive, of course. Everyone has his or her individual demons. However, the important thing is that any fear, if "fed" enough, can produce the expected results. Anxiety can indeed affect thinking. When they are sufficiently nervous, people may have trouble retrieving memories and expressing themselves. Their minds may actually go blank. Or they may be so concerned with their fears that they forget social niceties. Nervous people often do show their anxiety outwardly.

In other words, social fears can become self-fulfilling prophecies. The feared events exist in large part because they are feared! Conquer the fear, however, and half the battle is won.

Naming Your Demons

Before you can overcome the fears that are keeping you from feeling like a part of things, you need to identify those fears precisely or "name your demons." Having vague ideas about what you're afraid of is not sufficient. You must understand exactly what bothers you. Consequently, your first task is to be as open and honest with yourself as possible as you examine the situations you find uncomfortable or intimidating.

This process is easier for some people than for others. Some are able to examine their fears easily. Others find it difficult, largely because they try to hide their fears from themselves. They may deny their fears or blame others for them or simply refuse to think about them. Unfortunately, none of these strategies works very well. The fears, though never rising to the conscious level, nevertheless continue to haunt people and affect their behavior.

The following exercise will help you uncover the fears that play a role in keeping you apart from others. In doing this exercise, it is important that you not hold back. Although it may make you uncomfortable, you need to home in on your fears. You can't overcome fears that you don't acknowledge. But if you are able to name and recognize them, you can then use your knowledge to defeat your demons.

Exercise
Pinpointing Your Fears

For this exercise, as well as the other exercises in this book, you will need to set aside a block of time—in this case, about 45 minutes to an hour. You will need a place to sit that is quiet and where you will not be interrupted. You will also need paper and a pen or pencil, since this, like many of the other exercises in the book, involves some writing. I recommend that you get a notebook and use it for all the written exercises, so that you can keep them together.

You will be using the information you uncover in this exercise in later chapters. In your notebook, head the first page "My Fears."

1. Get comfortable and try to relax and clear your mind. Let go for now of anything that is worrying you. You can always come back to that later; for now you need to focus on the task at hand.

2. Think back to the last social situation you were in that felt uncomfortable, tense, or anxiety provoking. Or think back to the last event you avoided or declined attending. Let yourself remember in detail the physical details of the invitation, the setting, the other people involved.

3. How did you feel? What thoughts were you having? What were you afraid might happen? Did you worry about your appearance, the way you talked, what other people might think of you?

4. Under the heading "My Fears" in your notebook, list all the things you were anxious about or worried might happen. You may have one, a few, or many fears.

5. When you've listed all the fears you had about that first situation, think about other social situations you've been in recently that have made you uneasy or uncomfortable, or think about a general type of situation that you habitually avoid because of the way it causes you to feel or act. Identify what it is you fear about those events, and add those fears to your list.

6. Continue this process until you have a list that presents your fears in some detail.

Grouping Your Fears

You have now taken the first major step in your journey toward belonging: identifying the specific fears holding you back. You are now facing your fears head on. The next step, a relatively minor one compared to what you have just accomplished, is to group your fears in categories.

Grouping your fears may be unnecessary if your list is brief. However, if there are a number of fears on your list, some of them are probably related to others. Let's look again at the list of fears I gave earlier:

- Saying the wrong thing
- Dressing inappropriately
- Being thought stupid
- Being ignored or rejected
- Breaking something
- Being thought unattractive
- Laughing too much
- Being thought odd
- Not being able to dance
- Shaking uncontrollably
- Being thought dull

As further examples, I have had clients mention the following fears:

- Vomiting
- Crying uncontrollably
- Fainting
- His or her mind going blank
- Spilling food or drink
- Getting hiccups
- Having a quaver in his or her voice
- Being maneuvered into an unwanted commitment
- Losing his or her temper
- Being asked to participate in a sport where he or she feels incompetent
- Being forced into an argument
- Developing a facial tic
- Being asked to speak before the group

For the sake of illustration, let's say that all of these fears make up the list of someone using this book to overcome her loneliness—let's call her Sandy. Several of the fears listed appear to be variations of a few basic fears, so these the fears can be grouped under a few "themes":

Theme A—Fear of Being Judged
    Saying the wrong thing
    Dressing inappropriately
    Being thought stupid

Breaking something
Being ignored or rejected
Being thought unattractive
Laughing too much
Being thought odd
Being thought dull
Not being able to dance
Being asked to speak before the group
Spilling food or drink
Being asked to participate in a sport at
    which he or she feels incompetent

Theme B—Fear of Loss of Self-Control
Shaking uncontrollably
Vomiting
Crying uncontrollably
Fainting
Her mind going blank
Losing her temper
Getting hiccups

Theme C—Fear of Being Controlled
Being forced into an argument
Being maneuvered into an unwanted commitment

Theme D—Fear of Revealing Anxieties and Weaknesses
Quaver in voice
Developing facial tic

By grouping her fears into logical categories, Sandy was able
to reduce her long list of fears to four basic fears, or themes.
Clearly, Sandy could have put some individual fears in two or
more categories. For example, most, if not all, of the fears in Theme
B could have been listed under Theme A.

This fact illustrates how personal the categorization process
is. For Sandy, the most fearful aspect of shaking, vomiting, crying,
and so on (or the possibility of doing so) was the loss of self-
control. With these particular scenarios, the idea of losing control
scared her more than the idea of being judged. In contrast, what

she most feared about saying or wearing or doing the wrong thing was what other people would think of her.

Exercise
Putting Your Fears in Their Place

In the following exercise, you will categorize your fears and then rank each theme in terms of how fearful it is to *you*. The important thing here is that there is no right or wrong way to do this. Only you know your fears—both what your themes are and how frightening each theme is vis-à-vis the others. Rely on your own judgment, but also take the time to examine each fear carefully.

If several fears seem to fall into two categories, perhaps the two are really a single theme. If you have more than five themes, your categories may be too narrow. See if any of them seem to be related. If you have only one category, it may be too broad. Make sure you don't really have a couple of themes grouped together. In my experience, most people have two or three themes, with three or four fears under each theme.

The categories I've used above may or may not work for you. Feel free to call the themes anything you like, so long as you know what each name means.

1. In your notebook, turn back to the page titled "My Fears" and read through your list of fears.

2. Find common themes running through the fears, and give each theme a descriptive name. Write the theme names in the top margin of the "My Fears" page, as a key.

3. Put an A (or some other designator) by fears with one theme, a B by those with another theme, a C by those with still another theme, and so on. Assign each of the fears to one, and only one, theme. If a fear could fall under more than one theme, assign it to the category that seems strongest or most frightening.

4. When you are satisfied with your themes and the way you have sorted your fears, it is time to rank the themes. The most fearsome theme will receive a rank of 1, the next most fearsome 2,

and so on to the least fearsome. Write the appropriate rank by each theme name in the key at the top of the page.

In our example, Sandy ranked her themes like this:

Rank	Theme
1	Fear of Loss of Self-Control
2	Fear of Being Judged
3	Fear of Revealing Anxieties and Weakness
4	Fear of Being Controlled

Note that for Sandy, it was not the theme where she had the most fears that was the most powerful. This may or may not also be the case for you.

You've Made a Start

You have already made significant progress in your quest to overcome loneliness. You have identified fears that keep you apart from others, and you have grouped them into logical themes. In a later chapter you will begin to work on dismantling those fears using relaxation and imagery. In the next chapters, however, we will begin to explore the origins of those fears and to change some of the thinking patterns that give your fears power.

2

Changing the Way You Think

The only real difference between you and someone who is relaxed and spontaneous relating to other people lies in the way each of you thinks. People who seem to "fit in" easily are not innately smarter, funnier, or more attractive than you. They simply, unquestioningly, *believe* they belong, so they also feel and behave as if they belong. Consequently, everyone else believes and accepts that idea as well.

Likewise, for you to feel normal and natural in social situations, you also must believe that you belong. In this chapter you will learn to recognize the beliefs and thoughts that keep you apart from other people. Then you will begin to dismantle and discard the old hurtful patterns of thinking and replace them with new patterns that can help you in your quest to belong.

This is not a chapter you will be able to read through and work through all in one sitting. Some of the exercises require you to keep a record of your thoughts and feelings over a period of time, at least a few weeks. Several others require an ongoing awareness and a commitment to change. While you can and should read through this chapter now, you will probably also need to come back to it after reading later chapters of the book.

Thoughts—Seeds of Behavior

As you think, so you feel and act. You may not be entirely aware of this cause and effect, because not all thinking is totally conscious. Some thoughts occur so quietly or so fleetingly that they are at the borderline of consciousness—not entirely conscious but not unconscious either. However, they are there to examine if you know how to look for them.

In this chapter, we will be dealing with three kinds of thoughts: self-talk, automatic thoughts, and beliefs. *Self-talk* is the running commentary most people almost unconsciously make about their moment-to-moment actions and feelings. Self-talk can run the gamut from encouraging yourself to try something new by saying "I can *do* this!" to berating yourself for making a mistake by saying "That was so stupid!" Much of the time, self-talk is more subtle than either of these, yet it can have a powerful effect on your behavior and emotions. Negative self-talk can hold you back, or you can develop positive self-talk as a tool for change and growth.

Automatic thoughts are a type of self-talk that occurs invariably, or automatically, in certain situations. Even more than other self-talk, automatic thoughts may escape notice. They are very brief, fleeting, and may be no more than a single visual image. Nonetheless, automatic thoughts profoundly affect your emotions and ultimately your behavior.

Beliefs are thoughts that have over time become so ingrained that they no longer seem to be thoughts at all. Beliefs are so fundamental that they color the way you see yourself and the world around you. Yet beliefs can be false, and they can color things falsely, turning light to dark, possibility to threat. They become a kind of lens through which the world is viewed. Fortunately beliefs, like self-talk and automatic thoughts, can be revised in ways that have positive results.

Automatic Thoughts

People who are uncomfortable in social settings are guided by automatic thoughts. Before they even enter a crowded room or meet someone new, they predict that they won't do well. Furthermore, they tell themselves that they cannot do anything about it. Disaster will come, and they are helpless to fend it off.

This may sound overstated at first. But, if you refer back to the fears you identified in chapter 1, you will probably see that, in fact, you too expect things to go wrong. Although you are not yet conscious of your automatic thinking, the fears you listed there are fueled by it.

It works this way: Any of us, if we hear something enough times, begin to believe the message, particularly if there is a bit of truth in it. This is true even when we are the ones doing the telling—when it is our own thoughts talking. Repeated enough times, eventually the message becomes accepted as the truth, even when it is irrational or implausible.

Once the thought becomes a "truth" it pops up involuntarily and spontaneously in a particular situation. By then, it has become a bona fide automatic thought. And, however innocuous it may seem, an automatic thought is powerful enough to control mood, emotions, and actions.

Over time, automatic thoughts tend to condense into an abbreviated form. A brief phrase, perhaps only a word or a brief visual image, is all that flits across the edge of consciousness. Despite its brevity, it evokes the same emotional reaction as the entire message.

For example, after several sessions, Aaron, a young man I worked with who was uncomfortable at school functions, traced most of his anxiety to an automatic thought in the form of of an image. When he thought of going to social events, an ultra-brief image of people laughing at him flashed across his mind.

With further effort he fleshed out the full picture of the image: He is concentrating on executing the steps of the current dance craze, when he catches a glimpse of laughing faces and suddenly realizes that he is the center of attention. He feels that everyone is snickering at him. He has made a fool of himself, and his friends will be ashamed to be seen with him.

Over time, the full image had telescoped into a brief flash of people laughing at him while he was in the spotlight. What was the source of the image? Aaron had never had such an experience, yet this automatic thought had come to dominate an important aspect of his life.

Eventually, Aaron concluded that the image itself was a distillation of influences and experiences in his childhood—an inhibited, retiring mother who never felt accepted except by her closest relatives and a few friends; a hypercritical father and grandmother. As a result of his family's attitudes, Aaron had developed a fear of doing anything in public unless he could do it perfectly—which of course he couldn't.

Before he began therapy, Aaron had never connected his anxiety with automatic thoughts. He had always believed that social situations made him nervous, but in fact it was *he* who made himself anxious. Because of his erroneous conclusion, Aaron naturally avoided situations where he felt uncomfortable. He knew he couldn't change these situations, so he tried to stay away from them. It never occurred to him that it was his thinking that needed changing.

The good news was that Aaron's inaccurate and mistaken thinking could be changed. It was nothing more than an overlearned habit, which could be eliminated or modified like any other habit, given motivation and hard work.

What Are You Saying to Yourself?— The Ingredients of Automatic Thoughts

What-If Statements

Each person's automatic thoughts are unique and specific to the individual. But the kind of automatic thinking that causes loneliness has the common thread of predicting some sort of misfortune: *What if* this happens? *What if* that happens? I'll look like a fool! I'll be a laughingstock! I'll never live it down! Or worse—my friends will be so ashamed they'll turn their backs on me! My spouse will reject me.

Does this sound at all familiar? The following are further examples of *what-if statements* I have encountered in my practice:

- What if I have a coughing fit at the table?
- What if I start crying and can't stop?
- What if I slip and fall?
- What if I can't think of a thing to say?
- What if they see how nervous I really am?
- What if I can't remember their names?
- What if nobody will talk to me?
- What if I don't know what silverware to use?

These what-if statements, although they may seem ridiculous and improbable to outsiders, are nonetheless powerful negative messages to the only person who hears them. The people haunted by these thoughts took them very seriously—seriously enough either to be miserable at social events or to avoid them altogether.

Negative Self-Evaluations

The what-if statement is only part of the automatic thought. What makes the thought so powerful is the *negative self-evaluation* that is connected to the what-if statement. This negative self-evaluation is usually more difficult to detect than its what-if companion. Here are some examples:

- I always make a fool of myself. What if I have a coughing fit at the table?
- I can't control my emotions. What if I start crying and can't stop?
- I'm so clumsy. What if I slip and fall?
- I'm awful at parties. What if I can't think of a thing to say?
- I'm so transparent. What if they see how nervous I really am?
- I'm terrible with names. What if I can't remember their names?
- I'm so boring. What if nobody will talk to me?

- I never know what to do. What if I don't know what silverware to use?

You may recognize some of these statements as being similar to thoughts you have had. Whether or not they seem familiar to you now, it is almost certain that you sometimes make what-if statements something like these, and that they are connected to negative thoughts about yourself.

Everyone talks to herself or himself, but not necessarily in a negative way. It is likely, though, that you have developed the unfortunate habit of evaluating yourself negatively (as we will explore further in the next chapter). What's more, you have probably come to accept these evaluative statements as true. You avoid people because you fear that they too will judge you and find you lacking. However, neither this idea nor your negative self-evaluations are necessarily true.

Catastrophic Consequences

An automatic thought doesn't stop with a negative self-evaluation and a what-if statement. There is also some kind of *catastrophic consequence* connected. Who wouldn't be nervous thinking that their behavior would bring on a personal catastrophe? Naturally, someone expecting doom would feel very uncomfortable attending social occasions, and might be inclined to avoid them altogether.

Here are the catastrophic consequences that are part of the automatic thoughts we have been using as examples:

- I always make a fool of myself. What if I have a coughing fit at the table? I'll gross everybody out and never get invited back!
- I can't control my emotions. What if I start crying and can't stop? They'll know I'm such a weakling!
- I'm so clumsy. What if I slip and fall? Everybody will laugh at me and think I'm a stupid klutz!
- I'm awful at parties. What if I can't think of a thing to say? My friends will see me for the bore I really am and they'll drop me!
- I'm so transparent. What if they see how nervous I really am? I'll never be respected again!

- I'm terrible with names. What if I can't remember their names? They'll think I don't like them and they'll hate me!
- I'm so boring. What if nobody will talk to me? I'll stand there like a fool and they'll stare at me and laugh to themselves!
- I never know what to do. What if I don't know what silverware to use? Everybody will know I'm from the wrong side of the tracks and they'll reject me!

It will be clear to you by now how closely these statements connect to the fears discussed in chapter 1. You may even have already begun to think about the kinds of automatic thoughts that create and reinforce your own fears. In the next section you will do a couple of exercises to help you bring your automatic thoughts into the open, where they will begin to lose much of their power.

Uncovering Your Thoughts

Occasionally, I run into people who feel that it would be better not to dwell on any kind of negativity. They believe that it might make them feel worse to concentrate on their negative thoughts.

There is a certain, limited truth to this. Change is not always pleasant; it can be like a trip to the dentist. Discomfort, even pain, may be a by-product of the treatment, but the treatment is necessary to save the tooth and prevent worse future problems, thus preventing greater pain in the long run. Negative thoughts are like abscesses. They too must be treated, and they cannot be treated if they are ignored.

The harmful negative statements that you make to yourself are subtle and quick. Even though you may be completely unaware of them, you can ferret them out if you know how and where to look. You can learn to listen for automatic thoughts on the edge of your conscious thinking and to transmute them into powerful, positive thoughts.

Exercise
Listening for Automatic Thoughts

Most of your thoughts are innocuous; only a small portion of them are truly harmful. As you've learned, the thoughts that keep you from belonging generally follow a specific format:

Negative   What-if   Catastrophic   Harmful
evaluation + statement +   consequence =   automatic
of self   thought

As a rule, self-statements of this type precede a recurring painful emotion.

Look back at the fears you listed in your notebook under "My Fears" (the first exercise in chapter 1). No matter what they are, these fears are elicited by automatic thoughts. Thus you have already begun the work you need to do to uncover your harmful automatic thoughts by identifying the fears that crop up again and again in social situations. You'll start with these fears in this exercise, trying to identify the what-if statement, negative self-evaluation, and catastrophic consequence for each one.

For this exercise, as for the previous ones, you will need your notebook, a period of uninterrupted time, and a quiet place to work. Before you begin, turn to the "My Fears" page in your notebook and select the five fears that have been most troublesome for you. Copy those fears onto the next page or two in your notebook, leaving several lines for writing beneath each one. If you listed fewer than five fears in the "My Fears" list, then copy all your fears onto the next page or two in your notebook.

Read through all of the instructions below before starting. Then get comfortable and clear your mind so that you can concentrate.

1. Starting with the first fear you have written on the new page in your notebook, visualize the situation in which the fear is most likely to occur—at a social event, receiving an invitation or announcement, and so on.

2. Allow the situation to run through your mind (repeatedly, if necessary) until you become aware of the fear.

3. Allow the fear to grow until you become aware of a brief automatic thought behind the fear. This may be an image, a single word, a fleeting impression of some kind. Whatever it is, "catch hold" of it as it goes by.

4. Keep concentrating on the brief thought until you hear the full version: what-if statement, negative self-evaluation, catastrophic consequence. Keep in mind that an automatic thought anticipates the worst and overestimates the probability of the worst occurring.

5. Record the three components of the automatic thought in the space you allowed beneath the fear statement in your notebook.

6. Rate the degree to which you believe the thought using the following scale, and record the rating beneath the three components of the automatic thought:

1 = Never believe it
2 = Believe it occasionally, enough to be a minor problem
3 = Believe it about half the time
4 = Believe it in most situations
5 = Believe it always.

7. Continue with the second fear you have selected to work with, and so on until you find you are no longer detecting new automatic thoughts, but merely variations on the same theme. When that happens, stop the exercise. (Bear in mind that you don't need to complete this exercise all in one sitting. If you have identified several fears, you might find it more productive to try two or more sittings over several days.)

Your first entry will look something like this:

Fear 1: Breaking something

Negative self-evaluation:	*I'm always so clumsy when I'm nervous.*
What-if statement:	*What if, when the hostess hands me something, I drop it and break it?*
Catastrophic consequence:	*Everyone will laugh at me except the hostess, and she'll be furious and never invite me back again.*
Degree of believability:	*4*

If you find that this exercise doesn't work for you, that you aren't able to hear your automatic thoughts this way, you might want to read chapters 5 and 6, which cover deep relaxation and self-hypnosis, to begin to learn ways to tune in on your thoughts.

Whether or not you were able to complete this exercise, go on to the next one. It uses a similar format, but in the real world, to enable you to tune into and record your automatic thoughts.

Exercise
Keeping a Log of Automatic Thoughts

In the preceding exercise you identified one or more automatic thoughts that have kept you from belonging. Your eventual goal is to eliminate these thoughts and replace them with adaptive thoughts—thoughts that will help you to belong. First, though, you'll need to keep listening for other automatic thoughts and determine precisely when and where they occur.

To do this, over the next several weeks, while you continue to read and do other exercises in this book, you'll keep a log, making entries when you feel your fears (either those you've already identified or new ones) popping up. Be sure to record any new automatic thoughts or new fears as you become aware of them.

I've provided a chart for you to use to record information about your automatic thoughts on the next page. You may want to photocopy this chart and carry it with you, or you could use a small notepad that fits in your pocket or bag to jot down notes about automatic thoughts as they occur.

This exercise is open-ended. Start keeping your Automatic Thoughts Log now, and continue with it until you feel that you have exhausted the possibilities of finding different settings for automatic thoughts. This will probably take three or four weeks.

- The three components of each of your automatic thoughts
- The situation you were in when the thought occured
- The date and time when it occured
- The degree to which you believe the thought (using the five-point scale on the following page)
- The amount of fear or tension (using the ten-point scale on the next page)

Automatic Thoughts Log

Belief Scale

1 = Never believe it

2 = Believe it occasionally, enough to be a minor problem

3 = believe it about half the time

4 = Believe it in most situations

5 = Believe it always

Fear or Tension Scale

1..........2..........3..........4..........5..........6..........7..........8..........9..........10

No fear or tension   Moderate fear or tension   As fearful or tense as you have ever been

Automatic Thought	Situation	Date and Time	Belief Rating	Fear Rating
Negative self-evaluation:				
What-if statement:				
Catastrophic consequence:				
Negative self-evaluation:				
What-if statement:				
Catastrophic consequence:				

Exercise
Eliminating Automatic Thoughts

Using the information you have gained by doing the previous two exercises, starting on a new page in your notebook, you will list your automatic thoughts that have believability ratings of 3 and above. Each of the three parts of each automatic thought will be dealt with separately in this exercise, and in reverse order:

- Catastrophic consequence
- What-if statement
- Negative self-evaluation

In that order, list each part of each automatic thought, allowing room beneath it to write (as shown in the example below).

1. First, question the accuracy of the catastrophic consequence by:

   a. Asking yourself what is the absolute *worst thing* that could result in the situation that elicited the thought

   b. Rating *how probable* it is that the worst outcome would occur on a scale from 0 (completely improbable) to 10 (almost certain to occur)

   c. Recording what is actually *likely to occur*

2. Next, question the accuracy of the what-if statement in the same way: How probable is it that the "what-if" will occur? What is more likely to happen?

3. Finally, examine your negative self-evaluation objectively. Take a step back and try to view yourself from the viewpoint of someone who likes and cares about you. Your friends and family probably see you very differently from the way you see yourself. Would they agree with your negative self-evaluation? If not, what do you think they would say that would contradict it? (If you don't know, why not ask them?)

Note that this exercise will probably require more than one session to complete, and may be ongoing for as long as you continue to uncover new automatic thoughts.

Here's an example of how one person, Jay, completed the exercise for this automatic thought: "I'm awful at parties. What if I can't think of a thing to say? My friends will see me for the bore I really am and they'll drop me."

Catastrophic Consequence:	*My friends will see me for the bore I really am and they'll drop me.*
Worst outcome:	*My friends will desert me.*
Probability of worst outcome:	1
More likely outcome:	*My true friends already know what I'm like, and they are still my friends. They'll remain my friends even if I can't think of a thing to say at this party.*
What-If Statement:	*I won't be able to think of a thing to say.*
Probability of worst outcome:	4
More likely outcome:	*I'll think of things to say to some people but not to everybody.*
Negative Self-Evaluation:	*I'm awful at parties.*
Objective evaluation:	*My friends like me and they keep inviting me to their parties, so I can't be all that bad. Even if I were, maybe that's not so important to them. Maybe they like it that I'm a good listener and don't talk all the time. Maybe if I weren't so worried about finding something to say, I'd be more relaxed and would have a better time.*

Thoughts That Lead to Loneliness

Not all harmful thinking is on the edge of consciousness. Much of it is entirely conscious and is just as powerful as automatic thinking in shaping behavior. Like automatic thinking, these conscious thought patterns tend to be repetitive. They pop up spontaneously in the form of self-talk and lead to emotional responses, which in turn affect behavior.

Illogical Thought Patterns

Of course, not all self-talk is negative. We often use self-talk to guide our actions and help us make decisions—which is fine as long as the self-talk is sensible and grounded in logic. However, when it is distorted and illogical, self-talk can be a straitjacket that limits accomplishment and satisfaction. Illogical self-talk plays a major role in keeping you from belonging. It reinforces your loneliness by making you feel unworthy, unfit, or unwanted. It limits your possibilities and makes you feel that limitations are what you deserve or what you are likely to get.

The examples of the nine people described below illustrate nine types of distorted thinking that unnecessarily limit social choices and enjoyment. While you read through them, keep an open mind about your own thinking.

Mind Reading

Kirk tended to make snap judgments about people and then to react to his conclusions as if they were fact. His judgments were usually based on facial expressions. He would, for instance, interpret a grimace on a man's face as a sure sign of dislike for him.

Why is this an example of illogical thinking? Kirk saw whatever he wished to see in other people, which was usually negative. He never considered the range of possibilities behind others' behavior. The man with the grimace may not have been reacting to Kirk at all. He could have been fired that day. He might have just left a painful dental appointment, or he could have simply been experiencing heartburn. Yet Kirk was sure that he knew what was on the man's mind.

Mind reading was Kirk's nemesis. He made judgments about people based on what he thought, although he assumed he knew what they thought. What's more, his judgments became facts as far as he was concerned. As a result, Kirk often limited his social possibilities by writing off someone who might have turned into a good friend or a valuable ally.

People who read minds have no evidence to back up their judgments—only feelings and conjectures. Yet, they convince themselves that they know why other people behave as they do. Of course mind readers would never admit to anyone, least of all themselves, that they *know* what others are thinking.

Mind reading is perilous to friendship, because mind readers treat other people not as they truly are, but as they are assumed to be. And there is no factual basis for the assumptions, which often sound something like this:

- She thinks she's too good to be seen with me.
- He's kissing up to me because he wants my support.
- I know she likes me a lot, but she's been hurt too often to get involved.
- They're ignoring me because they're jealous.

You can see how mind readers cut off social opportunities for themselves. They "know" someone dislikes them, so they avoid the person or treat him or her with disdain.

Shandra didn't make snap judgments as Kirk did, but she was just as much a mind reader. She was inclined to blame other people for her negative emotions. If she felt angry with someone, for instance, she convinced herself that it was the other person's fault.

Shandra told herself that she was justified in reacting to the anger that she *knew* the other person felt. Consequently, she never examined her anger or tried to solve the conflicts behind it. Instead, she tended to stomp off in a huff, which often alienated the other person, who may or may not have actually been angry in the first place.

How can you know if you are reading minds? Ask yourself if you are treating people as if they think the same way you do. For example, if you're hurt when an old friend forgets your birthday, you might assume that anyone would be devasted if you forgot his or her birthday. Or, if you believe that good friends never disagree, you might feel that your friends would reject you if you expressed an honest opinion that differed from theirs.

People who read minds don't pay close attention to the words and actions of others. They are not aware of the vast range of differences among people. They believe that the people with whom they come in contact think largely as they do. It never occurs to them that other people can operate on a very different, and equally valid, set of beliefs and assumptions.

Overgeneralization

Martha, unlike Kirk, had actual evidence of being disliked. She had been rudely snubbed by a small group of acquaintances when she was a guest at a ritzy country club. Martha's face burned whenever she thought of the incident, and ever since then she avoided private clubs—as either a guest or a member.

The illogical aspect of Martha's thinking was that she assumed the same thing would happen to her again, even though she had been treated rudely only once and that was years ago. In fact, there was no particular reason for her to believe such an incident wasn't an isolated occurence. Assuming the experience would recur seriously limited Martha's social possibilities.

Martha let *overgeneralization* exclude her from a whole range of social possibilities. Unlike mind readers, people who overgeneralize have some evidence of what people think. Unfortunately they focus on one or two instances of negative evidence to the exclusion of many pieces of positive evidence. Martha focused exclusively on the one instance of being snubbed, but she never considered that she was accepted by almost everyone in most every social situation.

Because she was treated badly in a particular place, Martha associated her discomfort with that place. It didn't occur to her that the group of people who snubbed her might have done the same in any other setting. Martha associated rejection with the country club, so she came to feel rejected by the club itself, and then by all such clubs. Her social life became more restricted, as it usually does with people who overgeneralize.

People who overgeneralize think such illogical thoughts as these:

- Nobody at school likes me.
- Everyone in this church is so snooty.

- They'd never let somebody like me in that club.
- If they really knew what I was like, they couldn't possibly accept me.
- I'll never let anybody hurt me again.
- I don't trust anyone.

Examine your train of thought when you feel anxious about people or social occasions. Are you using words like *never, always, all, none, everyone,* and *anybody?* If you tend to use such all-inclusive words in your self-talk, you are probably overgeneralizing.

All-or-None Thinking

Francine either loved someone or hated them, and she believed that people reacted to her in the same way. There was no middle ground for her. As a result, Francine had a very small circle of good friends, a large number of enemies, and few social acquaintances.

All-or-none thinking was Francine's problem. For her, everything was black or white, with no shades of gray. In fact, she tended to think in absolute terms in most areas of her life. For example, she was never able to eat in moderation. It was either feast when she was not on a diet or famine when she was.

Francine approached people in much the same way. They were wonderful or terrible, angelic or pure evil. She had little tolerance for human frailties. Let a friend hurt her once and that was it. That person was shifted from the friend side of her mental ledger to the foe column. The ex-friend was given no chance to explain, and there was no possibility of forgiveness.

Similarly, Francine never gave an acquaintance the opportunity to become a friend unless he or she matched perfectly Francine's idea of what a friend should be. Needless to say, Francine was friendless more often than not. People in her circle were aware of her penchant for discarding and trashing friends, so not too many of her acquaintances tried to get close to her.

Perhaps equally as limiting for her, Francine also judged herself in all-or-none terms. She could not abide her own mistakes any more than she could endure the mistakes of others. One error on her part and she became an incompetent wretch who could do nothing right. As a result, she was prone to frequent mood swings, and people avoided her when she was in one of her recurrent dark moods.

If your friends tend to move in and out of favor, ask yourself if you are inclined toward all-or-none thinking. Ask yourself whether you have more enemies than friends. Be especially vigilant for this type of illogical self-talk if you often come down hard on yourself. Look within yourself for difficulty forgiving not only other people but also yourself.

Confusion of Possibility with Probability

Despite never having hosted a social disaster, Merrill always felt one was imminent. Of course, not every party he threw had gone perfectly, but all of them had been at least acceptable. Many of them had in fact been outstanding. All the same, he was always on the lookout for failure and was thus tense and constrained when people were in his home.

Although Merrill was not aware of it, his tension put a damper on his parties, so that his illogical thinking sometimes became a self-fulfilling prophecy. Because of his discomfort, Merrill entertained less and less over the years. In effect, he punished himself for having parties, and, as we all do, he avoided situations that were punishing for him.

Merrill's social opportunities grew more limited because of *confusion of probability with possibility*. Sure, it was *possible* for any party that he hosted to be a disaster. With proper planning and preparation, though, it was not very *probable*. However, Merrill did not differentiate between low probability and high probability. His distorted thinking led him to believe that bad things *would* happen just because they *could* happen.

This is the type of thinking that is behind many fears, not just social ones. People who are phobic about flying, for instance, believe the probability of being killed in a plane crash is very high. In fact, very few people die in aircraft accidents, as compared with automobile accidents.

Merrill not only consistently overestimated the odds of calamity, he didn't consider that he had the power to lower the probability of a bad outcome. He couldn't see that a little attention to food, drink, music, and guest list was very likely to avert almost all possiblity of social disaster. As a result, he became more and more anxious about his abilities as a host.

Do you dwell on negative possibilities? Do you usually anticipate the worst? Are you a worrier? If your answer to these questions is "yes," you may also sometimes confuse probability with possibility.

Filtering

Miranda didn't enjoy entertaining any more than Merrill did. For much of her adult life she had been able to see only the negative—about her parties, her appearance, her behavior—so that she could rarely focus on having fun. She not only gradually ceased entertaining, but she became more likely to turn down invitations than to accept them. The eventual result was a nonexistent social life.

Miranda was similar to Merrill in that she expected social failure. Her thinking was distorted by *filtering*. When she was entertaining, she focused on every little sign of potential trouble, but she paid scant attention to signs of success.

Miranda saw only the disgruntled man sitting alone at her party, not the throng of happy people around him. She saw the one plate of uneaten hors d'oeuvres but disregarded the compliments about her food. She agonized about the two or three people who left early, never thinking about those who enjoyed her hospitality until midnight.

Because she filtered out the positive and concentrated only on the negative aspects of her social life, Miranda dreaded entertaining and avoided it when she could. She also avoided being a guest, because she was always uncomfortable about her appearance and her actions. Miranda only thought about her negative qualities and magnified them out of proportion to reality.

Because her thinking was out of balance—almost exclusively negative with very little positive—it was punctuated with extremely negative words. Her self-talk was peppered with *hopeless, terrible, awful, stupid, worthless,* and other pejorative words. If you use these kinds of words in your self-talk, you too are at risk for filtered thinking. The words you use in your self-talk both reflect how you see the world and reinforce your vision of it. If the image in the mirror is distorted, then your worldview is distorted. You believe what you tell yourself and you shape your behavior accordingly.

Emotional Reasoning

A successful investor, Len was objective and clearheaded in his work, which primarily involved analyzing data using a personal computer. Except when his wife intervened, Len had an almost nonexistent social life. He was uncomfortable with people in the flesh, and he preferred spending his free time "interacting" with his computer and "chatting" on the Internet. He jokingly referred to himself as a nerd, and, indeed, his appearance and behavior did fit the stereotype.

Len felt like a social outcast; therefore he assumed he was a social outcast. He felt dull and boring, so he assumed he was dull and boring. His wife's best friend seemed to dislike him; therefore, she must dislike him. Len essentially believed that what he felt was true. It didn't occur to him that feelings aren't necessarily true just because they feel true.

Len's self-talk was based on *emotional reasoning*. His judgments about the motivations and actions of himself and others stemmed from his feelings, not from objective reality. And it was this emotional reasoning that kept him from belonging. Much to the distress of his wife, Len was happier on the Internet than in face-to-face encounters. To no avail, she pointed out that his wide-ranging knowledge made him an exceptional conversationalist.

If Len's thinking had been perfectly clear and logical, his feelings might have reflected reality. As with most of us, though, there was some distortion in his thinking. Thus his feelings were sometimes distorted, which resulted in distorted judgments about himself and others.

Do you tend to go with your negative feelings when you make decisions? Do you give more weight to negative emotions than to facts? If so, you may also be a dupe of emotional reasoning. This kind of thinking may have compromised your ability to feel comfortable with other people.

Catastrophizing

Patricia had started off married life going out with her fun-loving husband. She also had people in her home every week or two, mostly at her husband's behest. As time went by, however, she began first to dread, then to avoid, going out, though she still invited a few people to her home and occasionally visited a few friends. When her husband asked why she didn't want to come out with him, she laughed it off, saying he would be better off without her, since she was so clumsy and nervous in groups.

Catastrophizing is the kind of self-talk that kept Patricia from belonging. This distorted pattern of thinking is almost identical to the catastrophic consequence portion of automatic thoughts. Instead of being on the edge of consciousness, however, it is entirely conscious.

Patricia continually told herself to expect disaster. She always expected the worst and focused her thinking on "terrible" and "horrible" outcomes. Not only did she foresee catastrophe, she believed that she would be unable to handle it when it occurred.

Patricia believed her self-talk, so she avoided places and situations where she could be caught up in disaster. She avoided dinner parties because she was sure to spill something and everyone at the table would think her a clumsy fool. Plays, concerts, and church were out. Patricia was prone to urinary tract infections, and she just couldn't disturb people with her goings and comings to and from the ladies' room. They might even think she couldn't control her bladder and start to talk about it behind her back and laugh at her.

Large parties made her too nervous. She hated feeling confined by crowds of people. She grew all sweaty and twitchy, and everybody could see what a twit she was. How could they possibly respect her after that? She wouldn't have a friend left, and that would be unbearable!

Catastrophic thinking of this type is often linked to confusion of probability with possibility. If you consistently overestimate the odds of calamity, you may also tend to catastrophize. You may not only expect the worst, but may also believe that you would be helpless in the face of calamity. Do you use such words as *terrible*, *unbearable, horrible,* and *insufferable* in your self-talk? These are fairly reliable indicators of catastrophic thinking.

Personalization

William avoided socializing with people whenever possible. He was constantly comparing himself to those around him, and consequently never felt relaxed with them because he never felt that he could measure up.

The fallacy in William's thinking was a belief that his self-worth derived from events outside himself. He looked to others as measures of his value. If his wife seemed angry or depressed, William wondered what he had done wrong. If one of his children behaved badly, William questioned his parenting skills. If his mother complained, he automatically felt guilty.

Personalization was William's bane. Because of his tendency to relate everyone and everything in his environment to himself, he felt uncomfortable in many situations. He couldn't appreciate the talents and accomplishments of other people, because in comparison he always fell short. If a person was witty, William felt bad that he couldn't make people laugh. Being around an athlete made him feel oafish, while a well-read person made him feel stupid.

If you find yourself carefully weighing the reactions of others—their comments, their opinions, their facial expressions—you may also be personalizing. Do you look to others to set your worth? Are you inclined to compare yourself with friends, acquaintances, and coworkers?

It's draining to look to every conversation for a clue as to your value. Anyone who does so is likely to be tense around others. Tense people are inclined to avoid situations that make them tense. People who are prone to personalization are thus unlikely to seek out the company of other people.

Exercise
Recognizing Your Negative Self-Talk

Merrill, Len, Francine, and the others have one thing in common: It is their self-talk that keeps them from belonging. They don't belong because they tell themselves they don't belong. Their negative self-talk shapes the way they feel about themselves, and their negative feelings determine how they interact with other people.

Ultimately, loneliness is a state of mind brought on by illogical, distorted thinking. Could negative self-talk be keeping you outside or on the edge of belonging? This exercise will help you gather data to answer this essential question. You will need your notebook, as usual.

1. From your "Log of Automatic Thoughts" identify five social situations in which you felt the most fearful or tense and record them on a new page in your notebook. Title the page "Self-Talk."

2. In order to identify your self-talk, you'll need to encounter the situations you identified. Make an effort to go into each situation as soon as is feasible. For each situation, you might want to write in your notebook a statement of intent, such as "I will accept the next invitation to a party that I receive."

3. The next time you intend to go into each situation, pay careful attention to your self-talk while you are anticipating the occasion, for example, for several days before. Make notes about any self-talk you hear. Rate the self-talk for believability, as you did for your automatic thoughts, using the 5-point scale below. Also use the list below to determine what category of illogical thinking your self-talk falls into. Use the letters in parentheses to code each of your self-talk statements.

4. While you are actually in the situation, pay attention to your self-talk. As soon as possible afterwards, make notes on the self-talk you heard, rate it for believability, and categorize it as you did before.

Belief Scale
1 = Never believe it
2 = Believe it occasionally, enough to be a minor problem
3 = Believe it about half the time
4 = Believe it in most situations
5 = Believe it always

Illogical Thought Patterns

- Mind reading (MR)—Making judgments based on assumptions of what other people are thinking
- Overgeneralization (OG)—Assuming that a single bad experience or a few isolated experiences will recur in other situations or circumstances
- All-or-none thinking (AN)—Thinking in extremes (good or bad, friend or enemy, success or failure) with no middle ground
- Confusion of probability with possibility (CPP)—Vastly overestimating the odds of a bad outcome
- Filtering (F)—Focusing on the negative aspects of a situation while overlooking the positive aspects
- Emotional reasoning (ER)—Making judgments based on feelings while disregarding facts
- Catastrophizing (C)—Foreseeing the worst possible outcome in a given situation and feeling helpless to cope with it
- Personalization (P)—Making judgments about self-worth based on the actions of other people, which results in constant comparison with others

Exercise
Transforming Self-Talk

This exercise is designed to help you counter the negative self-talk you identified in the previous exercise by devising new positive statements to replace the old statements, similar to the way you countered your automatic thoughts in an earlier exercise.

1. Choose a specific instance of illogical self-talk that you identified in the preceding exercise to work on, and copy it onto a fresh page in your notebook. (Eventually, you will do this with each instance, but for now, choose one to work on.)

2. Devise counterarguments for the self-talk, as you did for your automatic thoughts earlier: Question the logic of the statement. Rate its believablilty again, since this may have changed since you first recorded the self-talk. Then write down positive state-

ments that logically refute—not just contradict—the negative self-talk (see the examples below).

3. Then compose and record your new helpful and realistic self-talk for each illogical statement. The statements should be brief, positive, and believable.

4. If you tend to think in images instead of words, your "self-talk" may be brief images of yourself and others in social situations. If this is the case, your positive statements should be visual as well—you'll come up with a new picture to replace the old.

5. Repeat this process for each type and instance of illogical self-talk that you identified or that you identify in the future.

Here are a couple of examples:

Mind Reading

Social situation:	*Thinking about accepting an invitation for a weekend tennis game.*
Illogical self-talk:	*He only invited me so he can win.*
Counterarguments:	*It's true that he's a better tennis player and almost always wins, but it's also true that we have a good time on the court. It's just as likely that he invited me because we always laugh a lot. Maybe he invited me because he belongs to a tennis club and I don't, and he knows that I enjoy the game but don't have many opportunities to play.*
Realistic, positive self-talk:	*He invited me because we have fun together.*

Confusion of Probability with Possibility

Social situation:	*Refusing to make eye contact with a business acquaintance across the room at a large cocktail party.*

Illogical self-talk:	*I've got to stand near the exit so I can get out of here quickly if I feel faint.*
Counterarguments:	*I fainted in public on two occasions but that was years ago. I have been in public hundreds of times since then and haven't fainted. I am in good health, and there is no reason I know of that I should faint.*
Realistic, positive self-talk:	*The chances of my fainting in public are extremely low—no more than 2 out of several hundred.*

Think of this exercise as open-ended. You will no doubt identify other instances of negative self-talk as you go through life. Be vigilant for illogical thinking any time you feel uneasy or negative about a social situation.

Phantom Conversations

As he worked to eliminate negative self-talk, Luke became aware of a disconcerting habit—having conversations with himself. These conversations almost always had negative overtones and usually occurred when Luke was angry. Sometimes the conversations were silent, but more often Luke spoke both sides aloud, usually when he was alone in his car. The conversations nearly always involved the two people he had the most difficulty confronting, his wife and his boss, who also happened to be a good friend.

A typical phantom conversation would be triggered by some perceived reprimand by his boss and friend, Albert:

"Well, Luke, I have your draft of the Jensen proposal on my desk, and I must say that it didn't convince me. How can you expect it to convince Mr. Jensen?"

"I thought it was pretty good. I worked all weekend on it. Maddie was in a real snit because I was glued to my desk all day Sunday."

"If you'd organize your work better, Luke, you wouldn't have to work overtime. Seems to me that you're also letting that wife of yours get the upper hand. Why don't you stand up to her?"

The fact is, Albert said no such thing. He actually said, "Luke, we're having more and more trouble hanging onto the Jensen account. Your proposal would be fine for most of our accounts, but we've got to go the extra mile with Jensen. Can you do another draft with the sales trends for the entire year, not just last quarter? And it would probably be good to include the latest projections for next year too."

Albert's suggestion was disappointing, but Luke knew that it was reasonable. Albert never mentioned Luke's wife, Maddie, nor Luke's work habits. Luke was angry, though, because of the disruptions to his schedule and because his wife had been annoyed with him for devoting another Sunday to work. Luke was also more than a little put out because Albert had once again caught him being a little slack.

Luke knew, of course, that Albert had not actually said the things Luke had him say in the phantom conversation. Yet Luke's emotions were genuine, and he felt much angrier after this two-way self-talk than he had before it. The point is that he *felt* angrier with Albert and thus *acted* angrier. The result was that another wedge was driven between two coworkers and friends all because of negative self-talk.

Luke's friendship with Albert was perilously close to serious disruption when he realized what he was doing. Luke had lived with illogical thinking so long that it had come to seem normal and natural.

The following exercise will help you identify and eliminate your own phantom conversations.

Exercise
Eradicating Phantom Conversations

In this exercise, you will monitor your behavior and thoughts for self-talk in which you talk through both sides of imaginary conversations. As with automatic thoughts and other types of self-talk, you will need to do this over a period of weeks.

1. In your notebook, record the following information about all phantom conversations with negative content:

a. The time and place of the phantom conversation

b. The other person involved

c. The emotion that lead to the conversation (such as anger, fear, anxiety)

d. A summary of the content of the phantom conversation

e. A summary of actual conversations on the same subject that you have had with that same person. Also make a note if no actual conversation has occurred.

2. After two weeks of recording phantom conversations, begin thought-stopping procedures:

a. Stop any phantom conversations as soon as you recognize what you are doing, and remind yourself that you are engaging in potentially damaging self-talk.

b. Think through actual conversations you've had with the person on the subject under consideration. Be realistic and do not exaggerate.

c. If there have been no prior conversations, remind yourself to base your opinions on observable facts, not on conjecture.

Mistaken Beliefs—The Source of Illogical Thinking

In the preceding exercise you identified the types of illogical thought patterns that have kept you from belonging. You are now aware of the negative self-talk fueling your loneliness. But what is the source of this distorted thinking? Why have you developed such self-defeating habits?

Your illogical, distorted thinking didn't spring forth spontaneously. Ironically, there is logic behind your illogical thinking. You think the way you do because you were programmed to do so. During the crucial early years, when you were learning how life works, every experience you had—all the praise and criticism, every interaction, every discovery—led you to form beliefs about how the world operates.

Over time, and with reinforcement, these beliefs became so deeply ingrained that they no longer seemed to be the assumptions that they actually were. They became instead unquestioned truths—laws of human nature governing your behavior—so integral to your worldview that you likely have not even been consciously aware of them. Thus, despite the anguish they caused, you continued to accept these beliefs and to act on them as if they were factual.

Hopefully, you are now beginning to recognize that some of the beliefs you have held about yourself and other people may be mistaken.

One of the most common mistaken beliefs is that one's value depends upon the recognition of other people. People with this type of belief tell themselves that they must constantly impress and please other people. They mistakenly believe that self-worth comes from outside themselves rather than from within. When they can't impress or please, they feel awful about themselves. They feel like failures. Their mistaken belief leads to distorted thinking and negative self-talk.

Remember Aaron, the young man who was so fearful of making mistakes in public that he avoided school dances? As he progressed through therapy, Aaron learned that he really didn't *have* an opinion of himself. His opinion was merely a reflection of the opinions of the people around him, especially that of his hypercritical father. Most of the time Aaron despised himself because he believed that his father's criticisms were valid. He felt worthless because he was told that he was worthless. It never occurred to him that his father's judgments could be questioned.

It was a major milestone in therapy when Aaron was able to look at himself objectively. He didn't like everything he saw, but he was able to decide for himself what he didn't like. Even more important, he began to recognize that he was persistent, diligent, and dependable—traits he had never seen through the derogatory eyes of his father.

Mandy, another high school student, tried continually to impress people. When she was the center of attention, she felt good about herself. She thrived on compliments, but felt bad about herself when she was not in the spotlight. When there was no one around to feed her ego, Mandy felt lost and unworthy, which made it difficult for her to tolerate being alone.

From an early age Mandy had adopted the erroneous belief that admiration by other people was the only true gauge of one's value. As a result, she spent an enormous amount of time and money on her appearance. She also expended a great deal of energy trying to be in the limelight. This one erroneous belief shaped her life.

Although your mistaken beliefs may not be as dramatic as Aaron's or Mandy's, they have nevertheless interfered with your venturing out socially. They will not be easy to recognize, for they are probably subliminal, below consciousness. If you are looking for them, however, they are retrievable.

A friend of mine recently told me about a belief of this type that she stumbled upon. She was open to the idea of having mistaken beliefs and thus recognized one when it popped into her mind. She said that lately she had been irritated by a briefcase that she often carried. Apparently it was off balance in some way, because it kept falling over every time she set it down.

One particularly stressful day, it happened again. My friend told me she felt as if "the damn thing was falling down on purpose," as if the briefcase had intentionally set out to frustrate her. With that, a metaphoric lightbulb lit above her head. It dawned on her that her life was being affected in a major way by the mistaken belief that the whole world and everybody in it was determined to frustrate her.

The following exercise lists some mistaken beliefs that tend to keep people from belonging. Use it to identify any that might have led to the illogical thinking and negative self-talk that you identified earlier in the chapter.

As you go through the list, pay close attention to any of the items that stir up emotion, such as anger, fear, annoyance, sadness, guilt, or disgust. You can often find irrational beliefs lurking behind repeated emotional reactions, just as my friend did when she was repeatedly irritated by the behavior of her briefcase. Any time you find yourself experiencing the same negative emotion over and over again in similar situations, look closely for an irrational belief behind it. You might want to use the list in this next exercise as a prompter.

Bear in mind, however, that this list doesn't exhaust the possibilities of mistaken beliefs. All of yours may not appear there. The list illustrates the general types of assumptions that tend to alienate people from others.

Exercise
Identifying Mistaken Beliefs

Instructions: To the left of the following statements, check off those that apply to you. Then, in the first space to the right, rate each statement you checked for believability using the 5-point scale below. (Leave the spaces in the second column empty for now.)

Belief Scale
1 = Never believe it
2 = Believe it occasionally, enough to be a minor problem
3 = Believe it about half the time
4 = Believe it in most situations   5 = Believe it always

		Believability Rating	Type of Belief
___	1. I am unintelligent, unattractive, or boring.	___	___
___	2. I cannot cope with terrible events.	___	___
___	3. I must do things perfectly to be acceptable.	___	___
___	4. Other people look down on me if I make mistakes.	___	___
___	5. I will be hurt if I trust other people.	___	___
___	6. I am a victim and cannot change that.	___	___
___	7. I can feel it when I'm making a bad impression.	___	___
___	8. People are basically unkind.	___	___

		Believability Rating	Type of Belief
___	9. People who seem distracted think I am boring.	___	___
___	10. Most people are out for themselves.	___	___
___	11. I know when people like me and when they don't.	___	___
___	12. If disaster can happen, it will happen sooner or later.	___	___
___	13. Anger is always unacceptable.	___	___
___	14. People won't accept me because I am an outsider.	___	___
___	15. I must accomplish things on my own without help.	___	___
___	16. I am either acceptable or unacceptable to others.	___	___
___	17. People never forget and rarely forgive.	___	___
___	18. People judge me by my appearance.	___	___
___	19. I must never show that I am irritated, annoyed, unhappy, or disappointed.	___	___
___	20. People judge me by my accomplishments.	___	___
___	21. People despise a failure.	___	___
___	22. People will reject me if they know what I am really like.	___	___
___	23. Pleasing other people will make them accept me.	___	___
___	24. People always disappoint, hurt, or abandon me in the end.	___	___
___	25. It's my fault if people don't like me.	___	___

		Believability Rating	Type of Belief
___	26. People who frown at me don't like me.	___	___
___	27. It's not worth the risk of rejection to try for friendship.	___	___
___	28. Friends are too much trouble.	___	___
___	29. I am ashamed of myself.	___	___
___	30. People are more inclined to speak ill than well of others.	___	___
___	31. I would be accepted if only I had the money, beauty, brains, education, or social background to fit in.	___	___
___	32. I'm not very important.	___	___
___	33. My opinions don't count much.	___	___
___	34. I have no right to speak up.	___	___
___	35. I don't have the right to have fun.	___	___
___	36. I am acceptable only if I am productive.	___	___
___	37. I must be nice and pleasant to be acceptable.	___	___
___	38. If something happened once, it's likely to happen again.	___	___
___	39. If you are not my friend, you must be my enemy.	___	___
___	40. Nobody listens to me.	___	___
___	41. I never measure up.	___	___
___	42. If I make a mistake, I will be scorned, rejected, or disliked.	___	___
___	43. I can usually tell what people think of me.	___	___
___	44. You are either for me or against me.	___	___

You have identified the automatic thoughts and self-talk that make you feel wary or unworthy of belonging. The negative thoughts that control your behavior have power over you because of your beliefs. You cannot abolish negative thinking until you delete these mistaken beliefs and replace them with realistic beliefs about yourself and other people.

Transforming Beliefs
About Yourself and Other People

Habit Beliefs

Not all beliefs have an equal hold on you. Some of them are more powerful than others in controlling your behavior. The least powerful beliefs are no more than habits. You've become accustomed to these *habit beliefs,* but you are not deeply committed to them. Like all habits, though, they take some effort to overcome.

Nora, for example, held the habit belief that nobody listened to her. She was a shy person who found the belief easier to tolerate than speaking up. This mental habit justified her remaining silent when she felt uncomfortable about offering her opinion. However, as a result she was chronically irritated at other people for not anticipating her wishes and needs.

In the short term the belief was convenient for Nora, although ultimately it was self-defeating. It led to such negative self-talk as "Why bother? They never do anything I want to do," which made her less likely to accept or issue invitations.

Once Nora decided to come out of her shell, she forced herself to be aware of her tendency to tell herself that nobody listened to her. When she felt the urge to fall back into the habit, she said to herself instead, "Speak up. My opinion is as valid as anyone's." In addition, she repeated this statement to herself from time to time throughout each day.

In time, the new statement became stronger and stronger, replacing the old habit belief, which in turn became weaker and weaker. Furthermore, much of the negative self-talk originally deriving from the belief began to fade away. Nora was no longer inclined to tell herself that being with people was boring because she always had to agree and do what they wanted to do. The net result was a more social and happier woman—all from changing a simple habit.

Emotional Beliefs

Other beliefs are more deeply ingrained than mere mental habits. Some beliefs hold credence emotionally but not intellectually. You know they are not actually true, but they seem true. These *emotional beliefs* feel true. Despite knowing that they are probably erroneous, you cannot shake them. You act upon them as if you had full faith in their veracity.

Although emotional beliefs are more tenacious than habit beliefs, they are not intractable. They have a firmer grip on you, because they *feel* true. You know they are not entirely logical, but they seem real. They are rooted more in your gut than in your head.

Raul, a mid-level executive in a multinational firm, concluded that it was he, not his opponents, who was holding himself back. An up-and-coming financial wizard and Cuban exile, Raul had the ability to rise high in a company with a vast Spanish-speaking market. He had the talent, technical skills, credentials, and Latino background to climb the ladder in his employer's Latin American operation and then to move into corporate headquarters. It wasn't happening, though.

After much soul searching, Raul admitted to himself that he *felt* that he did not deserve the success that was on his doorstep. He had a great deal of guilt about his parents and siblings living at poverty level in Cuba, while his income was rising. He knew that his family could eat a small portion of meat only once a month, while he was eating on expense account in the finest restaurants in Buenos Aires and Mexico City. He lived in a stylish townhouse and had a fine European car; they lived in a crumbling tenement and rode bicycles.

When the guilt became too great, Raul acquired the emotional belief that he did not deserve success. He didn't believe this intellectually. He certainly did not think that he should be washing dishes and living in a cold-water flat. All the same, it felt wrong to have so many material advantages.

As a result of his emotional belief, Raul's automatic thoughts and self-talk became quite negative. Among other negative thoughts, he told himself that he did fit in well with his Anglo colleagues. He told himself that he was a token minority who had a place with the company only as long as he was relegated to Central and South America.

In time Raul's behavior began to conform to his negative thinking. He withdrew from his associates, even from those who had been genuine boosters of his career. Because his social life was completely intertwined with his business life, Raul became more and more isolated. Loneliness became an increasing problem for him, and he was on a long slide into depression.

Fortunately, Raul sought treatment and profited well from therapy. There was no serious damage to his career, and he soon allowed himself to have friends and fun again. Along with other treatment goals, Raul learned to identify and change mistaken beliefs. In therapy Raul faced up to the guilt that was the impetus behind the belief that he did not deserve success. He didn't have to question whether or not his belief was factual, for he knew it was not. He knew that success was there for him to earn; that was one of the major reasons he risked imprisonment to come to the United States.

Raul learned in therapy that it is helpful to discover the origin of each emotional belief. Being aware of the origin helped him to accept emotionally the inappropriateness of the mistaken belief. Raul grew to realize that his being poor would not profit his family in Cuba in any way, while his accumulating wealth might possibly benefit them in the future.

Definite Beliefs

A third category of beliefs really do appear to be true to you. You are definitely committed to them both intellectually and emotionally. You might prefer not to have these *definite beliefs*, but you are convinced they are gospel and you react accordingly.

Mitchell, for example, definitely believed that anger is always unacceptable. He was convinced of this truism because he had seen people subvert themselves by losing control. He had friends who had alienated other friends because of their anger, and he had seen people at work lose ground because of their tempers. Mitchell believed that expressing anger was always bad. He knew it and he felt it.

Mitchell also realized that he himself had pushed away more than one friend and coworker because of his own angry outbursts. Try as he might, he couldn't prevent an eventual eruption, despite being able at times to control his temper for many months. Anybody who experienced or witnessed Mitchell's explosions grew wary of him. Over the years he had unwittingly but effectively erected a barrier around himself that few acquaintances were willing to cross.

As one step in challenging his mistaken belief, Mitchell looked for its origins. The source of his misconception was not difficult to find. Growing up with an abusive father, Mitchell had seen firsthand the damage anger can cause. Furthermore, he had been told over and over by his mother that anger was terrible, and he had been punished both subtly and overtly for expressing it.

Concurrently Mitchell questioned his belief logically. He looked at the other side of the issue—the benefits of expressing anger—as well as he could, examining as many arguments as he could think of against his belief. He looked for and read books on the subject, and he allowed himself to be objective.

Mitchell decided that he had been looking at anger in all-or-none terms. Certainly explosive outbursts were highly damaging, but a small degree of anger can be motivating. It can serve as an early warning signal that something is amiss and needs to be attended to. By ignoring his anger, Mitchell allowed it to grow because the underlying conflicts were never resolved. Mitchell kept ignoring the warning signals until it was too late.

Like steam building up in a boiler with no escape valve, the anger erupted explosively when it could no longer be contained. Ironically, the final provocation for an outburst was usually quite benign in proportion to the degree of anger expressed, which made Mitchell's anger all the more puzzling and unacceptable to the person on the receiving end.

Once Mitchell was able to see that anger handled constructively can be a stimulus for positive action, the intellectual underpinnings of his belief began to crumble. As appropriate as this was,

Mitchell still needed to replace his negative belief about anger with a positive one.

That led to the third step in countering his mistaken belief about anger—constructing and using a positive self-statement, or *affirmation*. His affirmation was brief, worded positively, and ultimately believable: "My anger will fade when I solve the problem behind it."

Categorizing Your Beliefs

It will take time to modify your old mistaken beliefs. It has taken a lifetime to form these assumptions about life; you can't expect them to fade away without some resistance. Keep in mind that beliefs are patterns of thought, and you have ultimate control over your thoughts. Because your beliefs determine your reality, you must change them to change your life.

Go back now to the preceding exercise and examine each belief you checked very carefully. It will take some thought, but you will probably be able to sort each of them into one of the three categories of beliefs. As a general rule, *habit beliefs* should have the lowest believability ratings in column A, *emotional beliefs* should be in the middle range of the ratings, and *definite beliefs* should have the highest ratings. The relationships between the categories and the ratings may not be quite this neat, but by and large they will hold.

Use the following code to label each of your beliefs in the second column of blanks in the Identifying Mistaken Beliefs exercise:

H = Habit belief
E = Emotional belief
D = Definite belief

The Positive Power of Private Thoughts

The next and final exercise in this chapter will help you tackle the task of modifying mistaken beliefs. The general principles for changing beliefs are to stay conscious of the belief and to substitute an affirmation for the belief.

There is power in positive thinking only if the thoughts are grounded in reality. Repeating a positive statement won't do a thing for you unless you really believe the affirmation. No matter how hard you work at it, you won't accept a positive untruth to the extent necessary to reprogram your behavior.

To be truly effective, a positive affirmation must be based upon truth, logic, and realism. That is why preceding exercises have emphasized finding alternative interpretations of what you had always considered to be reality. Affirmations must be based on changed perceptions of reality; they are not mindless mantras.

Exercise
Modifying Your Beliefs

This exercise is designed to help you substitute adaptive beliefs for the old beliefs that have held you back from belonging. You'll begin with habit beliefs because they are the easiest to change. Then you'll go on to your emotional belief, and finally you'll work on your definite beliefs.

Part 1: Habit Beliefs

1. Copy the beliefs that you labeled "H" in the questionnaire in the preceding exercise into your notebook on a page headed "Habit Beliefs." Leave several lines blank beneath each belief.

2. For each of these mistaken habit beliefs, compose and record a positive affirmation. The affirmation should be:

   a. Brief.

   b. Worded positively—for example, "My opinion is as valid as anyone's," not "They don't know any more than I do."

   c. Potentially believable, even though you might not believe it at the moment.

3. Say the affirmation to yourself every time that you are aware of behaving according to the old habit belief in your daily life. Tell yourself the old habit belief is not true.

4. At periodic intervals during the day, such as on the hour, repeat each affirmation to yourself. You may find it helpful at first to write them on cards or in a small notebook and carry them with

you. Another useful technique is to post cards with the affirmation written on them in places where you will see them often, such as on a mirror, the refrigerator, the dashboard of your car, inside your top desk drawer.

Keep doing steps 3 and 4 until you are free of your old habit beliefs. You can be sure this has happened when your behavior is guided by the new affirmations instead of the old mistaken beliefs. Don't wait to reach that point, however, before beginning to dispose of your emotional beliefs.

Part 2: Emotional Beliefs

To combat your mistaken emotional beliefs, look carefully for the origins of each one of them. (Reading the next chapter can help you get started if you have trouble.) Some of your emotional beliefs may have the same origin, or each may have separate origins. Whatever the case, discovering the source of a belief will allow you to relate to it on an emotional level. Once you have accomplished this, you will replace the hurtful belief with a helpful positive affirmation.

1. Copy the beliefs that you labeled "E" in the questionnaire into your notebook on a page headed "Emotional Beliefs." Leave several lines blank beneath each belief.

2. Search for the origin of each of these mistaken emotional beliefs. Again, reading the next chapter and doing additional reading can help. Record your conclusions about the origins in your notebook.

Note: If you have difficulty finding the origins of your mistaken emotional beliefs, you may want to skip over to chapters 5 and 6 where you will be instructed in the techniques of deep relaxation and self-hypnosis. These techniques can be very useful for uncovering information of this type. Once you become proficient with them, you could, for example, give yourself the following suggestion: "The origin of my mistaken belief that [state belief] will become apparent to me. I will become aware of it now, or it will come to me soon in the form of a memory, an insight, a dream, or a hunch."

3. For each of these mistaken habit beliefs, compose and record a positive affirmation. The affirmation should be:

   a. Brief.

   b. Worded positively.

   c. Potentially believable, even though you might not believe it at the moment.

4. Think of the origin of the emotional belief every time that you are aware of behaving according to the belief in your daily life. Then repeat the affirmation to yourself several times.

5. At periodic intervals during the day, such as on the hour, repeat each affirmation to yourself.

Part 3: Definite Beliefs

It will take some time to replace your negative emotional beliefs with positive ones. Keep persevering—it will happen. In the meantime, go ahead and start the assault on definite beliefs. The task of changing these mistaken beliefs will be more difficult, for you are committed to them both emotionally and intellectually. They not only feel true, they seem logical to you.

1. Copy the beliefs that you labeled "D" in the questionnaire into your notebook on a page headed "Definite Beliefs." Leave several lines blank beneath each belief.

2. Search for the origin of each of these definite beliefs the same way you went about uncovering the origins of your mistaken emotional beliefs. Record your conclusions.

3. List arguments in opposition of each belief as you did earlier for your automatic thoughts and self-talk. Think about these counterarguments and underline all that you conclude have validity. Each definite belief should have at least one valid counterargument.

4. For each of these mistaken habit beliefs, compose and record a positive affirmation. The affirmation should be:

   a. Brief.

b. Worded positively.

c. Potentially believable, even though you might not believe it at the moment.

5. Think of the origin of the definite belief every time that you are aware of behaving according to the belief in your daily life.

6. Also think of the logical counterargument, and repeat the positive affirmation to yourself several times.

7. At periodic intervals during the day, such as on the hour, repeat each affirmation to yourself.

Be Patient, Be Persistent

You will need to invest time in countering illogical thinking and overcoming mistaken beliefs. After all, you have repeated negative thoughts to yourself thousands and thousands of times over a period of many years. It will take more than a leisurely weekend to transform these deeply ingrained thought patterns. You'll need to keep repeating the new thoughts to yourself until they become second nature.

It will probably take weeks for new patterns of logical thinking to replace old patterns of irrational thought. It could take months to change very deeply held assumptions about life. Even years may not be out of the question in a few rare instances. But don't be discouraged. Think instead how this investment in time and effort will literally change your life.

From time to time, particularly when you are under stress, you will fall back into old beliefs and negative patterns of thinking. On those occasions, it is important to be honest with yourself and recognize what has happened. Label your thinking for what it is (mind reading, personalization, and so on) and think through your counterarguments for that particular type of thinking. Then spend more time than usual practicing realistic positive self-talk and repeating your affirmations.

3

Overcoming Shame

As you read the last chapter you may have been surprised by some of your thoughts and beliefs, particularly those you have about yourself. You have lived with these ideas for a long time and you must have been aware of them to some extent. All the same, it may have been disturbing to face head on how negative a picture you have of yourself and the world around you. If this was the case for you, shame may be a barrier between you and other people. It may be thwarting your efforts to belong.

This chapter focuses on shame, because shame leads to self-defeating thoughts, including a compulsion to withdraw and hide. Shame has a major impact on the way you feel about yourself—on your self-esteem. If you feel you must conceal yourself from other people you cannot belong. And you cannot belong if you don't feel worthy of belonging.

If you discover from reading this chapter that you are affected by shame and thus low self-esteem, I suggest that you read further in this area. (See the references section at the end of the book.)

The Effects of Shame

Shame, to one degree or another, is at the root of low self-esteem. Althought it is similar to guilt, shame is deeper and more tenacious. Guilty people feel bad about something they have done; shamed people feel bad for who they are. They feel that something is inherently wrong with them. As will be discussed shortly, shame has many origins—some in childhood and some in adulthood. The effects can be relatively slight, or they can be nearly crippling. It takes more than willpower to dispel shame, the most personally painful of emotions. Yet it can be overcome, given enough positive, healing experiences. And with commitment and hard work, it is in your power to create those experiences for yourself.

Avoidance and Social Deficiency

When shame originates in early childhood, avoidance tends to become a way of life: Avoidance prevents the child from having many social experiences; social skills cannot develop without social experiences; and social experiences are unlikely to be successful without social skills, which encourages further avoidance. Thus a downward spiral soon evolves. The most detrimental effect of this spiral is an enduring inability to acquire intimacy with other people. When relationships do form, they tend to be superficial.

I saw this firsthand in a middle-aged man whose parents escaped from communist Poland in the 1950s. They had immigrated to the United States when my client, Max, was a very young child. He had no memory of his parents' dramatic and courageous flight. If he had been able to remember, he might have felt pride in his parents instead of shame.

For reasons they couldn't control, Max's parents settled in a small city in a region with very few immigrants. A combination of a habit of distrust, a lack of facility with the English language, and the fact that they were Catholics in a Protestant neighborhood kept the family isolated. The parents also likely suffered deeply as a result of the losses of home, family, and friends they had endured, and possibly also from the long-term effects of overwhelming stress. In any event, they never adjusted to their new country.

Max grew up ashamed of his reclusive parents, and that shame gradually extended to himself. Over the years it was reinforced by the severe teasing of other children and the disdain of biased adults. He grew up avoiding his peers when he could and continued the habit into adulthood. He chose a vocation where he worked alone. He had elected not to have children, and he was reluctant to join any organizations. Yet eventually Max came to realize what he was missing and to wish that he could connect with others. This desire and the realization that the few relationships he had were all shallow brought him to therapy.

When I first saw Max, I was astonished at his lack of social skills. Having a conversation with him was like carrying on two parallel monologues, because he had never learned the give-and-take of verbal exchange. Instead of responding to another person's comments, he would remain silent for a few moments and then continue his soliloquy as if the other person had never spoken.

Max needed to acquire the simple social skills that most children absorb from parents, peers, and other significant adults. Reaching this objective in therapy was a major step toward his larger goal of acquiring self-respect and abolishing the self-hatred that had resulted from shame.

Self-Hatred and Projection

As stated above, there are degrees of shame. Shame always affects the bearer, but to a greater or lesser extent depending upon how shameful he or she feels. When it is severe, shame can be devastating. Severely shamed people "project" their own feelings onto other people on the invalid assumption that we all think and see things the same way. Since they despise themselves, they cannot believe that others don't detest them as well. Thus their self-denigration is so great that they find it impossible to accept respect and affection from others. Once again, the net result is avoidance of close relationships.

Renee, for example, could not accept affection from her husband, love from her children, friendship from old acquaintances, or even approval from her coworkers. Although she pretended to accept their regard, inside she actually rejected closeness or positive regard from everyone. During adolescence and early adulthood her shame was covered by a gauze-thin layer of bluster and exaggerated competence. By middle age Renee was unable to keep up the front. She avoided people more and more until she became unable to leave the house. At that point her husband insisted that she seek help.

Within a short time of beginning therapy Renee was able to discuss the deep shame she felt. It took considerably more time, however, to unravel the source of that shame, because it was associated with a forbidden topic. Despite the immense impact it had had on her family, for more than 35 years no one had mentioned the death of Renee's sister, Debbie.

Debbie had died when Renee was 10 years old, on Christmas Day. Despite emergency medical care and hospitalization, she had succumbed within hours to an asthma attack. Throughout the years since the death, Renee had suppressed an unacknowledged but deeply held belief that she was responsible for her sister's death.

The two girls had argued on Christmas Eve about whether or not to open a couple of presents. It was the family's custom to wait until Christmas morning to unwrap gifts, but the younger sister, Debbie, just couldn't resist. Over Renee's protests, she had torn open a package when her parents weren't around, which lead to a major altercation between the sisters. Renee was furious, and told Debbie that she wished she would die. Less than 24 hours later, Debbie was indeed dead.

Added to Renee's guilt over what she had said were the reactions of her parents. Renee was certain that her father felt responsible himself for Debbie's death, for not getting Debbie to the hospital sooner. His reaction (or Renee's perception of it) supported her belief that Debbie's death had been preventable. And since she believed she had caused the death, she also believed she had caused her father's anguish.

Even more damning for Renee, her mother, who was devoutly fundamental in her religious convictions, believed a sin "in your heart" to be as unacceptable as a sinful act. To her, thoughts were the same as behavior. Throughout her childhood Renee was told to "keep your thoughts pure" and warned that sinful thoughts had dire consequences. Thus, to her, wishing Debbie dead was the same as killing her.

Although Renee buried the belief that she "murdered" her sister, the abhorrent conclusion did not disappear. It affected her profoundly and daily. The shame of killing her little sister and her parents' beloved daughter destroyed any respect or love she had for herself and in turn her ability to accept respect and love from others.

Over time, Renee had found it impossible not only to become close to people emotionally, but even to meet and converse with them. This grievously shamed woman grew to believe that others saw her in the same light that she saw herself—a horribly sinful woman unworthy of attention or affection. It took a long time for Renee to revise her understanding of the past and begin to overcome her shame.

Self-Sabotage and Loneliness

Isolation is one of the consequences of serious shame. How can you belong when your instinct is to fade into the woodwork? If you are a deeply shamed person, you cannot will yourself to approach people for friendship. Although you might be successful in the short term, you can't keep up the act indefinitely. To overcome loneliness, you must first break though the barrier of shame.

Although shame originates in many ways, it is always perpetuated in much the same way. Self-deprecating and self-condemning attitudes, as well as negative self-talk, reinforce the shame. Harsh judgments like the following become part of shamed people's automatic thoughts:

- I never get anything right.
- Of course nobody loves me.
- I'm dumb and stupid.
- Who would ever listen to me?

Just as similar kinds of illogical thinking can reinforce fears (as discussed in chapter 2), this kind of self-defeating thought pattern leads to self-loathing and ultimately to self-sabotaging behavior. How can a person possibly succeed in anything with such ruinous thinking?

For example, Connie was a hard-working secretary who was appreciated by her supervisor and admired by her associates. Everyone could count on Connie, not only to do her work, but to take up the slack for others in the office. Although she enjoyed her work, she had the nagging feeling that it was interfering with other aspects of her life.

Connie was aware that she turned down too many invitations for lunch and worked too many weekends because of the demands of her job. She was aware that working made her feel good, while social invitations made her apprehensive. It was not obvious to her, however, that her penchant for work had sabotaged her social life.

It was only after much self-analysis that Connie realized that she was playing the same nose-to-the-grindstone role that she had played throughout her school years. She began to see how she had always told herself that she was "a hard worker but not very good with people." In fact, she could almost hear her mother's voice saying the same thing about her to her grandmother and other significant people in her life.

Like Connie, Ashley was responsible for subverting her own social life, and, like Connie's, Ashley's self-defeating behavior stemmed from harmful automatic thoughts. Although Ashley did not have a diagnosable eating disorder, she had been overweight as a child and was preoccupied with her weight as an adult.

Anytime Ashley felt overweight, which was most of the time, she was haunted by brief but powerful images of being unattractive and rejected. These cognitive flashes quickly ignited negative emotions, mostly shame, which caused Ashley to withdraw.

All of us can be self-critical at times. Sometimes it is justified, and even useful—in small doses it may motivate us to make positive changes. In large doses, however, it numbs and paralyzes. Think of shame as a continuum; below a certain point it may be helpful, but the further it is above that point the more detrimental it is. The following exercise will help you evaluate whether shame is keeping you from belonging.

Exercise
Calculating Your Shame Quotient

Instructions: Using the scale below, score how much of the time each statement is true for you. When you have responded to all the statements, multiply the score for each one by the indicated correction factor and record the corrected score. Then add up all your corrected scores to determine your shame quotient. A scoring key appears at the end of the exercise.

Belief Scale

0 = Never   **1** = Sometimes
2 = About half the time   **3** = Often   **4** = Always

	Score	Correction Factor	Corrected Score
1. I blush when someone speaks to me unexpectedly.	____	x 3 =	____
2. I blush when I am meeting a stranger or talking to someone I don't know well.	____	x 2 =	____
3. I blush when I talk in front of a group.	____	x 1 =	____
4. I can feel my heart pounding when someone speaks to me unexpectedly.	____	x 3 =	____
5. I can feel my heart pounding when I am meeting a stranger or talking to someone I don't know well.	____	x 2 =	____
6. I can feel my heart pounding when I talk in front of a group.	____	x 1 =	____
7. I feel as if I am a child when I meet a stranger or talk to someone I don't know well.	____	x 2 =	____
8. I have a desire to be somewhere else or to be invisible when I have to meet someone I don't know.	____	x 1 =	____

	Score	Correction Factor	Corrected Score
9. I avoid acquaintances when I can, so I will cross the street or move to another aisle in a store to hide from them.	____	x 2 =	____
10. I have thoughts about being ashamed, humiliated, or embarrassed.	____	x 1 =	____
11. I think about being weak, unable to defend myself, or unable to take care of myself.	____	x 1 =	____
12. I feel I am worthless or a failure.	____	x 3 =	____
13. I feel I am pitiful.	____	x 2 =	____
14. I feel I am disgusting, filthy, dirty, or soiled.	____	x 2 =	____
15. I feel I deserve punishment.	____	x 1 =	____
16. I feel I deserve criticism or disapproval.	____	x 1 =	____
17. I feel I am bad or awful.	____	x 2 =	____
18. I feel I have a basic flaw in my personalityor character that makes me contemptible.	____	x 2 =	____
19. I feel I am unwanted or unloved.	____	x 3 =	____
20. I feel uncomfortable when I receive praise or recognition.	____	x 1 =	____
21. I reject praise or compliments.	____	x 2 =	____
22. I attribute good things in my life to luck, divine intervention, or the actions of other people, rather than to my efforts or talent.	____	x 1 =	____
23. I believe that people who admire me don't really know me.	____	x 1 =	____
24. I prefer to be alone.	____	x 2 =	____
25. Although I smile and go through the motions of being social, it is pretense.	____	x 1 =	____

	Correction	Corrected
	Score Factor	Score

26. I feel awful when I make a
    mistake.   ____ x 1 =   ____

27. I feel ashamed of one or more sig-
    nificant people in my life (spouse,
    parent, child, lover. etc.).   ____ x 1 =   ____

28. Although I manage to make eye con-
    tact when I am speaking to people, I
    feel uncomfortable doing so.   ____ x 1 =   ____

29. I avoid eye contact when speaking
    to people.   ____ x 2 =   ____

30. I feel that I cannot connect with other
    people emotionally.   ____ x 3 =   ____

31. I try to stay out of sight when I am at
    a social gathering.   ____ x 3 =   ____

32. I criticize other people.   ____ x 1 =   ____

33. I become enraged when I feel slighted. ____ x 2 =   ____

34. I become enraged when I believe I
    have been treated unjustly.   ____ x 1 =   ____

35. I feel I am a serious problem to a
    significant person or persons in my
    life.   ____ x 2 =   ____

36. I act as if I am a perfectionist.   ____ x 1 =   ____

37. I want to call attention to myself.   ____ x 1 =   ____

38. I act outrageously because I don't
    care what people think.   ____ x 2 =   ____

39. I am afraid that I will be abandoned
    by a significant person or persons in
    my life.   ____ x 3 =   ____

40. I try to be whatever or whoever
    other people want me to be.   ____ x 2 =   ____

41. I try to please other people even
    when it may be detrimental to me or
    not in my best interests.   ____ x 1 =   ____

	Correction	Corrected
Score	**Factor**	**Score**

42. I am neglectful of my physical needs in that I don't eat a balanced diet, don't exercise properly, don't take proper care of hygiene, don't see a physician when I should, or don't comply with doctor's orders.   ____ x 1 = ____

43. I am neglectful of my appearance.   ____ x 1 = ____

44. I am self-abusive in that I actually try to hurt myself physically, such as by cutting or burning my arm.   ____ x 3 = ____

45. I get into trouble or harm myself because I forget to do important things, such as taking medication, meeting deadlines, or keeping professional or social appointments.   ____ x 2 = ____

46. I take great pains with my appearance.   ____ x 1 = ____

47. I feel self-conscious when I am with a group of people.   ____ x 1 = ____

48. I feel self-conscious in one-on-one conversations.   ____ x 2 = ____

49. I worry about doing the wrong thing when I am with other people.   ____ x 1 = ____

50. I believe that other people are aware of my flaws.   ____ x 1 = ____

51. When things go wrong, I believe that it is my fault.   ____ x 1 = ____

52. I have difficulty saying no, even to unreasonable requests.   ____ x 1 = ____

53. I don't like to ask for help or to take any assistance.   ____ x 1 = ____

54. I am concerned about being selfish or self-centered.   ____ x 1 = ____

	Correction	Corrected
	Score Factor	Score

55. I worry about what people think of
    me.   ___ x 1 =   _____

                                                          =====

      Shame Quotient (total of corrected scores)   =   _____

Key

Shame Quotient	Interpretation
50 or below	Shame is not a problem for you.
51 to 100	Shame may be a minor problem for you, but it probably won't interfere with your following the procedures in this book.
101 to 175	Shame is probably interfering with your social relationships, and you need to work on increasing your self-esteem in addition to completing the other suggestions in this book.
176 to 275	Shame is a problem for you. You may be able to overcome the effects of shame on your own by following the procedures in this chapter and using other resources, such as those listed at the end of the chapter. You may also want to seek professional advice about the possibility of entering therapy.
276 and above	Shame is having major detrimental effects on your life. It is important that you take any steps available for you to repair your self-esteem, including consulting with a mental health professional about therapy.

The Origins of Shame

Unrealistic Expectations

American culture's emphasis on competition and success is a two-edged sword. On the one side it motivates people to excel, but when people fall short (and we all do sometimes) it can demoralize. Competing means that we compare ourselves with our peers, and when we feel we don't measure up, we tend to think something is wrong with us.

In fact, if you set your standards high enough, you can never measure up. I have encountered people who no matter what their accomplishments were still ashamed. They were ashamed of graduating from a state college, ashamed of living in an older neighborehood, ashamed of being a middle manager, ashamed of driving an American car, ashamed of having working class parents, ashamed they didn't belong to a mainstream church, ashamed that their bright, healthy sons didn't make the football team. The list goes on and on.

As a culture, we often value appearance over substance. On television and in magazines and movies, beautiful slim people hop in and out of the beds of other beautiful slim people. Perfection seems to be the norm. With few exceptions, heroes, lovers, victors, even sometimes villains, are flawless looking. To compare yourself to such paragons, you need a pretty solid self-image. Otherwise a little girth or cellulite, a balding head, a few wrinkles here and there, a largish nose or a smallish chin will leave you feeling ashamed.

Some people feel shame over illicit sex, but at least as many these days are ashamed because, "Everyone is doing it except me!" And, at least in the popular media, everyone does seem to be doing it, though that may not be true in real life. One of my adolescent clients, an abashed virgin at 17, told me that he felt disheartened every time he went to the movies because, "Everybody makes it on the first date, and I can't make it at all." He had a good laugh, though, when he anonymously reported the most outrageous sexual behavior on a national survey he participated in at school. He said that all of his friends did the same thing.

Married couples feel they need to measure up to the sexual performances portrayed in movies or reported on the talk shows. When I first entered practice, a husband or wife might feel ashamed because he or she wanted oral sex; now it's when they don't. Husbands worry if they don't want sex, no matter how tired or anxious they happen to be. And wives worry if their men aren't instantly turned on by them.

Many people feel out of step with what they believe to be the cultural norms. People unsure of themselves pay too much attention to surveys of questionable validity and reports of "true confessions." Vulnerable people tend to compare themselves with popular portrayals of happy and successful people. They don't stop to consider that the characters on the screen are products of someone's imagination, nor do they question whether the rich and famous are truly happy or fulfilled.

Media myths exist about other aspects of life as well. Houses and apartments, regardless of the occupant's supposed income, are large, airy, and stylish. Work is almost always glamorous and exciting, whereas in reality any job entails a good deal that is routine and eventually dull. Mothers work long hours as highly paid executives, come home to feed, bathe, and cuddle with their angelic children, and then have the time and energy to slip into something slinky for Daddy when he arrives.

It takes a certain amount of courage to buck these images. Not only do they seemingly come at us from every side in the media, but often friends, bosses, coworkers, and family accept the myths as well, and are just as desperately trying to measure. To continue to judge yourself by such unrealistic standards, however, is to perpetuate your isolation. The first step toward being accepted by others is to accept yourself.

Race, Religion, and So On

Although as a society we have moved a long way from much of the racism and other biases seen during most of our history, prejudices remain. The messages may be more subtle than previously, but they are still there for old people, poor people, fat people, unattractive people, people of color, people with chronic illnesses, recent immigrants, mentally ill people, homosexuals, and others. It takes a strong ego to withstand an onslaught of cultural bias. On the other hand, a sure recipe for shame is to combine doubts about yourself as a person with a conviction that you belong to an inferior group.

Regardless of the best of intentions, religion can foster shame. Being told repeatedly, for instance, that your feelings are sinful can make a person feel defective. Some churches go further; shame can almost be a prerequisite for membership. I remember particularly one woman who had "fallen from grace" in an extramarital affair. She wanted nothing more than to return to her family. But though her husband wanted her to come back as well, the disgrace heaped upon her by her fundamentalist church made that ultimately impossible. The couple's lives were too deeply intertwined with the church to leave it, yet she could not abide the scorn she felt from the holier-than-thou congregation and pastor. Finally, shame and the "punishment" of herpes drove her to leave both home and church.

As with the expectations of the larger society, it may be necessary for you to examine, question, and even change some of the beliefs your membership in a group or religion may have given rise to in order to repair damage to your self-esteem.

Residues of Childhood

Shame has many sources—some subtle, others conspicuous. Some events that cause shame occur during the critical first few years of life, when personality is being formed. Other shaming events, as you have seen, occur later in life. Although shame from those later experiences can obstruct the development of relationships, it is the shame that originates in early childhood that is the most persistent and damaging.

> "If my own family doesn't love me, I must not deserve to be loved."

> "How can I please anybody when I can never please the people who are supposed to love me?"

> "Something must be wrong with a child whose father walks out and never bothers to get in touch."

> "I must not deserve anybody's attention and affection because my mother never had time for me but she doted on my sister."

These are the kinds of messages that can become deeply embedded in a child's mind and lead to unremitting shame. Quite often the messages stem from misunderstanding. Because children need to see their parents as wise and powerful, and lack the experience to do otherwise, they see only the flaws in themselves. And, all too often, their flaws and mistakes are what parents and other adults focus on.

Blaming themselves for their parents' behavior can also give children a sense of power over a chaotic situation. They know they have a chance of changing themselves, and they know they cannot change the omnipotent adults in their lives. So, if they accept the blame and try to change, maybe they can make a hurtful situation more tolerable. Feeling they are at fault, then, can give children some hope of control. Like most people, children dislike being helpless. Believing they are defective is much better than believing they are helpless.

Thus, children in dysfunctional families often want to believe that the problems are their fault. Daddy drinks because of their bad grades. Mommy hits them because of their bad behavior. Well, they can work real hard and make good grades and be on their best behavior, and then everything will be okay. The sad fact is that little changes, no matter what they do.

In time, a child who has grown up in such a family may banish all conscious thoughts about his or her defects, but the impression of being somehow deficient or tainted remains. If the impression is strong enough, the child grows up feeling ashamed, without necessarily knowing why.

Following are examples of how shame evolves in childhood. There are, of course, other paths to shame, but these examples are representative. They illustrate the powerful impact of early childhood experiences on our perception of ourselves as adults. The seeds for your negative thoughts about yourself may have been planted in your early life, just as they were for Alberto, Sibyl, Toby, and the others you'll read about here. See if you recognize your personal experiences in any of these examples.

The Scapegoat

Alberto was well into his middle years before he pinpointed the source of his shame. He was "the big, dumb kid in the family" who grew up feeling "conspicuous and stupid." Alberto was the lightning rod who drew the ire of his mother. No matter which of the three children in the family was at fault, Alberto always ended up taking the heat.

For most of his life Alberto thought that the fault lay in his clumsiness and stupidity. It was only after he learned to put aside self-blame that he saw that his only offense was his appearance. He looked like his father—the hated husband who had deserted his mother when she was eight months pregnant. He was big and large featured, not at all like his delicately handsome, compactly built half-brothers.

Alberto doubted that his mother realized that she had made him into the family scapegoat. It was only when she was enraged, which was rare, that she compared Alberto to his wretched father. More often, she simply called him clumsy and stupid, and the rest of the family followed her lead. As a consequence, Alberto grew up ashamed of himself and emotionally estranged from the people he should have been closest to.

The Abused Child

I quickly learned that praise evoked angry denials from Sibyl. She could not believe that any compliment directed toward her could possibly be sincere. Sibyl had been sexually abused over a long period of time by her stepfather and for a lesser period of time by an older stepbrother. Grievously shamed, she expected me, her therapist, to hold her in the same contempt that she felt for herself and was certain her family felt for her.

Sibyl came to me because she was on the verge of sabotaging herself once more. She had recently been promoted to a responsible new job, and she felt terrible anxiety as a result. She felt as if she were an impostor who was sure to be exposed to the world at any moment. An experienced graphic artist, she had risen to a management position with a publishing firm purely through talent and hard work—shame, distrust, and fear kept her from networking or forming relationships with colleagues.

The basic message Sibyl had carried through life was, "I must truly be defiled and defective to have been treated so badly by my father and brother and unprotected by my mother." Sibyl had absorbed the blame for the transgressions of her family. Despite a strong desire to bond, she described herself as not deserving friendship, and indeed she came to therapy completely friendless.

The Child of Alcoholics

Referred for therapy by his employer, Toby believed treatment to be a condition for keeping his job. Although he had not been told exactly why he had been sent to me, he assumed it was related to outbursts of temper with coworkers. Toby's most obvious problem was indeed with anger, but he had a number of others, all related to growing up in a home with two alcoholic parents. Toby was a lonely, 36-year-old bachelor who seemed to alienate everyone with whom he tried to connect.

Toby, an only child, was never abused by his well-to-do parents, nor were his physical needs ever neglected. Reared by a succession of maids and sitters who cared little about him, Toby was largely ignored by his parents. They were either out of the home traveling or going to parties or they were "out" at home from abusing alcohol.

Toby could remember spending only a handful of evenings alone with his parents. He couldn't recall either parent staying with him more than an hour or so on his birthdays. He remembered the family being together on Christmas mornings and Thanksgiving dinners, but his mother and father were unavailable to him emotionally once they had begun on their Bloody Marys.

As an adult, Toby harbored intense anger, anger which was rarely directed at its true object, his parents. Instead, innocent bystanders—shopkeepers, waiters, subordinates—bore the brunt of it. But he only got into trouble when he began to lose it with business associates and people with a degree of power over him.

Perhaps more destructive for him personally, Toby truly believed that he was worthless. Although he managed to hide his shame from himself much of the time, it nevertheless had a profound effect on his emotions and behavior. How could he belong when he was worthless? He only felt comfortable on the periphery, never as part of any group.

The Guilty Child

Madolyn was the child of "progressive" parents who were proud that they never used physical punishment and rarely raised their voices with their children. But, oh how they could lay on the guilt trips! Lectures and finger pointing were their stock in trade.

A bit of guilt here and there wouldn't have been a problem. In fact, used correctly and sparingly, guilt can be a healthy motivator. But Madolyn's sole punishment was guilt. She was made to feel guilty about almost anything that went wrong throughout her childhood and adolescence. As a result, she felt consumed by guilt as an adult. She was ready to accept the blame for almost anything.

Guilt in such large doses breeds shame, and shame leads to withdrawal, which is what happened to Madolyn. Although she was cheerful and friendly on the surface, she never allowed herself to attach deeply. She was certain that any serious overtures toward others would be rejected because she was such a bad person, so she led a solitary, lonely life.

The "Different" Child

You don't have to grow up in a dysfunctional family, as Madolyn, Toby, Sybil, and Alberto did, to feel the effects of shame. Martin, a 19-year-old having trouble adjusting to college, was from a large, affectionate family. He felt accepted and loved by his parents and siblings, but he wasn't so sure that people outside his family were so accepting.

Martin always felt a little apart from his brothers and peers. Unlike his family and the other kids at school, his interests ran more to acting, drawing, and playing piano than to team sports, cars, and country-western—not that he didn't try to be like everyone else. To their credit, his family was rather proud that he was "brainy," and planned early for his education. They encouraged him to participate in the usual pursuits of males from a small town in the middle South, but they never pushed him to do so and they never ridiculed him when he didn't.

Unfortunately Martin ran into a teacher in his elementary years who tormented him with shame. Martin never realized that he was "effeminate" until he was assigned to her fifth grade classroom. He said that the most humiliating incident of his life occurred when she shouted to him down a flight of steps crowded with children, "Why don't you just wear a dress to school tomorrow!"

Years later, Martin remembered that incident as the turning point when he began withdrawing from other children. He vividly recalled the other children sniggering at him. He was never comfortable around other kids after that, and he was much too ashamed to tell his parents.

Shame-Spawning Relationships

Abusive relationships breed a shame that slowly disintegrates pride and self-respect. Such abuse can be physical blows, verbal jabs, or "just" constant disparagement, and the abuse can come from a critical parent, a bullying supervisor, or a carping spouse. Whatever the source, abuse leads to shame.

Abusers beat down their victims, physically or verbally, usually with the objective of gaining power over them. After a while—often a very short while—the humilation of the beating, the ridicule, the criticism, takes its toll: The victim begins to believe the picture the abuser is painting of things. Eventually, the victim comes to believe that he or she deserves or is otherwise *causing* the abuse.

At this point, the abuser has gained the power he or she sought. The victim is simultaneously responsible for and helpless to prevent further abuse, because any situation's outcome is up to the abuser. If the victim begins to feel worthless, as abuse victims often do, he or she may be unable to imagine a life other than the abusive relationship.

Fear of loneliness may also then play a part. Shame cuts the victim off from other people, so he or she is all the more dependent upon the abuser for companionship. The victim grows to feel that he or she belongs only in that relationship and cannot find the strength to look elsewhere. The relationship seems preferable to none at all, which seems to be the alternative.

Abusers are sometimes immature people who vent the anger that arises from stress in a destructive way. Sometimes they have grown up in a shaming home, and consequently know no other way to relate to another person intimately. Abusers are often unaware of being abusive. For instance, they may simply be attempting to pull others down to their own level of inferiority so that they can hold on, fearing that their loved ones will leave unless they too feel insignificant and contemptible.

Healthy people sometimes get into abusive relationships with spouses, lovers, or bosses unwittingly. They may then find themselves stuck there for a variety of reasons. Sometimes they are optimistic, trusting people who genuinely believe that the abuser will change. Sometimes they are misguided, believing it best for the children or their careers to stay in the situation. Sometimes they become financially dependent. Given enough time and mistreatment, however, and they are no longer healthy. They begin to believe that they deserve what they get.

People who grow up in shaming households may unconsciously seek out shaming partners. They may feel more comfortable with the familiar, or they may feel so defective that they don't believe they can or should do better. If they aren't there already, they soon find themselves on a downward spiral of believing that punishment is their due.

Few people want to believe they are in shaming relationships. First it means letting go of the illusions that have enabled them to make it from one day to the next. It can affect the way they see themselves, and their loved ones, negatively. It can also mean changing their lives substantially—home, work, economic status, marital status, social and family ties. It doesn't take much imagination to see how difficult it will be to unravel themselves from relationships, so they deny, overlook, excuse, accept blame, and hold onto false hope.

Ultimately, none of these strategies works. Abusive relationships don't get better by themselves. Like many illnesses, treatment is needed to promote healing. And the first step to treatment is diagnosis. The following exercise will help you decide if you are being shamed in a relationship. Be honest with yourself as you respond to the questions; left "undiagnosed" a shaming relationship can be a major obstacle to your belonging.

Exercise
Are You in a Shaming Relationship?

Instructions: Answer the following questions by placing a check mark under "Yes" or "No." When you have answered all the questions, refer to the key that appears at the end of the questionnaire.

	Yes	No
1. Does a significant person in your life (such as spouse, parent, adult child, sibling, or supervisor) criticize you often?	___	___
2. Are you in a relationship in which you feel respect is lacking?	___	___
3. Do you find yourself criticizing someone in your life often?	___	___
4. Do insults or "putdowns" seem normal to you?	___	___
5. Do you put someone down consistently under the guise of humor?	___	___
6. Is it difficult for you to imagine a relationship characterized by mutual respect and dignity?	___	___
7. Do you feel that a significant person in your life is trying to make himself or herself feel superior at your expense?	___	___
8. Does a significant person frequently question your judgment, intelligence, or common sense?	___	___
9. Are you screamed at often?	___	___
10. Do you feel that you have to scream to get your point across?	___	___
11. Does a particular person harangue or lecture you frequently on your shortcomings?	___	___
12. Do you have difficulty refraining from telling someone of their failings?	___	___
13. Does someone hit, shove, or otherwise hurt you physically?	___	___

	Yes	No

14. Do you hit, shove, or otherwise hurt someone physically because they make you so angry that you can't help yourself or because you think they deserve it or it will help them? ___ ___

15. Do you feel weak, vulnerable, or like a child when you are around one particular person? ___ ___

16. Do you usually feel capable and worthy whenever you are not around a particular person? ___ ___

17. Do you believe that a significant person ignores you either in public or in private? ___ ___

18. Do you have the impression that a significant person is ashamed of your appearance, manners, education, intelligence, or family background? ___ ___

19. Does a significant person keep secrets from you or refuse to share important events in his or her life with you? ___ ___

20. Do you frequently get annoyed looks and weary sighs from a significant person? ___ ___

21. Do you often feel publicly humiliated by a significant person? ___ ___

22. Does a significant person complain about your behavior or traits to friends or relatives? ___ ___

23. Are you frequently interrupted by a particular person while you are talking? ___ ___

24. Do you and a significant person quarrel frequently? ___ ___

25. Do you feel hurt more often than not after a conversation with a significant person? ___ ___

26. Does anyone routinely curse or swear at you? ___ ___

27. Are you only touched for punishment or sex by a significant person? ___ ___

Yes   No

28. Are you often told by someone to get lost,
    leave home, disappear, or die?   ___   ___

29. Are your choices and taste frequently
    questioned by a significant person?   ___   ___

30. Do you want to get out of a relationship but
    feel unable or incapable of doing so?   ___   ___

Key

"Yes" answers warn of shaming actions. The more questions you answered affirmatively, the more likely you are in a harmful shaming relationship.

If you found that you are or have been in a shaming relationship, the next exercise will help you examine how you acquired shame from that source. Even if you have not been in a shaming relationship, the following exercise will help you think about the possible sources of shame in your life in preparation for neutralizing your shame.

If you are currently in a shaming relationship, a section toward the end of this chapter offers some possible solutions for confronting and repairing the relationship, although seeking additional help outside of this book will probably also be needed.

Exercise
Identifying Sources of Shame

Using what you have learned from the reading and exercises you have done so far in this chapter, in your notebook or in a separate journal, write about any sources of shame you have identified. For example, if you had a boss who reprimanded you in front of others, write down what you remember about the incident: the setting, who was there, what was said, how you felt. If you have identified several sources describe each of them the same way.

If the source of your shame goes back to a recurring pattern in childhood, if you are or were in a long-term relationship that was shaming, or if your self-esteem is such that it has caused you to experience a series of similar or related sources of shame, it may take several days, weeks, or even longer to uncover all the sources.

It will likely be painful to confront those memories, but I urge you to stick with it. The value of this exercise is in part simply in acknowledging your feelings and in part in realizing that those feelings did not spring from nowhere—nor do they reflect an objective truth. Rather, feelings of shame are a *reaction* to circumstances or events. While you cannot always control events (certainly not those in the past), you can learn to control your reactions to them.

Antidotes to Shame

Overcoming feelings of shame can, indeed must, be accomplished using a variety of strategies. Your goal in reading this book—connecting with people and making friends—is one antidote to shame. Belonging erodes shame because acceptance by other people restores self-respect and pride. If your shame has been severe, however, you may first need to seek that kind of acceptance by consulting a therapist. Deeply shamed people require a safe haven, such as that provided by therapy, to overcome their fears of rejection and ill-treatment.

Unless you have been greviously abused, you will probably be able to dispel your shame on your own. The remaining exercises in this chapter, along with other reading or work you choose to do to build self-esteem, will help you begin to break through the shame barrier enough to begin connecting with other people. Once that happens, the process of healing gains momentum. It occurs easily and naturally as you begin to feel appreciated and valued for being the person you are.

Forcing Out Shame

Shame won't simply fade away. It must be pushed aside by positive feelings, such as those of dignity and self-worth, and by recognition of your accomplishments. Your first task, then, is to learn that taking pride in yourself is a good thing; it is not conceit. Modesty has its place—but not false modesty and not self-denigration. There is wisdom in the biblical admonition not to hide your light under a bushel.

Everyone has things he or she can be proud of, but often we take these things for granted, focusing instead on where we fall short of our goals or expectations. In one sense, this is what keeps us going from day to day, the quest to attain, achieve, grow. In another sense, it often keeps us from appreciating where we are today, what we have accomplished and learned, the people we have become. Think of it this way: Say your goal is to amass a million dollars. So far, you only have half a million. You can tell yourself you're a failure because you haven't collected the whole million, or you can say, "Well great, I'm halfway there, and if I got one half I should be able to get the other."

The following exercise will help you examine your achievements and positive qualities. For the exercise to be effective, you will need try to view yourself in a positive light, which may be no easy task if you are accustomed to viewing yourself through the negative lens of shame. If viewing yourself positively seems impossible, make a committment to being objective. No one is all good or all bad, so it stands to reason that you must have positive traits. Try to see yourself as an impartial observer would.

Exercise
Examining Your Positive Qualities

Put guilt and modesty aside and be objective about the positive aspects of your personality and behavior. Head a new page in your notebook "My Positive Traits," and use it to list your skills, your accomplishments, your admirable attributes. Push any negative judgments out of your mind while you complete this exercise. You can always come back to them later, if you feel you need to, but for now they are irrelevant.

1. List the things you are good at, such as gardening, working on the car, sewing, managing money, cooking, playing a musical instrument, fixing things around the house, painting, writing, dancing—whatever you do well and enjoy doing.

2. List what you do well in your daily work—job, homemaking, school, volunteering, and so on. Write down all the skills, abilities, character traits, experience, and strengths you have that combine to make you good at what you do.

3. Consider yourself in relation to the other people in your life, including strangers. What positive traits do you have as a friend, child, spouse, sibling, patron? This can include compassion, fairness, listening skills, firmness, generosity, affection, respect—whatever you bring to a relationship that makes it work better.

Here's an example of how one person completed the exercise:

My Positive Traits

1. I'm good at taking care of houseplants, fixing small appliances, baking, crocheting, watercolor painting. I walk the dog twice every day and give him a really good workout. I keep myself in pretty good shape that way too, so I look okay for an "old lady."

2. I'm very patient with small children, and help them figure out what books they need. And I try to be patient with the bigger ones too, even when they are rude. I know the library really well after all these years, and I know where to send people for things we don't have. I'm helpful and polite. I try to be very careful to say clearly what I mean.

3. I'm faithful. Before Mother died, I visited her every weekend. I've kept in touch with my friends from college whenever I could. Even though Judy and I don't always get along, I try to see her side of things and be objective. I'm respectful of the people I work with. I always try to give them the benefit of the doubt when they've made a mistake.

If you found yourself having difficulty identifying your positive traits in doing this exercise, pretend that the person you are considering is not you, but someone who simply has the same qualities as you. Give this other person a name. Then imagine this mythical person going through your daily routine. Head a new page in your notebook with the mythical person's name, and do the exercise again.

When you have finished doing the exercise for this alter ego, compare the responses you came up with for yourself and for the mythical other. This can can give you insight into how you apply harsher, more stringent standards to yourself than you do to other people.

This exercise can be ongoing. Continue to add to your list as new abilities, strengths, and positive traits occur to you over the next several days or weeks. You may be surprised how many positive qualities you can find in yourself when you look for them.

It can help to remind yourself of your positive traits when you find yourself in stressful situations. Choose a few of your most positive traits and add them to the affirmations you keep handy.

Exercise
Building a Positive Self-Image

Once you have recognized and recorded a number of your strengths and abilities, you can use your knowledge to begin to build a more positive image of yourself. This is an exercise you can do every day to increase your self-esteem and thereby overcome shame.

1. First thing in the morning, select three items from your list. It doesn't matter which three, so just start at the top on the first day. The next day, select items 4 through 6, and so on.

2. When you have time during the day (in the shower, driving to work, on your lunch break, while fixing dinner, before you fall asleep) recall a specific incident from your past in which you demonstrated the strength or attribute. Take the time to relive the memory in detail.

3. If the incident involved someone paying you a compliment or otherwise acknowledging your worth, and at the time you were unable to accept the praise, this time listen to what the person says without rejecting it. Imagine that you simply smiled modestly and accepted the compliment with a gracious "Thank you" or "It was my pleasure."

The goal here is to learn to *believe* in your positive qualities and integrate them into your self-image. Keep doing this exercise on a daily basis until you have gone through your entire list at least once—including those qualities you add along the way. If you like, once you've completed the list once, you can start over at the beginning.

Removing the Underpinnings of Shame

In the preceding exercises you have been pushing aside shame by replacing it with a more positive image of yourself. You now need to go a step further and probe the mistaken beliefs and illogical self-talk that support your shame. Distorted thinking is a result of shame, but it also reinforces shame by keeping you convinced that the shame is deserved. Thus, illogical thinking must be transformed into logical thinking before shame can be abolished.

The following two exercises build on work you began in the last chapter toward changing your damaging self-talk and beliefs.

Exercise
Changing Self-Talk

You have already laid the foundation for changing your thoughts by completing the exercises in chapter 2. You know from those exercises the kinds of negative self-talk that have seriously affected your emotions and behavior.

1. In your notebook, turn back to the page titled "Self-Talk." Take a red pen and circle each instance of personalization (P), emotional reasoning (ER), and mind reading (MR). These are the types of illogical thought patterns most commonly associated with shame. You can estimate from the number of red circles the degree to which your distorted thinking has been related to shame.

2. Now turn to the following pages in your notebook, where you devised counterarguments to your self-talk and rewrote it. Review your responses to self-talk statements reflecting personalization, emotional reasoning, and mind reading. Pay close attention to your counterarguments and realistic positive self-talk.

3. Underline the self-talk that debunks shame. Keep these realistic statements in mind when you are in situations that ordinarily elicit feelings of shame. They will help you recognize shame for the sham that it often is. It may also help to copy these state-

ments out and carry them with you, or to post them as affirmations in your home, car, or office.

Exercise
Revising Beliefs

You will remember from chapter 2 that distorted thinking originates from erroneous beliefs—you think the way you do because you were "programmed" to think that way. Many of your beliefs were formed during the crucial early years, when you were learning how people act and how the world operates, but some of your beliefs have formed more recently. To change thinking, you must reverse any harmful beliefs, of whatever duration or origin, that have arisen out of shame or that reinforce it.

1. You identified three levels of beliefs in chapter 2. Read over the pages in your notebook titled "Habit Beliefs," "Emotional Beliefs," and "Definite Beliefs." Decide which ones may have originated from shame or may be supporting shame.

2. Reread the positive affirmations for each of these beliefs. Then modify any of the affirmations that you feel should be made stronger.

3. Then, as you did with the positive self-talk, underline the affirmations that debunk your old shaming beliefs. If you have not already done so, add these affirmations to those that you carry with you or otherwise refer to on a regular basis. Be sure to refer to these affirmations any time the old, harmful beliefs begin to overtake you.

Confronting Shame in Relationships

If you discovered in the "Are You in a Shaming Relationship?" exercise earlier in the chapter that you are in such a relationship, you may be wondering what you should do. The answer is not necessarily to leave the relationship; you may have other options. Before you make any drastic changes, why not see if the shame can be eliminated from the relationship? The following are examples of how other people have dealt with similar problems.

The Public Shamer

A highly visible supervisor in a furniture factory, Meredith earned more than her husband, Randy, who worked in a less prestigious job elsewhere in the huge plant. Meredith had long been aware of her husband's discontent in his job, but it took longer for her to see that his dissatisfaction grew in proportion to her success.

Randy was not a particularly sensitive or considerate husband, but he took his responsibilities seriously and his family was his top priority. Despite his grumbling, he was a hard worker whose interests centered about work and home. He couldn't have been a better father.

Although Meredith had few specific complaints about her husband, she was often hurt by the way he treated her in public. He interrupted her conversations, contradicted her comments, and belittled her opinions. Sometimes his putdowns were disguised with humor; other times they were simply mean.

Meredith never considered leaving the marriage, because she felt that the pluses far outweighed the minuses. Nonetheless, the shaming had taken its toll on the relationship. Meredith's affection for Randy steadily decreased, while her anger increased. At the same time she was aware of growing doubts about herself. She was bothered most by dwindling self-respect stemming from the knowledge that she was allowing Randy to treat her badly.

As forthright and practical in her private life as she was at work, Meredith tackled the problem head on once she admitted to herself that there was a problem. She picked the right moment to approach Randy, a time when both of them were relaxed and comparatively free of stress. As unemotionally as possible, she related facts to her husband, giving specific examples of hurtful incidents and telling him how they affected their relationship and her self-esteem. She did not speculate about why Randy was treating her badly in front of people.

As Meredith had anticipated, Randy's reaction was denial and caustic laughter. Despite growing anger, she didn't allow herself to react with a temper outburst, for she knew that would only divert her from her goal of stopping the shaming. She wanted to stay focused and didn't want to risk being sidetracked into an argument.

Meredith told her husband that she had decided that she would no longer be humiliated in front of people. Therefore, she would not go anywhere in public with him until he agreed to stop the putdowns. And if he were to embarrass her in public, no matter where they were or what the circumstances were, she would simply leave without a word. She would carry her car keys so that she could take the car, or, if necessary, she would get a ride or take a taxi. But she would never again fail to react.

Of course, Randy tested her, either by design or by habit. And Meredith was true to her word. The net effect was that Randy, not Meredith, was embarrassed, and Randy soon changed his ways.

Shame can also occur in relationships other than personal ones. Doug, for example, thought he had at last found the job of his dreams when he accepted an offer to manage the training department of a national corporation.

Although Doug was technically accomplished, he was a bit naive about human relationships. He wanted the job so badly, and was so concerned with creating a good impression, that in their pre-employment meetings he failed to interview his potential associates, particularly his direct superior, a junior vice president of the corporation. Consequently, Doug entered the job knowing very little about the personalities and capabilities of the people with whom he would be working.

He soon learned that his superior's background included stints as a high school teacher and principal, and Doug quickly concluded that he was being treated more like a wayward student than as a credible, responsible subordinate. He found that he could do very little to the satisfaction of his superior. Even more disconcerting, criticism was often directed at him in the presence of his own subordinates.

Because Doug was resented as an outsider brought in for the job, his subordinates were quite willing to accept the vice president's fault finding. Feeling subverted and ineffective, Doug was aware that the vice president was actually running the department and Doug himself was relegated to ordering supplies and approving travel schedules.

Although it did nothing to make his position more tenable, Doug discovered that the vice president had in recent months been relieved of some major responsibilities. Corporate gossip held that he was being eased out of his position and into early retirement. Apparently the man was treating Doug much as he had been treated and was desperately clinging to the few responsibilities he had left.

As a new employee with no mentor or allies, Doug was not quite sure how to proceed. He tried talking with his superior, but nothing changed. He wanted to stay with the company, but the longer he bided his time, the more ineffectual he felt and the more withdrawn he became from his associates. Finally, he was shaken out of his lassitude by a poor performance rating that would become part of his permanent record.

Doug decided that he had to do something immediately or risk losing his remaining confidence and determination. After careful consideration of his options, he realized that he could use the performance rating as a vehicle to catch the attention of others in management. He appealed the rating, which gave him the right to go over his superior's head for a hearing.

As things worked out, Doug's performance rating was amended with a rebuttal, so that the record was straight, but Doug had an uncomfortable year until his boss retired. Doug didn't feel so shameful during the interim, however. He felt that he had gained some control over his fate, and he believed that others in management were sympathetic to his plight. That was enough to draw him out so that he could begin to connect with his peers.

Two-Way Shame

Terry had been married for ten years and had two children in elementary school. She felt that her marriage was basically sound. There was no physical abuse in the marriage, nor were there many noisy arguments. What there was, was a constant barrage of criticism. For years Terry's self-esteem had been slipping as a result of constant disparagement from her husband. She felt completely worn down by the fault-finding about every facet of her life, from her childrearing to her appearance. Finally Terry became unwilling to continue in the marriage unless her husband began to treat her with the respect and dignity she deserved.

Terry's husband, Lawrence, agreed to marital counseling more readily than she thought he would, which puzzled her until she learned that he was as dissatisfied with the marriage as she was. Although he had never labeled it as such, Lawrence perceived that he too was the victim in a shaming relationship.

Eventually, both Terry and Lawrence came to recognize that each of them was highly critical of the other—and of their children as well. Lawrence was more outspoken in his carping, but Terry was a master at insinuation and silent reproach. Previously, however, both of them had seen their role in this mutually shaming relationship solely as that of the vicitim.

After so many years of practice it was not easy for the couple to back away from their negative style of interaction. The reciprocal shaming was more than a habit; it had its source in a destructive power struggle between husband and wife. Once both Terry and Lawrence were able to acknowledge this, they began backing away from their old ways. The change gained momentum as each of them realized the other was sincerely trying to restore the marriage.

Although this example is of two-way shame in a marriage, such dynamics can also occur between parents and adult children, siblings, and friends. The kind of understanding Terry and Lawrence reached is essential to repairing the relationship no matter who the parties are. What is needed is open communication and cooperation and the willingness of both people to try to see the other's side.

Physical Abuse

Chrissie's marriage was marred by serious physical abuse. Her husband, whom Chrissie described as a "closet bully," had no interest in changing. She knew that there were grave risks in leaving the marriage—economic hardship, social displacement, a battle over child custody, physical harm—but she knew she couldn't survive as a stable personality if she remained indefinitely.

For many months Chrissie wrestled with fear, but she eventually gathered the strength to strike out on her own. Her standard of living did indeed decline precipitously, and she lost the social advantages of having a well-to-do husband. The threatened court battle and bodily harm never materialized, thanks to the intervention of a caring extended family.

The last time I heard from Chrissie she had a good job, but she still had to struggle financially. All the same, she was happier and more satisfied in her small apartment than she had ever been in the 3,500-square-foot house she had left. She had gained the greater advantages of self-respect and self-confidence and was testing the waters for the first time in a relationship with a kind, compassionate man.

Chrissie's story had a happy ending, which might not have been the case had she not had a supportive family. Yet there are growing numbers of social agencies prepared to help abused women, and the courts, as well as society in general, are becoming increasingly more sympathetic.

In my experience it is exceedingly difficult for a physically abusive relationship to evolve into a mutually supportive one. The actual blows may stop as the perpetrator grows older or for some reason discontinues the physical abuse, but the shame itself is likely to continue. All the same, I have seen bad relationships become good ones when both parties honestly worked at change.

It Takes Time

Chronically shamed people cannot have very high regard for themselves, and, as a rule, the greater the shame, the lower self-esteem is likely to fall. Fortunately, however, the relationship between shame and self-esteem runs both ways, so that the restoration of self-esteem is also an antidote to shame.

Be patient as you work through shame. It will not disappear quickly. It's a stubborn emotion that has probably been building for years. It can be overcome; I've witnessed it many times. You'll know you have conquered it when you no longer feel a compulsion to withdraw and hide. You will be aware then of a momentous change in attitude, and you will know that you are well on your way to overcoming loneliness.

4

Recognizing What
Doesn't Work

Thus far, in your quest to overcome loneliness, you have identified
the fears you have about mixing with people. You have made
progress in replacing self-defeating ways of thinking with healthy
thought patterns. And you have begun to repair and enhance your
self-esteem.

You have been concentrating to this point on changing your
thoughts. This has affected the way you feel about yourself and
will ultimately affect the way you behave. It's time now to reinforce
your new patterns of thinking with new ways of behaving.

As I'm sure you realize, the way you interact with other
people can create obstacles to your belonging. I am not talking
about shyness, awkwardness, or poor manners. Rather, I am referring to an entire style of relating to others that is damaging to relationships, yet may be overlooked or thought to be a personality
trait that cannot be changed.

People who have difficulty interacting with other people very often have a passive or unassertive style of relating. Although these people rarely see their lack of assertiveness as a problem, it frequently has serious detrimental effects on both close and casual relationships. Less common, but equally destructive, is an aggressive style of interaction. People who react aggressively may or may not see the negative impact of their behavior on relationships. When they do, they may feel powerless to develop more effective ways of relating.

This chapter will help you determine if you rely upon either of these destructive styles to relate to other people. If you decide that you do, you will find that there is another choice available to you: assertiveness.

Assertiveness is basically direct and honest communication. It is a "happy medium" between passivity and aggressiveness, because it involves expressing your thoughts and feelings without infringing upon the rights of others. It can give you the confidence to go anywhere and hold your own in any social encounter.

Chapter 9 in part II of this book presents examples and exercises to help you build assertiveness skills. First, though, read this chapter and complete the exercises to determine where you fall on the passivity-assertiveness-aggression spectrum.

The Pitfalls of Passivity

Passivity or unassertiveness is an acquiescent or submissive way of relating to other people. Although there are a variety of sources of passive behavior, one reason people are not assertive is a desire to be liked. They worry that if they voice an opinion or desire that differs from what someone else thinks or wants, they risk rejection. To avoid the possibility of confrontation or argument, unassertive people accept what other people dictate. They let others call the shots, thinking that is the way to keep others happy and avoid conflict. And it does, after a fashion. But in the long run, the effect of passive behavior is to *cause* conflict—an internal conflict that often goes unexpressed, building up to the point where it has seriously detrimental effects on relationships and even health.

Although unassertive people escape some unpleasant moments, their apologetic, indirect way of interacting tends to backfire. They often end up stuck with tasks they don't want to do for people they would rather avoid. Decisions go against them; people seem indifferent to their needs and desires; they can feel taken for granted or nearly invisible. Instead of true friends they may have acquaintances who find them useful.

Take Lynda, for example. Lynda served on committees. She hosted sales parties in her home. She collected money for charities. She volunteered in classrooms and sickrooms. She baked for causes all over town. Everyone could count on Lynda.

Like many of us, Lynda had a secret dream. Ever since she was 13 years old, she had wanted to learn to fly airplanes. But now that she could afford to take lessons, she didn't have the time, because she was too busy helping other people. She kept meaning to cut back on her volunteer work, to let others take a turn on committees, but somehow she always ended up doing everything herself. She couldn't say no and "let down" the person who had asked. But personally she paid a large price for her lack of assertiveness. In addition to deferring her dream of flying indefinitely, Lynda felt "spread too thin": touchy, harrassed, overcommitted to the point where she wasn't sure she was really much good to anyone.

Unassertiveness and Consideration for Others

On the surface, unassertive behavior may seem polite. Actually, it's not polite at all, because it's often dishonest or at least misleading. It leads the other party to believe something that isn't necessarily true. And when, as usually happens eventually, the other person finds out he or she has been misled, that person, justifiably, feels betrayed.

In their efforts to avoid confrontation, instead of working out a solution, unassertive people talk around a problem. When they absolutely must deal with someone directly, their statements are often kept vague and general, so as not to offend, or are so mildly stated that they seem of little importance. Minor or unimportant issues may be brought up in lieu of the real problem, which in the end is never addressed.

Very often, unassertive people will complain to someone else rather than dealing with the person they have a problem with. You may know someone like this, perhaps a coworker who complains ad nauseum about a colleague or the boss but wouldn't dare speak frankly to that person about the situation. Instead of trying to solve the problem, he or she is trying to relieve internal pressure—perhaps at your expense.

Unassertive people give only a token argument, if any at all, in support of their viewpoint. You may wonder how that can be a disservice to others—after all, they get what they want and meet little or no resistance in getting their ideas across. There is every appearance that things have gone their way. How can this be a problem?

The fact is, the second party in the interaction doesn't know whether he or she has gotten his or her point across or not. While the unassertive party may appear to acquiesce to the other's wishes, he or she may totally disagree with them and have simply hidden his or her true beliefs to keep the peace and avoid anxiety.

Without showing it, or even being aware of it, the unassertive party may be resentful or angry or feel that the agreed-upon ideas are foolish. These negative thoughts and emotions may then lead him to subvert what the two parties have agreed upon. Consciously or unconsciously, the unassertive party may procrastinate, "forget," or otherwise undermine the agreement. In the end, this per- son may get his or her own way—but at a cost of interpersonal damage.

This type of behavior is often referred to as "passive-agressive." Recently, a friend of mine related a fairly classic example of passive-agressive behavior. My friend's father is a widower and spends a lot of time with my friend and his family, including accompanying them on their vacations. The father comes across as a kind, agreeable gentleman who is willing to do anything to fit in with his son's family. To a close observer, however, he is something of a tyrant—happy only when he gets his own way and adept at getting it through indirect means.

For example, my friend says, try as he might he can never get his father to give a straight answer to any question involving a decision. Although he is always consulted about where to go and what to do, his father won't say what he wants. His stock response instead is "It doesn't matter to me. I'll be happy doing whatever you want."

But he isn't happy doing what others want to do. If the activity doesn't suit him, he sulks and makes sarcastic remarks, which spoils the occasion for everyone. In effect, he insists that his son read his mind and that the family's activities revolve around him.

Effects on Relationships

Clearly, an unassertive lifestyle takes a toll. Among other things, without realizing it habitually passive people lose respect for themselves. They begin to dislike themselves, and think that since they don't like themselves, neither will others. That kind of thinking leads to loneliness; people who think poorly of themselves aren't likely to reach out to others for companionship and support.

Ironically, unassertive people may eventually sever the relationships that they have been so desperate to preserve. Always giving in to accommodate others results in tension, anger, resentment, and hurt. These negative emotions accumulate but are rarely expressed. Then, like water behind a dam with no spillway, the anger and other emotions build and build—until something has to give.

Sometimes the dam gives way suddenly. The ever-increasing pressure becomes so great that it is released in an overpowering cascade. The usually passive person becomes, not healthfully assertive, but explosively aggressive, and blows up, usually in the wrong place at the wrong time and with the wrong person.

The result can be permanent damage in a relationship with a family member, a friend, an associate, or a supervisor. At worst, there can be violence. At best, there is an acceleration of the downward spiral in self-esteem. Whatever the case, there is likely to be increased loneliness, since people avoid those given to explosive outbursts.

Harold, an architect, was referred to me by his company's employee assistance program. Harold was generally a model employee. From time to time, however, he would lose his temper with people in the office. Because he was hard-working and talented, his occasional tantrums were tolerated, although they probably kept him from advancing within the firm.

Things went well enough for Harold, until one day in his boss's office he cut loose with fist pounding and shouting. His emotions were so strong that he couldn't control himself, nor could he remember later exactly what had made him so angry. Although he didn't realize it at the time, his anger was not the result of one event, but of a long accumulation of perceived injustices.

At our first meeting, Harold was the epitome of contrition. He felt terrible about his behavior, but he wasn't willing to accept total responsibility for it. He was inclined to shift much of the blame to his supervisor. After a few sessions, Harold revealed the fury he felt about being subordinate to someone he believed to be inferior to himself professionally.

Harold resented his supervisor, and he couldn't talk things over with him. Harold felt powerless when his boss took personal credit for Harold's ideas. He felt unable to say no when the department's scut work was dumped on him. He had hidden his talent behind a veil of acquiescence.

Despite being the good guy who did the dirty work, Harold was not especially well liked in the office. His coworkers were put off by his unpredictable and overblown outbursts. And though he was agreeable about taking on tasks, his resentment kept him from being very friendly. He was a busy man at work, but a lonely one.

Effects on Health

With some unassertive people, the dam never breaks; their tension is never released. These people hold in all of their anger and resentment with no relief. They neither work out their problems with other people nor release them in aggressive verbal outbursts. Instead, the dam holding back negative emotions gradually cracks and crumbles.

The suppressed tension invades the body, causing such problems as headaches, backaches, and stomach problems. It is known that chronic stress affects blood pressure and there is considerable speculation that it affects the immune system as well. I am reminded of Anna, a secretary who tried to please every friend, every coworker, and every member of her family. She was on five medications to control her dangerously high blood pressure, and she was plagued with a succession of ills with no obvious medical causes. Although there is no conclusive proof, I have seen too many chronically unassertive people with health problems to believe that those problems are not somehow connected to their passivity.

The following exercise will help you determine whether passivity may be playing a part in your interpersonal behavior.

Exercise
Are You Unassertive?

Instructions: Using the five-point scale provided, answer each of the questions listed below. A scoring key appears at the end of the exercise.

Unassertiveness Scale

If you have difficulty responding to some of the questions—for example, those about body language—ask a friend, family member, or your spouse for opinions. If you feel uncomfortable doing that, spend a day or two observing yourself as objectively as you can and then complete the exercise.

0 = Never   **1** = Sometimes
2 = About half the time   **3** = Often   **4** = Always

1. How often do you complain to others about a person's behavior, instead of discussing it with that person?   _____

2. How often do you hint about problems instead of speaking frankly about them?   _____

3. How often do you feel guilty if you don't help someone who asks, no matter how inconvenient it is?   _____

4. How often do you avoid saying things that you feel will upset people?   _____

5. How often do you try to keep relationships smooth, no matter what the circumstances?   _____

6. How often do you feel terrible if you offend someone?   _____

7. How often do you speak in a soft voice?   _____

8. How often do you use "minimizing" phrases when making requests (I was wondering, kind of, sort of, a little bit, could you possibly)?   _____

9. How often do you speak apologetically or in a pleading voice when asking for a favor?   _____

10. How often do you find direct eye contact uncomfortable in a conversation with a peer? _____

11. How often do you find direct eye contact uncomfortable in a conversation with a superior? _____

12. How often do you find direct eye contact uncomfortable in a conversation with a subordinate? _____

13. How often do you go along with other people's suggestions for a restaurant, even when you dislike the food there? _____

14. How often do you postpone reporting unpleasant news?_____

15. How often do you keep silent when controversial issues are discussed? _____

16. How often do you avoid making positive suggestions for improvement? _____

17. How often do you pretend to agree with other people when you actually don't agree? _____

18. How often do you buy items from friends when you don't need or want them? _____

19. How often do you worry about offending other people? _____

20. How often do you disguise your true feelings to be polite or tactful? _____

21. How often do you become annoyed when other people don't anticipate your wishes? _____

22. How often do you feel guilty when you ask for help? _____

23. How often do you compromise without saying specifically what you want? _____

24. How often do you fail to talk with other people about annoying habits? _____

25. How often do you allow other people to impose upon you when they consistently fail to return favors? _____

26. How often do you lend small sums of money to people who usually fail to pay you back? _____

27. How often do you bury a request in a sentence that discounts its importance? ("I know you are really busy

and don't have time, but could you possibly help me with this report?") ___

28. How often do you agree to do something and then find an excuse not to do it? ___

29. How often do you hint about what you would like to do in a social situation, rather than clearly stating your wishes? ___

30. How often do you feel selfish when you get what you want? ___

31. How often do you ignore issues when you run into resistance from other people? ___

32. How often do you delay handling problems with other people until you are really angry? ___

33. How often do you feel guilty when you say no to an unreasonable request? ___

34. How often do you go along with a salesclerk's suggestion because you feel obligated? ___

35. How often do you shrug it off when someone borrows and damages a personal possession without paying for it or repairing it? ___

36. How often do you turn aside sincere compliments with negative remarks about yourself? ___

37. How often do you withdraw or sulk when you are angry with someone? ___

38. How often do you inconvenience yourself rather than other people? ___

39. How often do you feel that you must respect the views of someone just because the person is older? ___

40. How often do you put off discussing problems until you can't avoid dealing with them? ___

41. How often do you look down or away when someone begins speaking with you? ___

42. How often do you worry whether you have a right to take a stand on a particular issue? ___

43. How often do you strive to be seen as a "nice guy" at the expense of standing up for yourself? _____

44. How often do you feel that you simply don't know how to act assertively? _____

45. How often do you cut yourself down in conversations? _____

46. How often do you worry that people won't like you if you take a stand in a controversy? _____

47. How often do you settle for compromises that benefit the other person more than you? _____

48. How often do you allow problems with friends or coworkers to escalate into crises? _____

49. How often do you do something for another person, expecting something in return but not saying what you expect? _____

50. How often do you feel nervous when you have a conflict with another person? _____

Total = _____

Key

In general, the higher your total, the more unassertive your behavior is.

Score	Interpretation
65 or below	Unassertiveness is not a problem for you.
66 to 140	Unassertiveness is occasionally a problem for you.
141 to 165	Unassertiveness is consistently a problem for you.
165 and above	Passivity is a major obstacle for you.

If you have found that passivity or unassertiveness is a problem for you, in whatever degree, chapter 9 will be invaluable to you in your quest to belong.

Aggression—A Caricature of Assertion

Assertion is sometimes confused with aggression, but there is about as much similarity between the two as there is between a television soap opera and real life. If soap operas were like people's true daily lives no one would watch them. Instead, soaps take the most extreme elements of peoples lives and multiply and exaggerate them into melodrama. Likewise, aggression has elements of assertion, but those are overblown and execessive.

Aggression is a blunderbuss approach to interpersonal relationships. It's a demanding, unyielding style of getting what you want. An aggressive person has little regard for the rights of others. The behavior of an acquaintance of mine, Mona, illustrates aggression. I got to know (and dread) Mona when we both served on the board of directors of a community agency.

Mona was bright and quick on her feet. Until you knew her fairly well, Mona seemed simply to be a go-getter who got things done. After working alongside her for a while though, she seemed more like a bulldozer in high gear.

Mona's favorite tactic was to appear to debate without actually allowing give-and-take. She took the time to marshal her facts in advance and prepared her case exceptionally well, bolstering her arguments with all kinds of facts and figures (real or made up). But beware the person who disagreed with her. She had a way of boring in to make anyone with another opinion look like an unprepared fool. She'd embarrass the person until he or she backed off, and the attack discouraged others from joining in the fray.

Mona's best weapon, however, was her lack of empathy. She didn't mind hurting other people, and she didn't seem to care whether anybody liked or admired her. Her goal was to win. She was in her element in large meetings where she could cut someone down in front of the group. She realized the more vicious the attack, the less likely she was to be opposed by anyone else.

Having treated clients who had similar behavioral styles to Mona's, I can guess that she was probably quite isolated and, if she admitted it to herself, very lonely.

The Price of Aggression

For people who, like Mona, aren't troubled by guilt or ethics, an aggressive style can be rewarding—but usually only in the short run. Aggressive people may indeed get what they want for the moment. They are likely to pay a costly price, however, in terms of lost friendships. Few people want to be around an aggressive person for long. Not many people seek them out.

People may give in to an aggressive person to save embarrassment or to prevent a hassle. Chances are, though, that they haven't really been persuaded to the aggressive person's point of view. Whenever possible, they are likely to subvert the aggressive person by doing a half-hearted job or otherwise sabotaging whatever they've agreed to do. Often people say yes to an aggressive person just to get away. Once out of sight, he or she is out of mind, and the "agreement" is quietly forgotten.

Aggressive people who rant and rave soon lose credibility. Given enough time, they are likely to lose any effectiveness they may have had. People pretend to listen, but they no longer take the outbursts, or the speaker, seriously. In a business or institutional setting, people tend to lie in wait for an aggressive person, particularily if he or she is a peer, and they retaliate when and where they can. They may, for instance, bide their time, watching for mistakes. In the meantime, the aggressive person becomes increasingly isolated.

The dynamic is similar in the personal realm. People seldom like having their friends dictate to them, call all the shots, put them down, shout or use physical force. Given the option, they won't stay friends with such a person, and acquaintances are put off by those behaviors as well. The aggressive person is not likely to have many friendships and is likely to be lonely.

Aggressive Behavior Is Resistant to Change

Because aggressive people frequently are rewarded immediately by their aggressive behavior, a desire to change seldom arises spontaneously. Some kind of external impetus is usually required for them to change their behavior. Because they get what they want and other people listen and seem to agree with them, often with no argument, aggressive people can't see the eventual results of their behavior. They don't connect their problems with their aggressive behavior. They only see that they bark and others jump.

Joe, for example, a client of mine, was similar to Mona in that he was inclined to disregard the feelings and contributions of other people. Although he sometimes knew when he was being too pushy, he couldn't stop his aggressiveness when he thought he was right. Joe's reward was getting across his ideas, and he'd push and shove verbally to do so. But because people don't like being pushed and shoved, Joe was a man with acquaintances but no close friends. His loneliness was the impetus for his entering therapy and eventually learning to modify his behavior from aggressive to assertive.

If you suspect that your loneliness might be caused by an aggressive style of interaction, the following exercise will help you find out. Chapter 9, on assertiveness skills, will then help you learn more effective ways of relating to other people.

Exercise
Identifying Aggressive Behavior

Instructions: For each question below, place a check mark in the Yes or No column, depending on whether you behave in the way described in the question. If you aren't sure whether or not you do (which may be the case especially in questions concerning body language), ask a friend, family member, or your spouse. Alternatively, try to observe yourself objectively for a few days before completing the exercise.

	Yes	No
1. Do you use blaming and accusing phrases? ("What *can* you do right?" "What's the matter with you?")	___	___
2. Do you imply that the other person doesn't care about the task at hand or about a third person? ("It may not matter to *you*." "I don't believe she means much to you." "You may not want to do it right, but I do." "If it were important to you, you'd help us.")	___	___
3. Do you attack with hurtful names or adjectives? ("How dumb can you get!" "Get off it, dingbat!" "Get serious, stupid." "Don't be ludicrous!")	___	___
4. Do you belittle ideas different from yours? ("How idiotic!" "That's the weirdest plan you've come up with yet." "I can't believe you mean that.")	___	___

Yes   No

5. Do you imply that the other person is foolish, stupid, or incompetent without saying so directly? ("Nobody else on the committee is being so stubborn." "It's certainly obvious to the rest of us that we should do it that way." "You're always worth a laugh." "Do you think *you* can?")   ___   ___

6. Do you continue to argue and push when it's obvious that the other person is committed to his or her own viewpoint?   ___   ___

7. Do you refuse to listen to other points of view or ideas?   ___   ___

8. Do you interrupt while others are talking?   ___   ___

9. Do you criticize character or personality rather than behavior? ("If you weren't so lazy, you'd have finished the assignment." "You're so asinine.")   ___   ___

10. Do you insist on quick answers, without giving other people time to develop informed opinions?   ___   ___

11. Do you ask questions that express or imply judgment? ("Will you ever get dressed on time?" which really means, "You're always late, you inconsiderate person.")   ___   ___

12. Do you make it appear that the other person's intentions are harmful or negative? ("You're always trying to tear things down, aren't you?")   ___   ___

13. Do you use strong, general threats, which usually can't be backed up, instead of appropriate warnings? ("If you don't get your act together, you're out on your rear, young man." "This club doesn't need people like you." "One more mistake like that and you'll be transferred so far into the boondocks you won't even be able to telephone headquarters!")   ___   ___

14. Do you act quickly without consulting other people or gathering all the facts?   ___   ___

	Yes	**No**
15. Are you seldom interested in compromising?	——	——
16. Are you more inclined to attack than to solve problems?	——	——
17. Are you more inclined to detemine who's to blame than to look for solutions?	——	——
18. Do you say the right thing but use an accusatory, reproachful tone of voice?	——	——
19. Do you stare at people in an intimidating way?	——	——
20. Do you display signs of impatience when another person is talking (drumming your fingers, tapping your foot, sighing, looking at your watch, acting restless, looking aimlessly around the room)?	——	——
21. Do you use aggressive body language (shaking a finger at the other person, getting too close and invading personal space, standing with your hands on your hips, waving your arms around, clenching your fists, keeping your body tense or rigid)?	——	——
22. Do you sometimes feel angry or outraged for no good reason?	——	——
23. Do you want to win for the sake of winning?	——	——
24. Do you make demands instead of requests?	——	——
25. Do you focus on the person, rather than on his or her actions, by using "you" in criticisms? ("You never take time to proofread your work" instead of "This needs to be checked carefully before you leave.")	——	——

Total "Yes" responses: ——

Key

If you answered yes to seven or more questions, you probably have a problem with aggressive behavior. Your behavior may be causing people to avoid you or deal with you only when they have to. To make progress toward belonging, you'll need to transform your aggressive approach into an assertive one.

False Assertiveness—
Alcohol, Drugs, and Casual Sex

Alcohol misuse can either be the cause or the result of loneliness, and the same applies to chronic overuse of prescribed tanquilizers, marijuana, cocaine, or any other mind-altering substance. Many lonely people retreat into alcohol for solace. If they misuse the substance or become dependent upon it, they soon discover that it makes them less attractive and interesting to other people. Impaired and inebriated people are boring and troublesome, certainly not fun and amusing. Thus the lonely person becomes even lonelier.

Shy and lonely people often self-medicate on social occasions. They rely upon alcohol and tranquilizers to lower their inhibitions and loosen their tongues. Actually, the great American institution of the cocktail party was created for that expressed purpose, and alcohol consumption is fine, if the alcohol is used instead of abused and you are not at risk for alcoholism.

But beware of relying upon chemicals to supply you with courage and wit. They won't. You may feel at ease and elated during the brief high they produce, but that's short lived, and your thinking is impaired more than you realize. What you think is wit may be perceived as silliness by others. And the false courage supplied by chemicals will soon desert you, leaving you feeling depressed and more inwardly focused than ever.

If you are already caught up in alcohol and other chemicals, I urge you to talk to someone from Alcoholics Anonymous or Narcotics Anonymous. He or she can steer you in the right direction for help. Just look in your local phone directory for the nearest AA or NA chapter. You'll find AA meetings, and perhaps NA as well, in your hometown.

As with alcohol and other substances, it's all too easy for a lonely person to get entangled in casual sex. Even in this day of AIDS and other sexually transmitted diseases, many lonely people rush into sexual relationships in a search for intimacy. Unfortunately, relying on sex to engender intimacy, instead of intimacy leading to sex, causes many lonely people to end up lonelier than ever.

Sex without commitment seldom leads to enduring involvement. It's more likely to result in broken dreams and shattered illusions. And it can get in the way of connecting with someone with whom you could build an authentic and abiding emotional attachment. Unlike portrayals in two-hour movies, it takes time to nurture relationships in real life. Sexual attraction may be there from the first, but trust, mutual respect, and genuine affection must germinate and grow; their development cannot be rushed. They are the foundations of the type of stable relationship that will banish loneliness.

It Takes Determination

You know by now whether or not you deal with people passively or aggressively. As you've learned, both ways of interacting with people are deceptive. In the short run either style may seem to be working to your advantage. Given time, however, these approaches to relating to people are self-defeating, for they alienate others.

If either style is yours, you'll need to learn and practice assertiveness. In chapter 9 you'll find all the essential ingredients of assertiveness. Learning the basics will be easy. Putting them into practice will take determination. If you've been unassertive, you will probably feel that your new behavior is artificial and "not you." You may be tempted to shrug off your new knowledge and revert to old habits. When people seemed surprised or puzzled, you may fear hurting their feelings or making them angry. Old habits die hard. Likewise with an aggressive style. Toning down aggressive behavior may cost you some degree of immediate gratification.

Don't give in to the urge to take a short-term, easy way out. Keep in mind that all changes, even beneficial ones, are difficult. The more you practice, the more natural assertive behavior will seem. When the rewards begin to come, you will find it difficult to believe you ever behaved in any other way. Assertive behavior will be natural, will be "you," and it will serve you well in your quest to overcome loneliness. Your efforts will be more than repaid in improved relationships.

Part II

Skills
for Belonging

5

Practicing Relaxation

The most basic skill you'll need as you learn to belong is the ability to relax. A relaxed body is essential to being comfortable with other people, since it is physiologically impossible to be relaxed and nervous at the same time. In particular, relaxation is useful in overcoming the fears that you identified in chapter 1, which have kept you apart from others.

Relaxation, for the purpose of overcoming fear, does not refer to watching television or going fishing. Rather, it is a set of techniques you will acquire to enable you to overcome the discomfort and tension you have in social situations. Physiologically, the skills you will learn in this chapter prevent adrenaline and 40-odd other activating hormones from flooding your system. In effect, you will "train your brain" to release endorphins and other naturally occurring tranquilizers.

Once learned, these techniques are invaluable—not just in social situations, but any time stress or anxiety is having a detrimental effect on the quality of your life. They will enable you to be happier and healthier, no matter what your current circumstances.

Progressive Deep Relaxation

Progressive deep relaxation, or *progressive muscle relaxation,* is a technique you will learn in this chapter for achieving the deep state of relaxation you need to overcome fear. You will listen to a series of audiotaped suggestions, first to tense and then to relax, the major muscle groups of your body.

Don't be deceived by the simplicity of the technique. Developed more than 50 years ago, progressive deep relaxation has been found to have beneficial effects on many harmful conditions, ranging, for example, from colitis to phobias. In its original form, the technique entailed 200 different exercises and literally took months to complete. Today's more streamlined version includes only 15 to 20 basic exercises, but it is just as effective.

The Benefits

Research has clearly shown that the technique of deep muscle relaxation produces physiological responses that are the opposite of those of anxiety. Among other effects, heart and respiration rates slow and blood pressure decreases. A simple instruction to relax can produce these responses to some extent. If someone is given the same instruction while in a hypnotic trance, the effect is more pronounced. But the responses are greatest following successful deep relaxation training.

The calming effects of deep relaxation are not due simply to changes in muscle tone. It has been demonstrated, for instance, that people under the influence of the drug curare, which relaxes all the muscles completely, often experience severe anxiety at the same time. In contrast, the lulling and soothing effects of deep relaxation seem to be related to the mental effort of letting go.

Deep relaxation is the foundation for overcoming acquired fears, but it also has a number of other benefits. The skill is very useful for coping with stress-related ailments, such as tension headaches, hypertension, and insomnia. Sometimes these side effects of stress can be entirely eliminated. Almost always they can be reduced to some extent.

I often use deep relaxation procedures in therapy to help people prepare for anxiety-provoking events. It is particularly useful in controlling stage fright. It seems almost like magic when people with a lifelong fear of public speaking are not only able to go on stage but actually enjoy it! Imagine how useful deep relaxation might be to a talented musician who hates the limelight or to a top business executive who quakes at the thought of the next board meeting.

I've seen relaxation help mothers of brides cope with weddings, sales managers gear up for major sales meetings, high school students take college entrance exams, and harried workaholics enjoy vacations. I've used deep relaxation procedures to help people who can't use anesthesia prepare for potentially painful dental procedures, and I'm convinced that it increases tolerance to pain.

To the extent that relaxation helps people cope with stress, it eliminates harmful ways of coping. As a by-product of their dealing successfully with stress, the need for nicotine, alcohol, and other drugs is often reduced. Who needs tranquilizers when thinking certain thoughts will do the same thing with no side effects and no possibility of developing dependence?

A person skilled in relaxation is a person better able to overcome fatigue. The tensions accrued from mental and physical effort can be released more efficiently through deep relaxation. Just about every pursuit you can think of can be accomplished better with less mental tension—getting along with people, working at any job, even having fun.

As a psychologist, I have been intrigued by the sense of control that deep relaxation gives people. In a relatively short period of time, they learn that they are in charge of their minds and bodies. They learn that they can control aspects of their fate that they never thought possible before. They can do it without pills or crutches. Thinking this way increases self-esteem, fights off debilitating depression, and subdues self-defeating anxiety.

So, you may legitimately ask, if deep relaxation is so wonderful, why isn't everybody using it? The answer is simple: It takes time and effort. It must be practiced, and it requires a certain amount of self-discipline. A quick, short-term solution, like popping a pill or taking a drink, is much easier than changing aspects of one's lifestyle. Unfortunately, such a solution—far from having the positive long-term effects of deep relaxation—can have highly negative effects on health and happiness in the long run.

Basic Procedures

To practice deep relaxation you will need several things: sufficient time and a quiet place to practice, comfortable clothing, a cassette recorder, and an audiotape. You will be making your own tape shortly, based on a script in this chapter. The following are some basic pointers on its use and the technique of progressive deep relaxation generally.

Time Requirements

Developing relaxation skills is not a hit-and-miss affair. You will have to practice regularly, just as you would in developing any skill, such as playing the piano or driving a golf ball. At first, it takes a great deal of discipline to put in the time necessary to acquire the skill. Later, after you have perfected the skill, less practice is necessary. In my experience people need an average of 21 sessions, three weeks of daily practice, to achieve the degree of mastery needed to overcome social fears.

It is best to practice every day at the same time, if possible. Select a time of day that best fits your schedule and temperament. Within an hour or so of bedtime is not usually advisable, because of decreased ability to concentrate and increased chance of falling asleep.

Roughly 30 minutes of practice each day is required during the initial stage. During the intermediate stage, 15 to 20 minutes daily is adequate. Once the skill has been mastered, 15 minutes or so two or three times a week may be enough, depending on the amount of stress in your life and your personal temperament. Generally, an easygoing person would require fewer practice sessions than a person who is more easily stressed. One rule of thumb: People who say they don't have enough time to practice are the ones who need relaxation training the most.

Environment

While you are learning the skill, it is best to practice in the same setting every day. As a rule, a comfortable armchair in a quiet room with low lighting is the most effective setting for practice. The problem with lying down or using a recliner is that you may tend to drift off to sleep, and you will need to remain alert and responsive but deeply relaxed. (This would not be the case, of course, if you were using the skill to overcome insomnia.) Keeping your eyes closed will help you concentrate.

Mental State

Although relaxation may seem to be a passive process, it's actually quite active. Paradoxically, it takes effort to let go. Just as stress causes mental tightening, relaxation requires mental loosening. Blocking out the cares and worries of the day requires mental exertion, while the progressive exercises take some physical effort.

As hard as you try to concentrate on the exercises, your thoughts will drift away from the task occasionally. When that happens, just bring your thoughts back to the exercises as quickly as possible. Don't dwell on your anxieties, and don't focus on pleasant thoughts. Keep going back to the exercise.

Tension and Relaxation of Muscle Groups

As you listen to your personalized relaxation tape, you will be instructed to tense and relax specific groups of muscles. The exercise is more effective if you tense the muscles quickly, then hold the tension as instructed, and finally release the tension quickly. Don't let the tension ease away slowly. Let go of it as suddenly as you can.

Some people have been so tense for so long that they have trouble willfully relaxing muscle groups. If you are one of these unfortunates, be patient and keep practicing. You'll require more time to learn the skill, but it will happen if you persist.

Similarly, it's not unusual for someone to complain of a problem with relaxing a specific muscle group, say the muscles of the back, neck, or shoulders. In this instance, the person has chronically channeled tension into that particular group of muscles. Patience and persistence will overcome this problem. If you find that you have trouble relaxing one group of muscles, spend extra time practicing with that muscle group after you have finished following the instructions on your personal relaxation tape.

If tensing a particular set of muscles is painful or difficult for you because of a physical condition, you can skip that part of the procedure. For example, clenching your teeth and biting down hard may not be advisable if you have had problems with cracks in your teeth. Likewise, if you have arthritis, clenching your fists may cause pain. Since the point of the exercise is to relax, causing yourself pain or injury would be counterproductive, so keep aware of your reactions and modify the exercise as you need to.

Breathing

As you do the exercise, try to breathe normally except when you are actually contracting muscles. Breathe in when you contract a muscle group. Hold your breath while the muscles are contracted. Then breathe out when you relax the muscle group. After a while you won't have to think about it.

Staying in Charge

Occasionally, I encounter highly anxious people who report strange feelings when they first begin to use relaxation procedures. These people have been so tense for so long that they are disoriented by the feelings produced by relaxation. As a rule, they have been rather desperately maintaining control in their lives. For them, tension has been associated with control, and they feel out of control when they lose muscle tension.

If you are such a person, bear in mind that you can terminate a relaxation session at any time. *You are always in control during these exercises.* Usually, just keeping this thought in mind will help in large part to overcome the fear of relaxation.

Using *Calm* as a Cue

At the end of each daily session, take a moment to assess your state of relaxation. If you find yourself truly relaxed, spend a minute or two saying the word *calm* over and over to yourself. The idea is for your unconscious mind to associate that word with a state of relaxation. (You can also use another word, if you prefer. Just be sure to use the same word consistently.) Later, after you have completed the relaxation training, you will have been conditioned to associate that word with a relaxed state of body and mind. In stressful situations, you will be able to reduce your tension simply by thinking *calm*—the word will cause a flood of soothing hormones to cascade into your bloodstream.

If you find this hard to believe, think about your favorite food. Chances are, you will find yourself salivating. That's because you have associated the thought of that particular food with eating and producing saliva. Given enough instances of association, the mere thought of the food (not its smell, taste, or sight) will cause saliva to flow into your mouth.

Exercise
Rating Your Tension Level

You'll need to rate your level of tension before and after each session to gauge your progress. It will help to keep you motivated to see the difference each session makes. In addition, you will be able to see how your general level of tension declines over time as you become more and more skilled at deep relaxation.

Research and clinical practice have shown that people are quite good at subjectively rating their levels of tension. You'll use the following scale to give it a trial run now.

Tension Scale

1 = Totally relaxed, no tension   **2** = Very relaxed
3 = Moderately relaxed   **4** = Fairly relaxed
5 = Slightly relaxed   **6** = Slightly tense   **7** = Fairly tense
8 = Moderately tense   **9** = Very tense
10 = Extremely tense (the most uncomfortable you could be)

1. Using the tension scale, rate the level of tension you feel at this moment: _____

2. Close your eyes and, for about two minutes, imagine you are in your favorite place (which may be real or imaginary).

3. Again using the scale, rate your new level of tension: _____

I expect that your level of tension decreased after spending only a minute or two concentrating on a pleasant thought. Just wait until you see the results of acquiring basic relaxation skills.

Producing a Basic Training Audiotape

The following is the script for your basic relaxation training tape: the first of three tapes you'll make during the course of completing this book. You will need to read the script aloud, all the way through, before you begin recording it. Consider it a guideline, and make any changes that seem more natural and comfortable to you. Put the script in your own words, if you like. The italicized print is what you will record. The words in brackets are instructions you should follow while making the tape.

Make the tape when you are not pressured for time. Be sure to speak slowly and calmly while reading the script aloud.

Basic Relaxation Training Script

Sit back in your chair and get as comfortable as possible. Close your eyes. [Pause a few seconds]

Take a deep breath and hold it. [Pause] *Hold it.* [Pause] [Repeat *Hold it* every few seconds, for as long as you think you can hold your breath comfortably]

Now open your lips slightly and release the breath through your mouth. [Pause] *And when you are ready, take another deep breath.* [Pause for as long as you can reasonably hold your breath]

Keep breathing this way until you feel the tension leaving your body. [Pause] *When you are ready, breathe more naturally through your nose.* [Pause long enough for your breathing to return to a normal pattern]

Breathe slowly but naturally [Pause] *through your nose.* [Pause] *Be aware of the cool stream of air as it enters your nostrils.* [Pause] *Imagine that you are breathing in cool calm and breathing out warm tension.* [Pause] *Breathing in cool calm and breathing out warm tension.* [Pause] *Breathing in cool calm and breathing out warm tension.* [Pause]

Concentrate on breathing in calm and breathing out tension. [Pause] *Let each breath relax you as you settle down and breathe in calm and breathe out tension.* [Pause for one to two minutes]

Now, while keeping the rest of your body as relaxed as possible, clench your right fist tighter and tighter. [Pause] *The rest of your body is relaxed but your right fist is tight.* [Pause]

Now tighten the muscles of your lower right arm. Make them even tighter than your fist. Feel the tension. Be aware of it. Concentrate on it. [Pause] *Hold it.* [Pause] *Hold it.* [Pause]

Now relax. [Pause] *Let go and relax all the tension in your right fist and lower arm. Feel the difference.* [Pause] *Feel how loose and limp your right hand is. Be aware of how loose and limp your lower arm is.* [Pause] *Concentrate on the relaxation.* [Pause]

Now, keeping your right hand and lower right arm relaxed, contract your upper right arm and hold it. [Pause] *Hold it. Feel the tension.* [Pause]

Now relax. Completely relax your upper arm. Feel the tension leave your upper arm. [Pause] *Relax.* [Pause] *Concentrate on the looseness and limpness in your arm.* [Pause]

Now tighten your upper right arm once more. Make the muscles hard and tense. Hold it. [Pause]

Now quickly let go. Let go of the tension in your upper arm. [Pause] *Concentrate on your entire right arm. Make it as loose and limp as possible. Relax your entire right arm.* [Pause] *Deeper and deeper.* [Pause] *Let the tension go.* [Pause] *Further and further.*

Now, while keeping the rest of your body as relaxed as possible, clench your left fist tighter and tighter. [Pause] *The rest of your body is relaxed but your left fist is tight.* [Pause]

Now keep your fist clenched and tighten the muscles of your lower left arm. Make them even tighter than your fist. Feel the tension. Be aware of it. Concentrate on it. [Pause] *Hold it.* [Pause] *Hold it.* [Pause]

Now relax. [Pause] *Let go and relax all the tension in your left fist and lower arm. Feel the difference.* [Pause] *Feel how loose and limp your left hand is. Be aware of how loose and limp your lower arm is.* [Pause] *Concentrate on the relaxation.* [Pause]

Now, keeping your left hand and lower arm relaxed, contract your upper left arm and hold it. [Pause] Hold it. Feel the tension. [Pause]

Now relax. Completely relax your upper arm. Feel the tension leave your upper arm. [Pause] Relax. [Pause] Concentrate on the looseness and limpness in your arm. [Pause]

Now tighten your upper left arm once more. Make the muscles hard and tense. Hold it. [Pause]

Now quickly let go. Let go of the tension in your upper arm. [Pause] Concentrate on your entire left arm. Make it as loose and limp as possible. Relax your entire left arm. [Pause] Deeper and deeper. [Pause] Let the tension go. [Pause] Further and further.

Concentrate now on the muscles of your forehead. Focus all of your attention on those muscles.

Wrinkle your forehead. [Pause] Tighter and tighter. [Pause] Hold it. Hold the tension in your forehead. [Pause]

Now relax. Relax all the tension in your forehead. Let go and relax. [Pause] Concentrate on the looseness in your forehead. Be aware of how relaxed the muscles in your forehead are. [Pause]

Once more, tense the muscles of your forehead. Frown. Feel your forehead muscles contract. [Pause] Concentrate on the tension in your forehead. [Pause]

Now relax. Let go and relax. Feel your forehead growing smoother and smoother. [Pause] Notice the difference between a tense forehead and a relaxed forehead. [Pause]

Now frown with the muscles around your eyes, nose, and upper cheeks. Focus on the tension there. [Pause]

Now let go of the tension. Relax. Let all the muscles of your face go loose and limp. Feel the smoothness in your face. Stay relaxed. [Pause]

Once again, tense the muscles around your eyes, nose, and upper cheeks. [Pause] Feel the tension. Be aware of it. See how different a tense face is from a relaxed face. [Pause]

Now relax. Release the tension. Feel your face go limp and loose. Focus on the relaxed feeling. [Pause]

Let your attention move down to your jaws and chin.
Clench your teeth. Feel the tension in your jaw. [Pause] *Hold*
it. [Pause] *Bite down hard and feel the tension spread*
throughout your mouth and jaw. [Pause]

Now let go. Let all of the tension leave your mouth and
jaw. Let your mouth grow slack. Feel the contrast. [Pause] *All*
relaxed now. [Pause]

Focus all your attention on your neck. Arch your head
backward and feel the tension in your neck. Feel the muscles
grow taut. Keep your neck tense. [Pause]

Now relax. Let go of the tension. Your neck is relaxed and
comfortable. [Pause]

Once more tense your neck muscles. Feel the tautness.
Arch your head back and be aware of the tension. [Pause]

Relax again. Your neck is suddenly relaxed. Smooth and
relaxed. Feel how loose it is. [Pause]

Push your shoulders up and feel the tension. [Pause]
Hold it. Hold the tension in your shoulders. Feel it. [Pause]

Now relax. Relax your shoulders. Let the tension go. Feel
how relaxation differs from tension. [Pause]

Again, push up your shoulders. [Pause] *Hold them up.*

Now let go. Let your shoulders fall. Let them go loose and
limp. Concentrate on the feeling of complete relaxation. [Pause]

While your body is relaxed, concentrate for a few moments
on your breathing. Focus on the warm stream of air leaving
your nostrils. Feel how warm the air is as it leaves your body
and how cool it is as it enters. [Pause]

Let your entire body go loose and limp. Feel as if you are
melting in the chair. Going more and more loose, more and
more limp. [Pause] *Enjoy the feelings of relaxation.* [Pause]

Focus your attention on the muscles of your abdomen.
Tighten them. Tighten them with all your might. [Pause] *Hold*
it. [Pause]

Relax. Relax the muscles of your abdomen. All tension
gone. Just loose and relaxed. [Pause]

Again, tighten the muscles of your abdomen. Tighten
them. Keep them taut and tense. [Pause]

Now let them go. Let the muscles of your abdomen relax. All tension gone. [Pause]

Tense your buttocks. Tighten the muscles and hold them tense for a moment. [Pause]

Now let go. Release all your muscles and relax. Completely relax. [Pause]

Tense your buttocks again. Keep the muscles taut. Hold it. [Pause] *Hold it.* [Pause]

Now relax. Relax. All muscles loose and relaxed. Focus on your entire torso—shoulders, abdomen, buttocks—totally relaxed. [Pause]

Focus on your legs and tighten the muscles of your thighs. Hold the tension in your thighs. Keep your thighs tight. [Pause]

Now let go. Let your thighs relax. Loose and limp. No tension. [Pause]

Tighten your thighs once more. Concentrate on the tension. [Pause] *Hold it.* [Pause]

Let go of all tension. Your thighs are now loose and limp. The muscles are flaccid. [Pause]

Tense the muscles in both calves. Tighten them as much as possible. Increase the pressure by pushing your feet down on the floor. [Pause] *Hold it.* [Pause]

Now let go. Let all the tension leave the muscles of your calves. Let them go loose and limp. Totally relaxed. [Pause]

Focus your attention on your right foot. Tense the muscles. Squeeze them. Press your right heel into the floor. [Pause] *Very tense. Very taut.* [Pause]

Now relax all the muscles in your right foot. The foot is loose, limp, and relaxed. All muscles smooth. [Pause]

Again, tighten your right foot. Press it downward. Push against the floor. [Pause] *Tight and taut.* [Pause]

Relax. Let your right foot relax. Go loose and limp. [Pause] *Right foot completely relaxed.* [Pause]

Turn your attention to your left foot. Tense the muscles. Squeeze them. Press your left heel into the floor. [Pause] *Very tense. Very taut.* [Pause]

Now relax all the muscles in your left foot. The foot is loose, limp, and relaxed. All muscles smooth. [Pause]

Again, tighten your left foot. Press it downward. Push against the floor. [Pause] *Tight and taut.* [Pause]

Relax. Let your left foot relax. Go loose and limp. [Pause] *Left foot completely relaxed.* [Pause]

Now that you have tensed and relaxed many of the major muscle groups in your body, take a few moments to let your entire body relax. [Pause] *It feels heavy. Very, very heavy. Completely relaxed.* [Pause]

Keep your body relaxed and think the word "calm" over and over for a minute or two. Associate this word with the deeply relaxed state of your body. [Pause]

Now slowly open your eyes. Take a moment to orient yourself.

Now you can go back to your daily activities.

Recording Your Progress

Your goal is to be able to achieve consistently a state of relaxation equivalent to a rating of 2 (very relaxed) or below on the Tension Scale after your daily relaxation session. This generally takes about three weeks of daily practice (21 sessions).

Use the Before-and-After Chart to rate your level of tension each day before and after you follow the procedures on your basic relaxation tape. The Before ratings will almost certainly be consistently higher than the After ratings. At some point the numbers in both columns should begin to decrease.

When your After ratings fall to 2 on two out of every three sessions, you will have achieved the state of relaxation training that you need to move on to the next step. Depending on your general level of tension and your reactions to stress, you may reach that goal sooner or later than the average of 21 sessions.

Before-and-After Chart

Instructions: Use photocopies of this chart to record your progress with relaxation skills. Rate your tension level using the 10-point scale below both before and after you do the relaxation exercises. Record any unusual circumstances affecting your level of tension under Comments.

Tension Scale

1 = Totally relaxed, no tension   **2** = Very relaxed
3 = Moderately relaxed   **4** = Fairly relaxed
5 = Slightly relaxed   **6** = Slightly tense
7 = Fairly tense   **8** = Moderately tense   **9** = Very tense
10 = Extremely tense (the most uncomfortable you could be)

Session Before After Comments

Session	Before	After	Comments
1			
2			
3			
4			
5			
6			
7			
8			
9			
10			
11			
12			
13			
14			
15			
16			
17			
18			
19			
20			
21			

Autogenic Training

Now that you're skilled at deep relaxation, you'll find it useful to learn another technique to enhance your abilities. *Autogenic training* uses repeated suggestions of heaviness and warmth to soothe the autonomic nervous system. Suggestions of heaviness cause the muscles to relax, while suggestions of warmth lead to dilation of blood vessels, which lowers blood pressure and redirects blood flow to specific muscle groups for even deeper states of relaxation.

We'll use autogenic training to supplement, not replace, the progressive relaxation procedures you've learned. By now, you know how well you are responding to progressive relaxation. If you are satisfied with your progress, scale back to three sessions per week—say, Monday, Wednesday, and Friday. On Tuesday, Thursday, and Saturday, substitute autogenic procedures for the muscle tensing and relaxing exercise. Take Sunday off. We'll scale back further as we go along.

Use an additonal copy of the Before-and-After Chart to record your tension level before and after autogenic training sessions.

Producing an Autogenic Training Tape

Your autogenic training tape will be shorter than the basic relaxation training tape you have been using. Once again, a script is provided here for you to record on audiotape. Feel free to modify the script if you would feel more comfortable with different wording. As before, read the italicized print aloud, slowly, but don't read the instructions in brackets. The script begins with the same breathing exercises you put on the basic relaxation tape.

Autogenic Training Tape Script

Sit back in your chair as comfortably as possible and close your eyes. [Pause a few seconds]

Take a deep breath and hold it. [Pause] *Hold it.* [Pause] *Hold it.* [Repeat *Hold it every few seconds* for as long as you think you can hold your breath comfortably]

Now open your lips slightly and release the breath through your mouth. [Pause] *And when you are ready, take another deep breath.* [Pause for as long as you can reasonably hold your breath]

Keep breathing this way until you feel the tension leaving your body. [Pause] *When you are ready, breathe more naturally through your nose.* [Pause long enough for your breathing to return to a nomal pattern]

Breathe slowly but naturally through your nose. [Pause] *Be aware of the cool stream of air as it enters your nostrils.* [Pause] *Imagine that you are breathing in cool calm and breathing out warm tension.* [Pause]

Breathing in cool calm and breathing out warm tension. [Pause] *Breathing in cool calm and breathing out warm tension.* [Pause]

Concentrate on breathing in calm and breathing out tension. [Pause] *Let each breath relax you as you settle down and breathe in calm and breathe out tension.* [Pause for one to two minutes]

And now, without moving any part of your body, think the following thoughts: Your right arm is growing heavier and heavier. [Pause] *You are concentrating on your right arm, and you feel it growing very heavy.* [Pause]

It is so heavy that it feels as if it is sinking into the arm of the chair. [Pause] *Your right arm is growing heavier and heavier.* [Pause] *The heaviness is moving down into your right hand.* [Pause]

You feel a heaviness throughout your right arm and hand. And now you feel warmth radiating throughout your right arm. [Pause]

It feels as if the warm sun is beating down on your right arm. You feel a warmth throughout your right arm. [Pause] *You feel the warmth moving down into your right hand.* [Pause]

The warmth moves down into your right hand. It feels as if your right hand is soaking in very warm water. Very, very warm. [Pause]

The warmth moves down into the fingertips of your right hand. [Pause] *There is a tingling sensation in the fingertips of your right hand. Tingling in the fingertips.* [Pause] *Feel the tin-*

gling in the fingertips. [Pause] *Your right arm from shoulder to fingertips is very, very warm.* [Pause]

And now, without moving any part of your body, think the following thoughts: *Your left arm is growing heavier and heavier.* [Pause] *You are concentrating on your left arm, and you feel it growing very heavy.* [Pause]

It is so heavy that it feels as if it is sinking into the arm of the chair. [Pause] *Your left arm is growing heavier and heavier.* [Pause] *The heaviness is moving down into your left hand.* [Pause]

You feel a heaviness throughout your left arm and hand. And now you feel warmth radiating throughout your left arm. [Pause]

It feels as if the warm sun is beating down on your left arm. You feel a warmth throughout your left arm. [Pause] *You feel the warmth moving down into your left hand.* [Pause]

The warmth moves down into your left hand. It feels as if your left hand is soaking in very warm water. Very, very warm. [Pause]

The warmth moves down into the fingertips of your left hand. [Pause] *There is a tingling sensation in the fingertips of your left hand. Tingling in the fingertips.* [Pause] *Feel the tingling in the fingertips.* [Pause] *Your left arm from shoulder to fingertips is very, very warm.* [Pause]

Feel the heaviness now on your face. The muscles of your face feel so heavy. [Pause] *Very heavy.* [Pause]

There is also a warmth spreading throughout your face. [Pause] *It feels as if the warm sun is beating down on your face. Feel the warmth spreading down your neck into your shoulders. Very, very warm.* [Pause]

Feel the heaviness in your shoulders. As if a weight is pressing down. Very heavy. [Pause]

Be aware of a heaviness growing in your right thigh. [Pause] *A heaviness is growing and spreading down your right leg.* [Pause] *Heaviness moving down into your right calf. So heavy. Feel the heaviness in the right calf.* [Pause]

Your right leg is so heavy. And the heaviness moves down into your right foot. [Pause] *Your right foot is pressing down.*

Growing heavier and heavier. [Pause] *The right foot is so very, very heavy.* [Pause]

Be aware of a heaviness growing in your left thigh. [Pause] *A heaviness is growing and spreading down your left leg.* [Pause] *Heaviness moving down into your left calf. So heavy.* [Pause] *Feel the heaviness in the left calf.* [Pause]

Your left leg is so heavy. And the heaviness moves down into your left foot. [Pause] *Your left foot is pressing down. Growing heavier and heavier.* [Pause] *The foot is so very, very heavy.* [Pause]

Now feel warmth growing in both of your thighs. It feels as if a wave of warmth is moving slowly down your thighs. [Pause]

The warmth of the sun is radiating down your legs. [Pause] *A wave of warmth moving down your legs into your calves.* [Pause]

Feel the warmth. It feels as if your legs are soaking in warm, warm water. [Pause] *The warmth moves down into your feet. A wave of warmth covering your feet.* [Pause]

The warmth moves down into your toes. [Pause] *You feel tingling sensations in your toes.* [Pause] *Tingling in all of your toes. Feel the tingling in your toes.* [Pause]

Once more become aware of your breathing. Breathing in cool calm. Breathing out warm tension. [Pause] *Concentrate on breathing for a few moments.* [Pause for 15 seconds]

Keep your body relaxed and think the word "calm" over and over for a minute or two. Associate this word with the deeply relaxed state of your body. [Pause]

Now slowly open your eyes. Become aware of your surroundings. [Pause]

Stay relaxed as you go about your daily routine.

Having Trouble Relaxing?

Don't lose heart if the autogenic procedures don't seem to be working for you. First, be sure that you have given yourself enough time to respond. Keep trying for a few sessions.

If you happen to be very tense on a particular day, you may have more success if you use the autogenic procedures after vigorous physical activity. Schedule your autogenic session after a period of aerobic exercise. A brisk half-hour walk would be excellent preparation for autogenic training.

If you continue to have trouble responding to the autogenic procedures, here is another route to take: On the days when you would have practiced autogenic training, substitute a "think through" of the deep relaxation tape instead. You should have it memorized by now.

Sit back as usual with your eyes closed. Go through the breathing exercises. Then go through the progressive relaxation exercises mentally, but *without moving your body.* Instead of contracting and releasing each muscle group, simply *think about* relaxing each group in turn, without first contracting it. Be sure to think the word "calm" over and over for a minute or two just before you end the session.

Fitting Relaxation into Your Daily Life

When you are convinced that you have mastered deep relaxation, you can shorten the length of your practice sessions and scale back the frequency. At this point, you are having progressive relaxation sessions with your basic tape on Monday, Wednesday, and Friday of each week, alternating with autogenic sessions on Tuesday, Thursday, and Saturday. The following are a few strategies for keeping in "peak relaxation training" using a more abbreviated schedule.

"Think-Through" Sessions

If your After tension ratings have consistently remained at 2 or below, you can begin briefer "think-through" sessions. Find a time when you won't be disturbed for 15 minutes or so. Then get comfortable; close your eyes; go through the breathing procedures briefly; and simply think about relaxing each major muscle group in the order that you have memorized from your audiotape. Be sure to think the word "calm" over and over for a minute or two just before you end the session. Start with 15-minute think-through relaxation sessions three days per week, trading off with think-through autogenic sessions.

Booster Sessions

In addition to think-through sessions, you'll still need to have occasional booster sessions in which you go through your basic relaxation tape in its entirety. You may also find it necessary to go through the autogenic tape from time to time. As a general rule, schedule booster sessions when your After tension levels begin to climb consistently above a rating of 2.

Decreasing the Number of Sessions

As time goes on and your skills become even better honed, you can decrease your number of sessions per week. Continue to use the Tension Scale as a guideline. Any time your After rating climbs above 2 for more than one session out of three, it's time to go back to lengthier and more frequent sessions for a while.

An Essential Part of Your Toolkit

If you have continued to associate the word *calm* with a state of relaxation, you have conditioned a deep relaxation response. It's time to begin using it in your daily life.

Monitor your body from time to time for tension; you should be an expert by now at recognizing it. If you find tension in any part of your body, take a moment to close your eyes. Think the word *calm* as you inhale, and imagine breathing out tension as you exhale.

Use the conditioned relaxation response several times during your day and you'll notice how much more relaxed you remain. It can work wonders too when you find yourself in a tense situation, such as an unexpected and unplanned presentation at a staff meeting. Don't close your eyes if that's awkward, but think *calm* as you inhale. The soothing hormones will flow! You now have a built-in, natural tranquilizer that you can use any time, any place.

6

Using Self-Hypnosis

By means of progressive relaxation techniques and autogenic train-ing, you have learned to induce a deep state of relaxation, and you have mastered the use of a conditioned relaxation response to cope with stress in your daily life. At the same time you have laid the groundwork for self-hypnosis, which will prove very useful in your quest to belong.

Although not a therapy in itself, self-hypnosis has proven to be an invaluable therapeutic tool for many purposes. In the context of overcoming loneliness, you'll use it to neutralize fear. You will also use it to enhance your confidence, strengthen your self-esteem, practice assertiveness, and perfect social skills—all ingredients in our recipe for overcoming loneliness.

The single most important factor in each of these areas is your mental attitude. As you have learned in earlier chapters, your thoughts, beliefs, and fears—and how you react to them—are what has been keeping you apart from others. And, as you may have discovered, changing your attitude isn't easy. It can be a long, arduous process, but there is a means available of speeding it up: hypnosis.

Most people can learn hypnosis on their own. Like many clients I've seen, you can use it to program yourself to overcome your fears and loneliness. Later in this chapter you'll learn the techniques for self-hypnosis. First, however, you need to learn something about the phenomenon, in order to avoid any misunderstanding or fear that might get in the way of your using hypnosis effectively. Experience has taught me that the more people know about hypnosis, the more willing and able they are to use it.

Understanding Hypnosis

Popular misconceptions about hypnosis abound. For our purposes, *hypnosis* can be defined as simply a state of consciousness involving focused attention. I have found it to be efficient and effective in helping people to change attitudes.

Since ancient times, healers have recognized the influence of thoughts and suggestions on the body. Written records of hypnosis go back as far as 1500 BC; evidence exists that the Egyptians, Greeks, Celts, and Druids, among others, practiced hypnosis. Yet, despite the experience of centuries, hypnosis remains largely a mystery. The phenomenon is an established fact, but how or why it works remains unknown.

If you are like most people I've seen in therapy, you may have serious doubts whether it will work for you. You may think someone must be weak-minded or psychologically fragile to be hypnotized, or perhaps you feel that a good hypnotic subject must be gullible or naive. The truth is, there is plenty of evidence that mentally healthy, strong-willed people can be hypnotized. In fact, it's a natural phenomenon that many people use—consciously or unconsciously.

Many professionals and businesspeople use self-hypnosis in their careers, even though they may not recognize it as such. Consider a salesman who psychs himself up just before calling on a major account or a neurosurgeon who focuses her full concentration on the delicate procedure ahead. Both these people are blocking out distractions and placing all of their attention on a single goal. That is the essence of hypnosis.

Some experts say that actors, orators, and musicians do their best work while in a hypnotic trance, because they are then completely focused on their work. Women using the Lamaze method of natural childbirth are relying upon self-hypnosis to alter their perception of pain. Bursts of creativity are likely preceded by a state of altered consciousness and focused attention.

Many world class and major league athletes retain psychologists to coach them in self-hypnosis. The object is to harness their powers of concentration. The athletes learn to guide themselves mentally through physical feats while shutting out all distractions. They visualize and feel themselves going through their routines perfectly. The enhanced concentration and positive frame of mind allow them to deliver peak performance on demand. Divers, for example, do this almost visibly. If you have watched olympic or championship diving events, you may have noticed the divers' concentration during the final secods before they launch themselves from the board. They pause and focus inwardly, shutting out the competition and the crowd as they visualize the perfect dive.

A Natural Form of Focused Attention

Hypnotic states are experienced naturally in everyday life. Most of us move in and out of hypnotic trance without realizing it. Daydreaming and twilight sleep are self-induced altered (or alternative) states of consciousness. The person lost in a book or movie is in a light trance.

As a commuter, I'm often aware, after the fact, of having been in a light trance. I'll find myself ten miles down the familiar highway with no recollection of having driven through one town or another. In fact, I have been perfectly in control of my car on one level of consciousness. On another level, though, I have been concentrating so intently on my thoughts or been so completely absorbed in music that the passing scenery has not registered.

This type of deep concentration is the essence of hypnosis. A trance is mysterious in one respect. In another, it's nothing more than attention compressed to a single point. It is like focusing sunlight using a magnifying glass or filtering out all but one substance from a chemical solution. It takes practice, but most people can learn self-hypnosis to the extent necessary to accomplish their goals.

Once you learn self-hypnosis, you'll use it to maintain a hyperalert state in a deeply relaxed body. In this state, you will tap latent abilities within yourself to attain your goals. You'll program yourself to overcome fears, misgivings, and misunderstandings that are holding you back. You'll use self-hypnosis to acquire new attitudes and new skills that will help you fit into any social scene.

Relaxed but Alert

Although stage hypnotists (and some therapists) use the command "go to sleep," that wording is inaccurate. Except for the relaxed state of the body, there's nothing about hypnosis that resembles sleep. The brain waves of a person in a hypnotic trance are similar to those of someone who is awake, alert, and relaxed. Research studies confirm a high incidence of alpha electrical activity during trance states. This is the output of a resting but vigilant brain, not of a brain that is asleep or unconscious.

Because they are not unconscious, most people remember what occurred when they were hypnotized. Indeed, novices typically have to be convinced that they have actually been in a trance. Only about 5 percent go into trances so deep that they cannot recall what happened.

In fact, some people can only manage the lightest of trances, despite having strong motivation for hypnosis. Their inability to enter deeper trances may be neurological instead of psychological. But even a very light trance can be helpful in bringing about change.

There is no chance, as some people fear, that hypnosis will cause you to sink into a trance so deep that you can't be recalled. On the contrary, it takes effort to maintain a hypnotic state—the natural tendency is to drift out of it. Occasionally a hypnotized person will move from a trance directly into natural sleep, from which awakening is a simple matter.

The Question of Control

People who don't understand hypnosis often fear that it will cause them to lose control or give up control to someone else. Too many movies have depicted hypnotists as evil manipulators. Perhaps that's good drama, but it's not reality.

It's only in fiction that the devious hypnotist extracts secrets from the helpless victim. It's also a myth that a person in trance babbles on about personal matters, as surgery patients sometimes do under anesthesia. People under hypnosis are able to control what they talk about. Furthermore, evidence supports that they cannot be forced to commit acts against their will.

Far from taking away control, hypnosis helps people gain more control over their behavior and tap into under-utilized abilities within themselves. It is simply a tool that can be used to help people relax, overcome fear, control anger, explore memories and motivation, enhance self-esteem, control pain, maximize performance in events, and, as we are doing here, overcome loneliness.

The Altered State

As a hypnotic trance is induced, heart rate and breathing slow. Blood pressure falls, and muscles grow limp. There is a feeling of languor and detachment.

People often have difficulty describing the sensations they feel under hypnosis. Most people I work with find it pleasant. A few find it exhilarating. A small group finds it disagreeable. For these people, hypnosis is sometimes not the right tool. (If after giving it your best shot, you find you are one of these people, proceed with the remaining chapters in the book. Hypnosis can be useful, but it isn't essential to overcoming loneliness.)

Trance Logic

As the conscious mind quiets, a way of thinking called *trance logic* emerges. The inclination to be judgmental gives way to an interest in observing.

Trance logic results in greater compliance with requests and willingness to accept change. It allows increased access to the unconscious mind—that vast storehouse of memories, feelings, and thoughts that operates on its own logic and strongly influences conscious behavior.

People under hypnosis are more likely to express true thoughts and emotions, since their usual inhibitions grow weaker.

They are less inclined to initiate actions on their own and more likely to accept suggestions from others. There is, then, a decrease in personal will, but not a total eradication of will.

Some time ago I saw a businessman in therapy who had difficulty being forthright in discussions about his personal life. Roger was a vice president in a national manufacturing company and had no difficulty being straightforward in business matters.

He felt, however, not just embarrassed but uneasy and guilty when he talked about himself or about private matters. As a result, Roger and his wife had drifted far apart and were headed for a divorce that he didn't want. He came to therapy at his wife's insistence.

Fortunately, Roger was open to new ideas and found hypnosis fascinating. When he was in trance, he put aside his inhibitions and had no difficulty discussing the most intimate subjects. He reminded me of a shy person at a cocktail party whose restraints give way after a drink or two.

By suggesting to Roger that he remain uninhibited in lighter and lighter trances, I was able to help him gradually let go of his inhibitions in the conscious state. It also helped for him to discover that he was confusing intimacy with selfishness, for which he had been severely punished as a child.

As a welcome by-product of therapy, Roger found himself less inhibited socially and more adept at making friends. In hindsight, he recognized that he had been a lonely man who was growing more and more isolated outside of his circle of business acquaintances. Roger's experience taught me that hypnosis could be a valuable tool in overcoming loneliness.

Memory

The mind reacts in a number of interesting ways during hypnosis. If a trance is deep enough, a hypnotized person can actually relive past experiences.

I remember one of my clients, who would invariably slide into a deep trance, usually within two or three minutes after we began hypnosis. I never encouraged her to do so, since it wasn't necessary for our purposes. Judy was simply one of those rare people who slip into deep trances spontaneously.

When she remembered events, Judy seemed to go back in time. Her voice, her vocabulary, and even the slang she used were always in character for the period in her life she was "visiting." It was as if she remembered and acted out every detail and nuance.

Unlike Judy, many people in trance recall events as if watching them on a video screen or hearing them on an audiotape player. It's even more common for people to recall memories much as they ordinarily do, only somewhat more vividly and in more detail.

Memory under hypnosis is fallible. Because they are more suggestible than usual, people in trance may "remember" what the therapist wants them to. Their recollections may bear little resemblance to fact, or fiction may be woven into facts. You can imagine how tricky that makes gathering legal evidence through hypnosis, which is why such evidence is not admissible in many courts of law. Hypnosis enhances imagination, just as it promotes creativity.

I suspect that Judy may have sometimes unconsciously embellished her memories in an effort to please me, since eagerness to please had gotten her into trouble more than once. Yet, despite my suspicions, I was never able to detect inconsistencies or fallacies in her recollections.

Time Perception

Time can contract or expand under hypnosis. Three minutes can seem an hour or ten minutes can pass in an instant. This change in time perception can be useful, for instance, to a person in pain or an athlete in an endurance event.

Pain Perception

In deeper trances, people can endure unnatural distortions of the body and physical pain. A minority of people can undergo surgical and dental procedures without anesthesia. Although most of us cannot eliminate pain, we can learn to diminish it through self-hypnosis.

A typical case is a client referred to me by a dentist. Margery was allergic to dental anesthesia, yet she had to have major dental work. Needless to say, she decided that hypnosis was a better alternative than bearing the pain, and she was highly motivated to learn self-hypnosis.

After a few sessions with me and many sessions alone at home, Margery became quite adept at pain control. She told me later that she was aware of pain in the dental chair, but it was as if it were "disconnected" from her. During the dental procedure she had placed herself on a tropical beach, with the sun of the dental light beating down on her and the sounds of the surf masking the drill. The pain was annoying, but no more so than hovering mosquitos.

Dreams

It's possible to affect dreams through hypnosis. Memories of dreams can be enhanced after the fact, or the content of the dreams can be influenced in advance. When people aren't able to recall a fact or event under hypnosis, I usually suggest that they will recall it at a later time and that the recollection will come to them when they are ready, as an insight, a hunch, or a memory in a dream. Quite often, the recollection will indeed come in the form of a dream.

How You Will Use Hypnosis

Most of the attributes of hypnosis will not concern you in your goal of overcoming loneliness. Two of them, however, will serve you well: detachment and suggestibility. Along with the relaxation techniques you have been mastering, they are cornerstones of your strategy for feeling comfortable socially.

Detachment

During hypnosis some people experience changes in the perception of their bodies, called *detachment*. These people feel like observers viewing themselves from exterior vantage points. In a more dramatic form of detachment, the shape and size of body parts may seem altered. The legs, for example, may seem to have grown very long so that the feet are far away. The head may seem perched on a long neck. Yet, whatever the altered perception, the hypnotized person is more likely to react with acceptance than with fear.

You will likely experience—and benefit from—a less extreme aspect of detachment. In effect, you will learn to view yourself from a distance. This will allow you to separate yourself emotionally from events that are ordinarily painful or fearful for you—a very helpful therapeutic process.

You will use detachment to overcome inhibitions that keep you from connecting with other people and to view yourself dispassionately in social situations that are usually alarming or uncomfortable for you. By doing this in gradual steps, you will "unlearn" the fear that you have associated with events that are actually harmless.

Suggestibility

It's not enough simply to overcome fear or discomfort. You must also replace negative ways of thinking and acting with positive ones. To do that, you will learn to make use of *suggestion*, the hallmark of hypnosis. You will learn to implant positive patterns of thinking into your unconscious mind, and you will learn new habits that will benefit you in your quest to belong.

Inducing an Altered State

Despite having mastered deep relaxation, you may have some doubts about your ability to induce a hypnotic trance on your own. Bear in mind the basic principle that *all hypnosis is self-hypnosis*. A trained hypnotherapist can talk a client through the hypnosis procedures, but it is the client and the client alone who actually causes a trance to occur. You can learn the procedures to talk yourself into a trance.

The first step is to create an induction method for yourself. I will give you some general principles for inducing a hypnotic trance and present a sample procedure. From these, you'll design a personalized procedure for yourself and record it on audiotape. As you did with deep relaxation, you'll then use the tape to perfect your hypnotic skills. Once you've become proficient in self-hypnosis, you'll be able to induce a trance quickly without using the tape.

Principles of Induction

Knowing deep relaxation as you do means that you have a head start in inducing a trance. The first principle of induction is settling into a comfortable position with a relaxed mind and body. You can sit or lie down. Sit up if you fall asleep easily, since being asleep is incompatible with being in a hypnotic trance.

Don't cross your arms or your legs. Crossing your limbs tends to increase tactile stimulation and curtail blood circulation, both of which can interfere with trance induction.

You will want to learn self-hypnosis in privacy, although later you'll be able to use it virtually anywhere. Many people find it easier to focus attention in a quiet room with low illumination. For example, I turn off the ceiling lights and use table lamps instead.

Although I have not found music to be helpful, you could experiment with soft, nonintrusive music if you like. In my office I use a white noise generator (which sounds like a waterfall) to mask noise from adjoining rooms. Some people aren't bothered by extraneous sounds but most are.

Elements of the Induction Tape

Vocal Quality

I have my clients use their own voices in making their self-induction tapes, because I believe that this makes it easier later for them to think through the procedures without the tape. After all, you think in your own voice, not someone else's.

Speak in a low, rhythmic voice when recording the tape, and project confidence through your tone of voice and choice of words. Speak in a positive manner, and don't use words like *perhaps* or *maybe*.

Repetition

Repeating instructions during the induction is important. The monotony facilitates the slide into an altered state, which is why some clinicians set a metronome for a slow beat where the client can hear it. Repetition also reinforces the instructions to the unconscious mind. The repetitions don't have to be precisely the same each time; rather, they can be variations on the same theme.

Deepening

Although you'll need only to enter a light trance for our purposes, you should include instructions on the tape to deepen the trance from time to time. Because there is a natural tendency to move out of a trance, it is necessary to work at staying there. Periodic deepening will ensure that you will stay as deep as necessary.

I've used instructions in the sample script that work for me, but you will want to incorporate deepening instructions that are tailored to you personally. Later exercises will help you do this. Three or four repetitions of deepening instructions will probably be sufficient. You may also use more than one type of deepening, if that seems to work better for you.

Personalizing Your Script

Unless you feel very comfortable with them, don't use the images I've suggested in the following induction script. I used, for example, an image of descending in an elevator. If elevators bother you in some way, you could substitute an image of riding downward on an escalator or walking down a ramp—whatever image suits you. It's essential that the images you use relax you.

If modifying the script, be careful to change *only the images.* Don't eliminate a section of the script or change any of the ideas or concepts. All of the elements in the sample script are necessary for inducing a light trance efficiently.

You will want to read through this script first, then do the exercises in the following section before making your induction tape. You will also want to write out in your notebook either an entirely new script or at least your personalized sections before recording.

Note that neither the section headings in the sample script, which are in boldface type, nor the instructions, which are in brackets, are to be read aloud. Only the italicized text should be recorded on tape. Where possible, the script is similar to your relaxation script in order to generalize your skills from one medium to another. The script assumes you are skilled in deep relaxation.

Sample Induction Script

Preparation

Take a few moments to get comfortable in your chair. [Pause for 10 seconds] *Now sit back and slowly close your eyes.* [Pause for 5 seconds]

Relaxation

Take a deep breath and hold it. [Pause] *Hold it.* [Pause] *Hold it.* [Repeat *Hold it* every few seconds for as long as you think you can hold your breath comfortably] *Now open your lips slightly and release the breath through your mouth.* [Pause] *And when you are ready, take another deep breath.* [Pause for as long as you can reasonably hold your breath] *Keep breathing this way until you feel the tension leaving your body.* [Pause]

When you are ready, breathe more naturally through your nose. [Pause long enough for your breathing to return to a normal pattern] *Breathe slowly but naturally through your nose.* [Pause] *Be aware of the cool stream of air as it enters your nostrils.* [Pause] *Imagine that you are breathing in cool calm and breathing out warm tension.* [Pause] *Breathing in cool calm and breathing out warm tension.* [Pause] *Breathing in cool calm and breathing out warm tension.* [Pause] *Think the word calm. Concentrate on calm.* [Repeat two times, then pause for a few seconds]

Relaxation Imagery

Imagine that a warm wave of relaxation is slowly sweeping up your body. Feel the relaxation moving over your body. [Pause] *The warm wave is moving slowly up your body bringing a deep, deep sense of relaxation.* [Pause, then repeat]

Imagine that you are floating in warm water. [or above the field of gravity or whatever image you find best suited for you] *As you float, all muscles let go. All muscles relax.* [Repeat, then pause]

Altering Consciousness

You're floating along. Letting go. Just letting go. Drifting. [Pause] *You are drifting. Letting go. Letting all thoughts leave your mind.* [Pause] *Just concentrating on my voice and concentrating on letting go.* [Pause] *Concentrating on letting go. Concentrating on my voice.* [Pause]

Drifting along, without a worry, without a care. Taking time out to drift. [Pause] *Concentrating on drifting, floating along.* [Pause] *Without a worry, without a care.* [Pause] *And if any worries or cares intrude, put them in a basket and let them float away from you downstream.*

Feel yourself drifting, floating. Without a worry, without a care. [Pause] *Taking time out to drift along.* [Pause] *Just concentrating on drifting and concentrating on my voice. Nothing else matters, as you drift along. Letting go.* [Pause] *Letting go so that you drift without a worry, without a care.* [Pause]

Altering Consciousness
with Deepening

Imagine there is a tiny faucet in your brain. A tiny faucet down low and toward the back of your brain. Picture the faucet and imagine that you turn it on. You turn it on and wondrous, soothing hormones begin to flow into your bloodstream. [Pause]

You turn on the faucet and soothing hormones flow. [Pause] *Soothing and calming.* [Pause] *The hormones move deeper into your bloodstream, bringing a sense of peace, tranquility, and contentment.* [Pause]

Feel the peace. Be aware of it. Feel the tranquility and the contentment. [Pause] *With each beat of your heart, the hormones move deeper and deeper, deeper and deeper. Bringing a sense of peace and tranquility and contentment.* [Pause] *With each beat of your heart, you feel more and more peaceful, more and more tranquil, more and more content.* [Pause]

Feel the peace spreading throughout your body. Peace and tranquility spreading throughout your body. Feel the contentment. [Pause]

Peace and tranquility and contentment spreading deeper and deeper. With each beat of your heart the soothing, calming hormones move deeper and deeper. [Pause]

Altering Consciousness with Deepening
(second iteration)

As the soothing hormones move deeper, you feel heavier and heavier. Feel the heaviness moving throughout your body. [Pause] *Your whole body growing heavier and heavier as you move deeper and deeper.* [Pause]

Be aware of the heaviness spreading throughout your body. You feel as if you're sinking downward. Feel your body moving

downward. Further and further. [Pause] *Deeper and deeper.*
[Pause]

Concentrate on the heaviness. In your arms. In your torso.
In your legs. Focus your attention on the heaviness. Con-
centrate on it. Be aware of it. [Pause] *Heavy. Very,*
very heavy.

Deepening

Now you are going deeper. Riding an elevator down,
down into the earth. Deeper and deeper. [Pause]

Now you are moving downward, downward. [Pause] *As I*
count, each number you hear will take you deeper. Think of des-
cending as I count. Each number takes you deeper and deeper.

Ten. [Pause 3 seconds] *Moving deeper.* [Pause 3
seconds] *Nine.* [Pause 3 seconds] *Growing heavier.* [Pause 3
seconds] *Eight.* [Pause 8 seconds] *Seven.* [Pause 8 seconds]
Six. [Pause 8 seconds] *Five.* [Pause 8 seconds] *Four.* [Pause
8 seconds] *Three.* [Pause 8 seconds] *Two.* [Pause 8 seconds]
One. [Pause 8 seconds]

First Suggestion

Calm. You are feeling calm. Calm. [Pause] *Calm. Think*
the word "calm." Visualize the word "calm." [Pause] *Let your*
unconscious mind associate the word calm with the way you
are feeling now. With a tranquil mind and a relaxed body.
[Pause]

You are calm. Feel the calm. Be aware of it. Think it.
Visualize it. [Pause] *Calm.* [Pause] *Let your unconscious mind*
associate the word calm with the way you feel now. Tranquil
mind. Relaxed body. [Pause]

Now and in the future, think the word calm and soothing
hormones flow. Soothing hormones cascade into your
bloodstream bringing peace and tranquility.

Deepening Using Imagery

Imagine that you are standing by a small pond. The water
is very clear and very still. The water is very deep. Everything
is in slow motion.

You throw a pebble and watch it arc downward into the pond. It falls into the pond and sinks downward. Slowly, very slowly. Watch it sink. Watch it move downward. Descending further and further.

Watch it sink. As it does, you too move downward. Further and further. Deeper and deeper. Very, very deep. Deep and heavy. Very, very heavy.

First Suggestion (second iteration)

Imagine now that you are sitting in a very comfortable chair. Before you is a big screen, like a movie screen. You see yourself on the screen. You are very relaxed, at ease. Tranquil and content. Calm. Very, very calm.

See yourself on the screen. Relaxed. Tranquil. Content. Calm. Very, very calm. Plant that image deep into your unconscious mind.

See the word calm on the screen. Hear the word calm. See the word calm and hear the word calm. Calm. Calm. Hear it and see it. See yourself and the word calm on the screen. See the two images, you and the word calm. You are relaxed, tranquil, content.

Let your unconscious mind associate the word calm with the image on the screen. A relaxed body and a tranquil mind. Relaxed body. Tranquil mind. Calm.

Now and in the future, think the word calm and soothing hormones flow. Soothing hormones cascade into your bloodstream bringing peace and tranquility.

End your tape here. When you use the tape, you will present other suggestions and imagery at this point, but in the form of thoughts, not aloud on the tape.

You then end the self-hypnosis session by imagining that your body is growing lighter and your mind more buoyant. You imagine that you are moving upward, and then tell yourself mentally: *Come back to this time and this place. And open your eyes when you are ready.*

Incorporating Imagery

Images enhance the effectiveness of suggestions in hypnosis. Normal thoughts include pictures and bits of data from the other senses, as well as words. For most of us, dreams consist primarily of pictures, with some words and other sounds, smells, tastes, and tactile sensations thrown in. Both conscious thought and dreams mimic actual experience in this way. Likewise, trance thoughts will be more "solid" and believable if they incorporate sensory images in addition to words. Your use of images in self-hypnosis is limited only by your imagination.

Several points are important to note about images. First, images are subjective. What is an effective image for one person may not work at all for someone else. For instance, my image of a peaceful scene would be sitting in soft moss leaning against a birch tree beside a mountain stream on a summer day. Yours might be sitting in church or lying on a tropical beach.

Second, images should be associated with the suggestion they accompany. Use your feelings as a guide. Since a feeling of well-being is generally associated with comfort and warmth, you might, for example, use images involving those sensations to help you overcome a state of uneasiness. If I were using imagery to induce a feeling of warmth throughout my body, I would probably picture myself lying in a hammock in warm sunshine on a beautiful autumn day. You might prefer to see yourself snuggled into a warm bed or soaking in a hot tub.

Third, you will want to use imagery on some occasions to distance yourself from an anxiety-provoking scene. Sometimes visualizing yourself in the actual situation would be too frightening, at least initially. To insulate yourself from the fear, you can picture yourself viewing an image on a screen. If you were, for example, working on overcoming stage fright, you'd see yourself first on a screen talking to an audience, rather than imagining that you are actually up before the group. You'll be using this technique in the exercises in the next chapter.

Sometimes the screen technique is used for another purpose, as it was in the sample induction script. Most people find it easy to imagine they are viewing a screen, probably because most of us have a great deal of practice watching television and movie screens. It often takes more practice for people to learn to visualize themselves in an actual situation.

Finally, images don't necessarily have to be visual. My image of sitting beside a mountain stream was primarily visual, but it also included tactile elements. I felt the soft moss and the warm sunshine. An image can even be entirely tactile, such as feeling yourself being massaged or imagining a cool breeze flowing over your body. It can be auditory, such as hearing music or the sound of a pounding surf or a howling wind. Some people are even proficient at olfactory imagery, conjuring up such aromas as the fragrance of a freshly cut gardenia.

Part of devising the most effective images for you personally is determining what types of things you are best able to imagine. For instance, I've found that I use auditory imagery best, followed by visual imagery. Next comes tactile imagery. I'm not able to use olfactory imagery, because I can't produce odors in my imagination. The first of the exercises that follows will help you identify the types of images that work best for you.

The second exercise below uses the information gained from the first exercise to devise images that will be effective at the points in your induction script where trance-deepening suggestions are used.

Exercise
Identifying Effective Imagery

Instructions: Spend a few moments inducing a relaxation response. Then read the first description of an image below. Close your eyes and reproduce the image in your imagination. Finally, rate the image using the Effectiveness Scale below. Then go on to the second image, and so on through each image in order.

Effectiveness Scale
1 = Unable to reproduce the image
2 = Questionable reproduction of the image
3 = Reproduced the image enough for it to be recognizable
4 = Fairly good reproduction of the image
5 = Reproduced the image vividly

Rating

1. You are walking through a wooded park on a bright autumn afternoon and noticing the blue sky and white clouds, as well as the colors of the leaves on the trees and on the ground. ____

2. You are sitting in a kitchen with your eyes closed and you are aware of a freshly baked loaf of bread on a table before you. ____

3. You are lying on your stomach aware of fingers kneading the muscles of your neck and shoulders. ____

4. You are in a concert hall listening to your favorite type of music. ____

5. You are sitting on a pier that extends out over the ocean. You lean back, close your eyes, and smell the briny, slightly fishy odor of the sea. ____

6. You are lying in the grass on a hillside on a hot summer day. Your eyes are closed and you are aware of a cooling breeze on your face. ____

7. You are walking along the shore of a lake watching the sun slowly sink behind western hills. ____

8. It's late at night. Everything is still and quiet, and you hear the sound of a train passing in the distance. ____

Key

Add together the rating numbers you gave questions 1 and 7. ____ + ____ = ____ Visual

Questions 1 and 7 primarily involve sight.

Add together the rating numbers you gave questions 2 and 5. ____ + ____ = ____ Olfactory

Questions 2 and 5 primarily involve smell.

Add together the rating numbers you gave questions 3 and 6. ____ + ____ = ____ Tactile

Questions 3 and 6 primarily involve touch.

Add together the rating numbers you gave questions 4 and 8. ____ + ____ = ____ Auditory

Questions 4 and 8 primarily involve hearing.

The type of imagery with the highest score is the one you should use most often during self-hypnosis. You can use the others also from time to time, provided the total score for that type of image was 6 or higher.

Exercise
Identifying Deepening Procedures

1. Take a few minutes to brainstorm several ideas of different images for taking yourself deeper into a trance and jot them down in your notebook. Come up with at least five ideas—more if you can—using the results of the preceding exercise as a guide to the types of images that are most effective for you.

   For examples, look back at the sections labeled "Deepening" in the sample induction script. Other examples include walking down a circular staircase, scuba diving in gradually deepening water, riding on a train going deeper and deeper into a tunnel, falling slowly down through progressively thicker layers of clouds.

2. Spend a few moments inducing a relaxation response. Then close your eyes and try to visualize the first of your ideas for a deepening image in turn.

3. After imagining the image, rate it using the same Effectiveness Scale you used before:

Effectiveness Scale
1 = Unable to reproduce the image
2 = Questionable reproduction of the image
3 = Reproduced the image enough for it to be recognizable
4 = Fairly good reproduction of the image
5 = Reproduced the image vividly

4. Repeat steps 2 and 3 with each of your ideas.

You'll want to use the images with the highest ratings in your induction script. Remember that you can use the same image more than once, or you can use variations of the same image.

Exercise
Making Your Personal Induction Tape

At this point, you have all the information you need to write your own induction script.

1. In your notebook, head a new page "Induction Script."

2. Refer to the sample script earlier in the chapter as an outline. You will substitute images that you have identified as effective for you personally for images in the script that make you feel uncomfortable or seem less satisfactory.

3. Write out a new script for those sections, remembering the principles of repetition and deepening.

4. When you have devised your own script following the outline of the sample, you are ready to record it. Remember to include the first two sections on preparation and relaxation from the sample. Also remember to keep the quality of your voice low and rhythmic, positive and confident.

Practicing with Your Tape

Your next task is to practice going into hypnotic trances so that you will, in effect, prepare fertile ground for the suggestions that will help you overcome fears and make progress toward belonging.

The process of hypnosis can be thought of as a gradual dimming of the houselights in a theater while a spotlight is focused on the stage. With that, the attention of the entire audience is shifted from many, many places in the theater to a single place. It's time now for you to learn to shift your attention from the world at large to a single subject.

In a sense, this is a refinement of things you do already. For example, you automatically block out extraneous noises. You breathe without thinking about it, and you are usually unaware of a host of tactile sensations, such as the texture of your clothing, the feel of the chair beneath you, and the weight of this book in your hand. In other words, you selectively focus your attention all of the time. Using hypnosis, you will just be further refining that ability.

Before you can effectively go on to the next chapter, in which you will use hypnotic suggestions in elminating fears, you need to reach a certain level of proficiency with trance induction. The Trance-Depth Chart is provided (at the end of the chapter) so that you can track your progress. (It is similar to the Before-and-After Chart you used with the relaxation exercises in the last chapter.) The criterion you will need to meet is to reach a trance depth of 2 to 3 or greater in roughly two out of every three sessions. There is no need to go deeper.

It's not possible for me to say how many sessions you'll need to obtain the trance depth necessary for our purposes, since it varies greatly from individual to individual. It may take you a matter of weeks or far less. However, the vast majority of people are able to reach a depth of 3 within a reasonable period of time.

Exercise
Trance Induction and Ratification

Do this exercise daily until you are able to reach a trance depth of 3 in two out of every three sessions.

1. Get comfortable and then listen to your induction tape. Make an effort to give yourself over to the instructions on the tape.

2. When you reach the end of the tape, before giving yourself the suggestion to resurface, *think* the following suggestion. Do not talk aloud, as that will tend to lighten the trance. The words you use need not be identical to those used below; for example, you can substitute the word *my* for *your* or *right hand* for *left hand*.

Trance Ratification

Concentrate on the fingers of your left hand. Focus all of your attention on the fingers of your left hand. Concentrate on them. Be aware of the fingers of your left hand. [Pause]

Feel a restlessness growing in the fingers of your left hand. Be aware of a twitching in the fingers of your left hand. Feel the restlessness—almost an electric feeling. A restless tingling sensation. [Pause] *Feel the restlessness.* [Pause]

Be aware of the tingling in the fingers of your left hand.
Feel the tingling. The tingling is growing. The tingling is
spreading. [Pause]

Feel the tingling in the fingers of your left hand. The tin-
gling is growing strong. It's spreading. Feel the tingling. [Keep
repeating similar thoughts to yourself until you feel the
tingling]

At this point you should indeed feel a tingling sensation in
the fingers of your left hand, which would indicate that you have
reached a trance depth sufficient for what you want to accomplish
here. The trance depth would be rated as 2 to 3 on a scale of 1 to
9, with 1 equivalent to the lightest possible trance.

3. If you wish, just for fun, you can continue this suggestion further to test for additional trance depth.

The tingling grows stronger and stronger. It moves up
into your left hand. Feel the tingling moving up into your left
hand. The tingling is spreading higher and higher. Feel it. Feel
the tingling spreading, moving higher. [Pause]

The tingling is changing. It's changing. It's changing to a
feeling of lightness. To a feeling of airiness spreading
throughout your left hand. [Pause]

Lightness and airiness spreading throughout your left
hand. Feel it. Be aware of it. Concentrate on the the lightness
and airiness throughout your left hand. [Pause]

And it moves higher. Feel the lightness, the airiness
moving up into your left arm. Feel it spreading all the way up
to your elbow. A lightness and airiness all the way from finger-
tips to elbow. [Pause]

Your left arm feels light and airy. Light and airy all the
way from fingertips to elbow. Very light and airy. [Pause]

Feel the buoyancy. Your left arm is light and buoyant.
Light and buoyant all the way from fingertips to elbow. Con-
centrate on the buoyancy. Be aware of it. Concentrate on it.
Feel it. Feel the buoyancy. All the way from fingertips to elbow.

[Continue along these lines until you feel a lightness in your left
arm]

*Now compare your left arm with your right. Your left arm
is light and airy. Your left arm is so buoyant, but your right
arm is so heavy. Feel the difference: light, buoyant left arm,
heavy, heavy right arm.*

By now your left arm should indeed feel light and buoyant,
indicating a trance depth rating of 4 or 5 on our scale of 1 to 9.

4. To test for further depth, which is interesting but not necessary,
   continue with the suggestion:

   *Concentrate on the buoyancy of your left arm. The light-
   ness and airiness of your left arm. It feels so light and airy.*

   *It feels as if there is a string attached to your left wrist
   and the string is attached to a balloon filled with helium. The
   string is tugging at your wrist as the balloon rises. It keeps tugging at your wrist as the balloon rises.*

   *Your arm is rising as the string tugs at your wrist. Feel
   it floating. It's floating. Feel your left arm rising and floating.
   Light and airy. Floating.* [Repeat approximately the same
   suggestion two or three times]

If your left arm actually rises at this point, your trance depth
is somewhere between 5 and 6. If your arm doesn't rise, you could
continue the suggestion a little further:

   *Your left arm is so light, so airy, so buoyant. It feels as if
   it is a balloon filled with helium. Your left arm is a balloon
   filled with helium.*

   *Feel it. Feel the buoyancy. Your left arm is filled with
   helium from fingertips to elbow. And it's rising. It's floating.
   Feel your left arm rising, floating. Floating upward higher and
   higher.* [Keep repeating with variations until you feel your
   arm rise]

Again, if your arm rises and floats, you have achieved a
trance depth of 5 or 6. Bear in mind that a depth of 2 to 3 is entirely
sufficient for the exercises in this book.

5. End the self-hypnosis session by imagining that your body is
   growing lighter and your mind more buoyant. You imagine that

you are moving upward, and then tell yourself mentally: *Come back to this time and this place. And open your eyes when you are ready.*

6. Using the Trance Depth Chart, record how deep you were able to go.

Principles of Hypnotic Suggestion

In the next chapter, you'll work with hypnotic suggestions to begin eliminating the fears that keep you apart from others. After experimenting with the trance ratification suggestions, you have probably already deduced some of the principles of hypnotic suggestion. You'll need to understand these principles in order to frame suggestions in a manner most likely to be effective. There are other principles, but you don't need to be familiar with them for your purpose here.

Repetition

Suggestions are more likely to flourish if they are repeated several times during a hypnotic session. For most purposes three repetitions are sufficient.

Variation

When repeating suggestions, vary them somewhat from one repetition to another. It may be more effective to vary them by using both a verbal form of the suggestion (thinking in words) and visual imagery (thinking essentially the same thought in pictures).

Think back, for instance, to the sample induction script. I used two iterations (repetitions with variation) of the suggestion for the word *calm* to be associated with a state of relaxed tranquility. First you thought of the word *calm* while associating it with a relaxed body and a tranquil mind. Then you associated calm with an image of yourself on a screen looking relaxed and tranquil.

Alternation

Where possible, alternate suggestions with deepening procedures, since suggestions tend to lighten trance depth. And remember, you'll have to keep working to keep the trance sufficiently deep, because there is natural tendency to rise out of the trance.

Positive Statements

Frame your suggestions in positive terms. You wouldn't, for instance, tell yourself, "I won't be nervous at Margie's wedding." You would say instead, "I will be comfortable and confident at Margie's wedding."

Confidence

Always keep in mind that, framed correctly and given enough time and the proper circumstances, most suggestions will indeed work. Think through your suggestions confidently, expecting them to work.

Bear in mind, though, that suggestions aren't magic. You must *work with* the suggestions in your daily life. A person who isn't motivated and isn't actively trying to stop smoking won't give up cigarettes just because he has been told to do so in a hypnotic trance. He has to work with the suggestion—not against it. He must structure his daily life to allow the suggestion to work.

Focus on Goals

It will enhance the effectiveness of any hypnotic suggestion to focus on your ultimate goal at some time during the session. This will reinforce motivation at a deep level. Because your goal is to overcome loneliness, you would want to see an image of yourself mixing happily and easily with others. At some time during the session, visualize yourself on a screen having a wonderful time at a party or with people in whatever circumstances you prefer.

Limited Number of Suggestions

Don't work on too many suggestions at one time. Limit yourself to no more than two or three per session. Often, you'll want to limit yourself to one important suggestion, iterated several times.

Simplicity

Keep your suggestions as simple as possible. Make the wording and images easy to understand and remember. Don't leave any room for misunderstanding.

Timing of Suggestions

As a general rule, place your most important suggestion toward the end of the self-hypnosis session. In other words, place suggestions into the session in order of importance, with the least important coming first.

Use of Will Power

Actually, this section could be titled "Nonuse of Will Power." Don't strain yourself mentally to make suggestions work. They don't work through the power of determination.

Simply focus your attention on a properly framed suggestion while you are in a sufficiently deep trance. Just let it happen. It's like going to sleep; determinedly ordering yourself to sleep will only keep you awake. The only successful strategy is to prepare yourself for sleep and let it happen.

It's Planting Time

Don't expect immediate results with hypnosis. Think of the suggestions you give yourself under self-hypnosis as seeds that need nurturing—water, sunlight, good soil. Even under the best of conditions an occasional seed fails to grow. More often, though, seeds that are planted carefully with the right nutrients flourish in season.

Before you can expect hypnotic suggestions to germinate, you must learn to focus attention on the seed that you are planting: water and feed it often. And then give it time to grow.

Trance-Depth Chart

Instructions: Photocopy this page and use it to keep a record of your progress. The following will help you rate the depth of your trances. When you consistently reach a depth of 2 to 3 (in two out of three sessions) you are ready to go on to the next chapter.

Trance-Depth Scale

1 = No tingling felt   **2–3** = Tingling in finger
4–5 = Arm feels light   **5–6** = Arm rises and float
7–8 = Pain is blocked   **9** = No recall of events during trance

Session	Depth	Comments
1		
2		
3		
4		
5		
6		
7		
8		
9		
10		
11		
12		
13		
14		
15		
16		
17		
18		
19		
20		
21		
22		
23		
24		

7

Neutralizing Your Fears

Your mastery of deep relaxation will prove indispensable in neutralizing your fears. It's a physiological fact that you cannot simultaneously be fearful and relaxed. Your body responds by releasing either hormones that soothe or hormones that activate—never both at the same time.

Fears are neutralized by training your body to release soothing hormones in situations where it has been releasing activating hormones. Your knowledge of self-hypnosis will allow you to reproduce these fearful situations in your imagination, so that you can transform them into benign situations.

This transformation is possible because the social situations you find frightening are not intrinsically harmful. It's not as if you literally fear for life and limb. Rationally, you know you are not likely to be injured in any way. Instead, the harm you fear is in your imagination. Of course, there is a risk of embarrassment or even humiliation, but physiologically you are reacting as if you were in physical peril.

Your fear, and the release of activating hormones, comes not from actual danger but rather from *thinking* that you are in danger. You will neutralize the fear by changing your thinking.

You would have discarded your fear long ago if you could have changed your thinking through will power alone. The fact that you have progressed this far in your quest to belong proves that you have the determination to dispose of your fear. You need more than motivation, however. You need the proper tools to change your thinking and neutralize fear. And you have two of those tools now: deep relaxation and self-hypnosis. In this chapter you will use deep relaxation and self-hypnosis to neutralize fear.

Breaking Fears into Manageable Pieces

In chapter 1 you faced your fears about social situations. You grouped those fears by theme and gave each theme a name. In this chapter you will learn to neutralize the fear underlying each theme.

To do this, you will break each theme down into ten *fear steps*, which together constitute a *fear staircase*. Each fear step is a little higher, or more threatening, than the one preceding it. Let's say that fear step 1 represents 10 percent of the potential fear the theme holds for you. Fear step 2 would then represent 20 percent; fear step 6, 60 percent; and fear step 10, 100 percent.

When you neutralize the fear behind fear step 1, fear step 2 also loses much of its power. Its fear level is reduced from 20 percent to 10 percent. In fact, the fear level behind all of the remaining fear steps is reduced by 10 percentage points, so that fear step 3 is now at 20 percent and fear step 10 at 90 percent.

Once fear step 1 has been neutralized, you move on to neutralize fear step 2, which is now at a 10 percent level of fear. When fear step 2 is neutralized, fear step 3, which started out at 30 percent and is now down to 10 percent, is the next to be neutralized— and so on until you work your way through all 10 fear steps. At that point all of the fear behind the theme has been discarded.

Note that you will never endeavor to neutralize more than 10 percent of your fear at any given time. In other words, you will chip away at your fear by degrees. By dismantling your fear in manageable increments, you will never feel overwhelmed by it.

An Example of a Fear Staircase

A widower with two children in college, Alex was a lonely man. He had been married for 22 years when his wife died in an industrial accident. Among many other problems, this shy man suddenly had no one to stimulate him socially. He found himself going to work, doing chores at home, and filling the rest of his time with reading and television. He hated it.

When Alex and I began his therapy, I had him work on identifying his fears and their underlying themes, as you did in chapter 1. After some soul searching, Alex identified five individual fears that had always held him back from belonging. He was able to group the five fears under two themes:

Theme 1—Fear of Being Judged
    a. Fear of being thought stupid
    b. Fear of appearing foolish
    c. Fear of being considered an intellectual fraud

Theme 2—Fear of Revealing Anxiety
    a. Fear of quaver in voice
    b. Fear of tremor in fingers

Rather than five individual fears, Alex actually had three variations on the fear of being judged and two variations on the fear of revealing his anxiety. By grouping his fears in this way, Alex had the more manageable task of neutralizing two basic fears rather than five individual fears.

Once he had identified his themes, Alex needed to take each of them and break them down into fear steps. He started with Theme 1—Fear of Being Judged, which had the higher rank of the two themes he had identified. That is, his fear of being judged was greater, or more powerful, than his fear of revealing his anxiety to other people.

Alex and I spent an hour or so discussing his fear of being judged. I explained that our task was to construct a hierarchy, or staircase, of ten fear steps related to his fear of being judged.

The fear steps were to be scenes that Alex could visualize. The events in the scenes should be plausible, even if they were improbable, and he should be able to imagine himself easily in each scene.

Start at the Top

Each fear step was to be somewhat more fearful than the one before it, just as the steps on a staircase go higher and higher. The fear steps, I explained to Alex, should range from the least fearful scene he could imagine to the most fearful; however, we would work in reverse order.

I asked Alex to describe his most fearful scene—a scene that would stir up 100 percent of his fear of being judged. He said that was easy, since he had already been in that scene in real life.

Alex, who had always been at the top of his class in school, had been selected to represent his high school in a televised competition with gifted students from several other high schools. Although Alex would have preferred to forget the whole thing, he felt he couldn't refuse the coveted invitation—it would have been equivalent to a talented athlete's having refused a chance to quarterback the football team.

When Alex accepted the invitation, the competition was months away. Although he felt anxious about it, he was able to block out the anxiety most of the time. But, despite an immense amount of preparation, he grew increasingly anxious as the date of the competition approached. When it finally arrived, he was so nervous that he couldn't retrieve the knowledge he had so carefully stored.

In short, Alex blew it. He came in last in the competition and felt that he had made a fool of himself in view of all of his friends, acquaintances, relatives, and thousands of strangers. Unfortunately, he was also teased unmercifully by some of the students who would have liked to have been in his place.

Since the competition 30 years ago, Alex had felt like an intellectual fraud. Already shy, he grew less comfortable in groups of people. He always felt that his memory would fail him, so that he would appear stupid, even when answering such harmless questions as "Who wrote that book you've been talking about?"

For Alex, then, fear step 10 was his disastrous performance at the competition. For him, recalling this scene evoked 100 percent

Fear Staircase

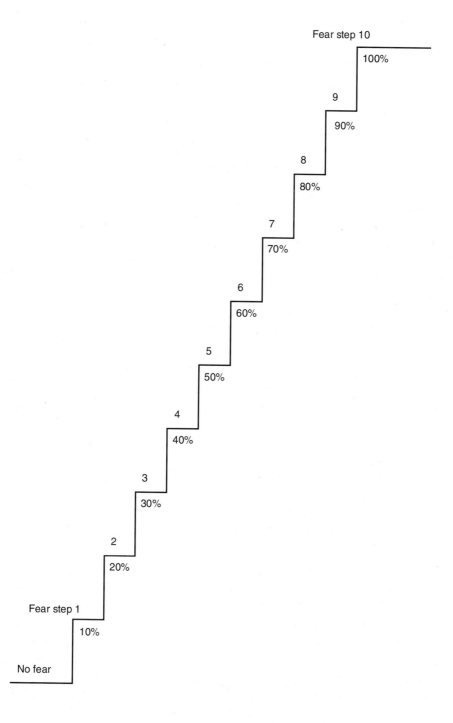

of the anxiety associated with the theme of being judged. He couldn't imagine a scene that would make him more uncomfortable.

Although Alex's ultimate fear step was a reenactment of real life, it didn't necessarily have to be. For many people fear step 10 is a scene that is dreaded but exists only in the imagination. Roxanne, for example, could think of nothing worse than fainting at a formal occasion. In fact, she hadn't fainted since she was an adolescent. Nevertheless, the thought of fainting at a wedding or funeral elicited 100 percent of the anxiety associated with her fear theme of losing control in public.

Go to the Bottom

Whatever its nature, fear step 10 is generally constructed first, followed by fear step 1. In this way, the extremes of the hierarchy—the top and bottom steps of the staircase—are used to create a framework—something like figuring out how tall a staircase in your house would need to be, before you begin to build it. Fear step 1 should be a scene that causes anxiety—but to the least extent possible. It should not be possible, then, to imagine a scene related to the theme that would elicit *less* fear.

I rate the small degree of fear associated with fear step 1 as 10 percent of the total fear possible. Another way of looking at it is that fear step 1 is only 10 percent as frightening as fear step 10.

With regard to being judged, Alex said that the least frightening scene, fear step 1, would be to have difficulty finding words—getting tongue-tied—when a third person witnesses a conversation he is having with someone else. In this scene, his mind goes blank trying to recall the name of a person, place, or thing. He said that this would make him feel foolish enough to be uncomfortable, although he wouldn't feel particularly uncomfortable if there were not a third person present. It was the presence of an audience that seemed to bother him.

Jump to the Middle

Next, I asked Alex to create fear step 5, which would be halfway between no fear at all and the worst imaginable fear. That is, 50 percent of the maximum anxiety would be evoked when he imagined this scene. After some thought, Alex decided that fear step 5 would involve being called on to give a toast at a wedding reception or family anniversary celebration. Once again, his fear was related to his mind going blank in front of an audience.

At this point, Alex's fear staircase for the theme of being judged looked like the chart on the following page.

Then Fill in Between

If it comes easier for you, you may prefer to construct the steps in your fear staircase in a different order from that shown here. But I have found that usually people can judge extremes and halfway points fairly easily—easier, say, than estimating 10-percent increments in order. Once the extreme and middle steps have been identified, it just becomes a matter of filling in the gaps. And by the time you get to the gaps, you've had enough practice for the task to be fairly simple.

For example, after Alex determined fear step 5, he worked out step 3, which is halfway between 1 and 5. Next, he went to fear step 2, midway between 1 and 3, and then step 4, midway between 3 and 5.

At this point fear steps 6, 7, 8, and 9 had yet to be worked out. As none of these were exactly halfway between completed steps, he used a slightly different approach. Alex constructed scenes that he estimated to be 10 percent more fearful than the scenes immediately preceding them. He completed fear steps 6, 7, 8, and finally 9, in this manner. Here's the order in which Alex's fear steps were constructed:

Order of Construction

10
1
5
3
2
4
6
7
8
9

Alex's Fear Staircase
Theme 1—Fear of Being Judged

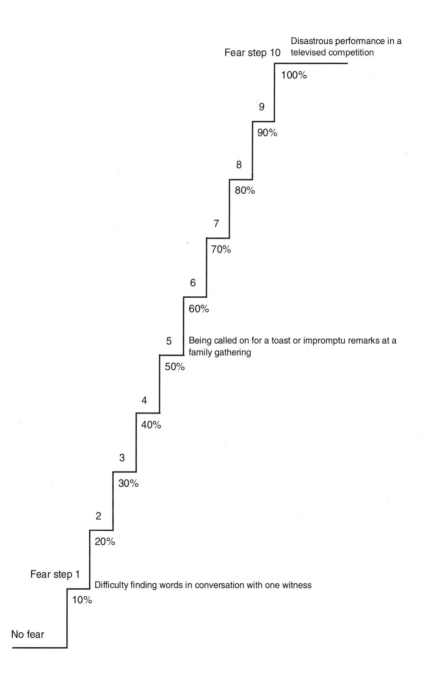

Fear step 10   Disastrous performance in a televised competition

100%

9

90%

8

80%

7

70%

6

60%

5   Being called on for a toast or impromptu remarks at a family gathering

50%

4

40%

3

30%

2

20%

Fear step 1   Difficulty finding words in conversation with one witness

10%

No fear

Alex's finished fear staircase looked like the one on the following page.

Needless to say, no one can complete a hierarchy with steps that are precisely 10 percent apart. The point is to strive for a series of graduated steps, in which each step is only a little more fearful than the one before it. If the amount of fear from one step to another is too great, the procedure for neutralizing fear will not work. The idea is to chew away at the fear in small bites. If the bites are too large, there is a danger of choking on them.

Constructing Fear Staircases

Defining the Dimensions of Your Fear

You may have noticed from Alex's fear staircase that his anxiety seemed to increase in several "dimensions." The size of the audience was important to him—the more people involved, the more nervous he was. His familiarity with the audience was another dimension; his discomfort grew as he went from events with extended family to events with friends to events with acquaintances and strangers.

The complexity of material to be recalled was also a dimension of fear for Alex. He became more anxious as he went from difficulty in finding words to recall of facts and then to composing and relating impromptu remarks and performing.

A fourth and final dimension of fear was the formality of the occasion, with fear growing as the events became more formal, perhaps because graceful "escape" from the event was less likely the more formal the event. Alex knew, for instance, that he could slip away, from a family reunion with less commotion than from a church service.

It will be helpful in devising your first fear staircase to define the dimensions of your fear. Perhaps, like Alex, the more people involved, the more fearful you become. It could be that the more you feel you are in the spotlight, the more uncomfortable you are. Time could be a fear dimension, with anxiety growing as the date for a major social event grows nearer. Similarly, physical space could be a dimension.

Alex's Fear Staircase
Theme 1—Fear of Being Judged

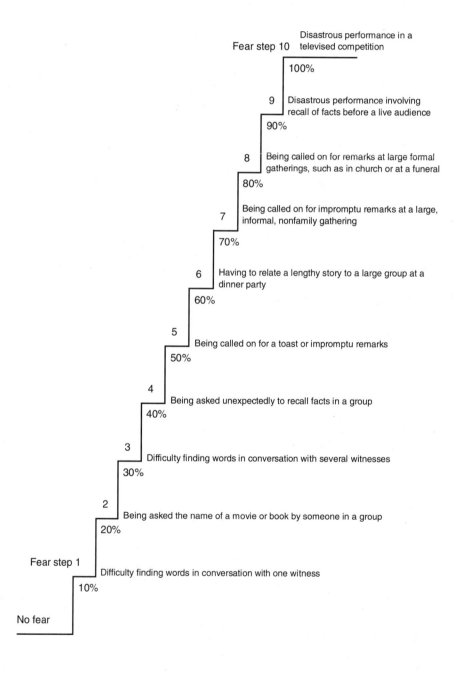

Fear step 10   Disastrous performance in a televised competition

100%

9   Disastrous performance involving recall of facts before a live audience

90%

8   Being called on for remarks at large formal gatherings, such as in church or at a funeral

80%

7   Being called on for impromptu remarks at a large, informal, nonfamily gathering

70%

6   Having to relate a lengthy story to a large group at a dinner party

60%

5   Being called on for a toast or impromptu remarks

50%

4   Being asked unexpectedly to recall facts in a group

40%

3   Difficulty finding words in conversation with several witnesses

30%

2   Being asked the name of a movie or book by someone in a group

20%

Fear step 1   Difficulty finding words in conversation with one witness

10%

No fear

You will use the dimensions of your fear that you identify in the following exercise to help you construct staircases for each of your fear themes.

Exercise
Analyzing Your Fears

Begin with the theme you ranked number 1—the theme that provokes the most anxiety. Later you'll do this same exercise for each of your other fear themes.

1. Turn back to the page labeled "My Fears" in your notebook, and refer to the key you created at the top of the page.

2. Determine which theme you identified as being the most fearful, and write the name of that theme at the top of a new page in your notebook. Subtitle the page "Dimensions."

3. Take some time to analyze the dimensions of your fears with that theme, referring back to the "My Fears" page as necessary. You may have only one or several dimensions for each theme.

4. List your findings on the "Dimensions" page for that theme.

When you are ready to create additional fear staircases, you will repeat this exercise for the other themes you identified.

Devising Your Fear Steps

At this juncture, you have identified the dimensions of the fears underlying your first theme. You will use this information to construct your first fear staircase, in the following exercise. Before you proceed, you may find it helpful to reread the section "An Example of a Fear Staircase." I estimate that it will take you about an hour to complete your first staircase.

Exercise
Building Your Fear Staircase

Using the fear dimensions you defined in the preceding exercise for theme 1 and the process described in "An Example of a Fear Staircase," build a fear staircase for your highest ranking fear theme.

1. Head a page in your notebook "Fear Staircase 1" and write down the name of your highest ranked fear theme (or make a photocopy of the blank Fear Staircase page and use it the same way).

2. Begin by identifying fear step 10: the worst possible scene you can imagine happening that involves that theme. This scene embodies 100 percent of your fear. Write a brief (one sentence) description of that theme.

3. Then identify a scene for fear step 1. This is an image that creates a mild anxiety, the least you can imagine, but not none at all. It should be roughly one-tenth as anxiety provoking as fear step 10. Record that step just as you did fear step 10.

4. Next, identify a scene that is midway between 1 and 10. It should cause a moderate amount of anxiety—approximately half of the maximum that fear step 10 represents. Record the step.

5. Fill in the rest of the steps in the following order: 3, 2, 4, 6, 7, 8, 9.

Later you will construct fear staircases for your remaining themes using this same process.

The Neutralization Process

Before you go on to devise your other fear staircases, you will begin to dismantle Fear Staircase 1. The neutralization process will involves your thinking about fearful events without allowing your body to react as if you were in danger.

Given enough time and the proper procedures, you will "unlearn" that those events are fearful. You will train your body at a very deep level to release calming hormones in situations where it has been releasing activating and mobilizing hormones. In effect, you will create a built-in tranquilizer for yourself.

Alex's progress was fairly typical, neither unusually fast nor unusually slow. After two weeks or so of working through the neutralization procedures, Alex began to notice that his fear was indeed diminishing. He did most of the actual work on his own, just as you will.

After I helped him construct his fear staircases and took him through a few trial runs, Alex did the relaxation and visualization exercises at home. My input then was mostly encouragement, which Alex needed during the period before he noticed much change in his anxiety level.

As I'm sure will be your experience, Alex's progress accelerated once he got through his first fear staircase. He spent about five weeks neutralizing his most fearful staircase, working almost every day in 30-minute sessions.

It was during the initial two weeks that Alex had the most problem with motivation. He said that it seemed to take forever to get through the first few steps of the first staircase. At some point, though, he said, "The tiny faucet in my brain turned on and released all those soothing hormones." It was as if Alex's efforts created some neurologic-endocrine change, which became more and more pronounced as he continued to practice the neutralization procedure. It was also, I believe, a matter of increased self-confidence.

Once Alex realized that he was indeed making progress, he found that he was eager to get on with the neutralization. He completed his second fear staircase, the one for his theme of Fear of Revealing Anxiety, in about two weeks. In only seven weeks, then, Alex had created a built-in tranquilizer for situations that had frightened him for about 30 years. A few weeks seems brief when you look at it that way.

You have completed all the necessary preparations for neutralizing the most salient fear that has been holding you back from belonging. It's time now to begin the neutralization process with Fear Staircase 1.

Continue on with this chapter and into subsequent chapters as you begin neutralizing your fears. It will probably take you three to six weeks to dismantle Fear Staircase 1, if you work at it every day for a half-hour or so.

Exercise
Dismantling Your Fear Staircase

Neutralizing your fears is only possible if you tackle them in small increments, which is what the fear staircase allows you to do. Take on too much fear at one time, and you will be overwhelmed and demoralized. Be patient and persistent as you follow these steps to dismantle Fear Staircase 1.

1. Use the Tension Scale below to rate your level of tension as you go through the neutralization process. Before beginning the neutralization process, rate the level of tension for all ten fear steps and record the ratings in the appropriate spaces on the Fear Staircase Record.

Tension Scale
1 = Totally relaxed, no tension **2** = Very relaxed
3 = Moderately relaxed **4** = Fairly relaxed
5 = Slightly relaxed **6** = Slightly tense
7 = Fairly tense **8** = Moderately tense **9** = Very tense
10 = Extremely tense (the most uncomfortable you could be)

2. Use self-hypnosis to relax and induce a trance sufficiently deep for you to visualize the steps in your fear staircase.

3. When you are very calm and deeply relaxed, visualize fear step 1. If you find yourself growing anxious, shift your visualization to a neutral, calming scene. When your tension level has declined to a rating of 1 or 2, shift back to fear step 1.

4. Keep working with fear step 1 until you are able to visualize it while keeping your tension level at a rating of 1 or 2, which may take more than one session. When you have met this criterion, record the date and final tension level in the space provided on the Fear Staircase Record.

5. You will work through the remaining nine fear steps as you did fear step 1. The only difference is that when you find your anxiety growing during visualization, you back up to the previous fear step instead of visualizing a neutral scene.

   If necessary, you can keep backing down the fear staircase until you reach a step for which your tension level is 1 or 2. If this happens, you probably have been moving too fast up the staircase without having completely neutralized previous fear steps.

6. When you have successfully dismantled your first fear staircase,

go on to the next most fearful theme. If you have not already constructed a staircase for that theme, do so by referring back to the preceding exercises. Then follow steps 1 through 5 above. Continue this process until all of your fear themes have been neutralized.

Fear Staircase Record

Instructions: Make a separate copy of this page for each of your fear staircases, and use it to record your progress. Use the Tension Scale to rate the level of tension you feel regarding each fear step before you begin the neutralization process for each staircase. Then rate your level of tension for that step after you have dismantled that step, and record the date.

Tension Scale

1 = Totally relaxed, no tension   2 = Very relaxed
3 = Moderately relaxed   4 = Fairly relaxed
5 = Slightly relaxed   6 = Slightly tense
7 = Fairly tense   8 = Moderately tense   9 = Very tense
10 = Extremely tense (the most uncomfortable you could be)

Fear Staircase ___

Theme: _____

Fear Step	Tension Level Before	Tension Level After	Date Achieved
1			
2			
3			
4			
5			
6			
7			
8			
9			
10			

It Gets Faster from Here On

Congratulations! You have achieved a major goal in your quest to belong—you have neutralized many of the fears holding you back. When you are ready, you can go on to construct and dismantle your remaining fear staircases. Keep in mind that the first fear staircase is always the hardest. You'll almost certainly find yourself picking up speed as you progress from one fear staircase to another.

Be sure to complete all of the exercises above for each of the fear themes you identified in chapter 1: analyzing the dimensions of your fears, building the staircase, and then dismantling it step by step. Not only will it take you less time to construct each succeeding fear staircase, but you can expect to spend less time neutralizing each step. The process picks up steam as you move ahead. Hang in there!

8

Learning Social Skills

Communication is the essence of social interaction, and conversation is at the core of communication. With good conversational skills you can function well in any social setting. Focusing on a conversation also means that you become less self-conscious; you take your attention off of yourself and place it where it belongs—on the interaction. More importantly, conversation is where the beginnings of friendships are formed.

As you learn to converse comfortably, you will begin to enjoy conversation, and you will find yourself initiating conversations rather than avoiding them. You will experience a growing confidence in your skills and begin to see yourself in a different, more positive light. Inevitably, as your liking for yourself grows and you come to appreciate your worth, others will be attracted to you.

The principles you will learn in this chapter can be applied in any setting, with minor modifications. You have opportunities to meet new people in any number of places—at work, in church, even at the car wash. I have concentrated on large social gatherings, such as cocktail parties and receptions, because lonely people seem to dread these most of all. Once you learn to meet people at these affairs, you'll find it a snap to approach people in settings where you have something built-in to talk about, say in a class, at a zoning hearing, or at a meeting of your local historical society.

First Impressions

Although they may be inaccurate or unfair, first impressions often result in attitudes that are slow to change. The influence of a first impression is far out of proportion to the influence of a second, third, or fourth impression. A brief first meeting can set the tone for social interaction, if not permanently, at least for a long time. You can use the power of first impressions to your advantage by following a few simple principles, which you may already know but, for whatever reasons, are not following.

Dress for Success

Which is right: "Don't judge a book by its cover" or "Clothes make the man"? Perhaps both are. In an ideal world people would reserve judgment until the inner substance and true worth of another was revealed. But in the real world people make hasty appraisals based on the evidence before them: speech, manners, posture, appearance.

There is probably some survival value in this tendency, despite the obvious injustice. If you were, for example, walking on a deserted side street in a big city, wouldn't you react differently to a well-groomed man looking straight ahead than you would to an unkempt man who was staring at you? We've all learned to expect certain things when people appear a certain way. That holds as true at a party as it does on a desolate street.

If you want to belong, you need to look as if you belong. Teenagers know this instinctively. As unfortunate as it may be, people are more apt to accept someone who looks like an "insider" than one who looks like an "intruder." To put it another way, people will be more attracted to you if you look and act like one of them. Of course, you want to be your own person—not just a "clone." But when making an initial impression you don't want to appear so different that you deflect interest. Once you connect, there will be plenty of time to let your individual traits emerge.

I remember well a move I once made from the coat-and-tie environment of a large eastern city to the shirt-sleeve informality of a small southern town. I didn't feel comfortable until I discarded the starched white shirts, and I suspect that I was regarded with suspicion until I learned to conform to local customs.

What is acceptable in one place can be absolutely wrong in another. Dress codes in Reno, Nevada, are different from those in Rochester, New York, and the differences are not all attributable to climate. Likewise, big cities are unlike little ones, and circles within a city can be very different from one another. Just because they share an island doesn't mean Manhattan academics dress or talk like Wall Street wheeler-dealers. If you've stayed in the same place for a long time, you probably know what is acceptable. If you're new to the area or even to a particular clique, you may not.

Because local customs vary so greatly in our vast country, your only recourse is to observe the people around you carefully. Start paying attention to how they act, how they dress, how they wear their hair, how they talk. A move from the deep South to the upper South once caught me by surprise because of the differences in speech. It had never occurred to me that, not only accents, but also word usage could be different four hundred miles up the interstate highway—not to mention the differences in foods, in the degree of formality, and in the types of parties people enjoyed.

Listen to What Your Body Is Saying

Apart from your dress and grooming, the very first impression anyone has of you is your body language. A glance at you across a room reveals a great deal about your attitude. The way you hold yourself can say "Whoa, back off. I'm not interested," while a few simple adjustments can communicate the opposite: "I'm eager to meet you. Come on over."

If you are shy or reticent around strangers, you may be giving off more negative signals than you realize. Despite sincerely wanting to belong, meeting and greeting strangers may be very difficult for you. The immediate discomfort for a long time may have been a stronger motivator than the eventual reward of having more friends. So, without having been consciously aware of it, you may have habitually avoided anxiety and discomfort by closing off your access to strangers. It's also possible that you have given off negative signals simply through bad habits.

Leave Me Alone!

Although we rarely think about these things consciously, there are universal signals in our culture that give us clues to another person's frame of mind. At a party, would you readily approach a stranger sitting with arms folded, legs crossed, frowning with a finger or two over his mouth? You almost certainly wouldn't because these are classic signs that say "Leave me alone!"

You may be thinking "But I always stand with my arms crossed. I don't mean anything by it. I'm just more comfortable that way." That may be, but crossed arms *do* covey a negative message. Such a posture tends to be interpreted as a sign of impatience or displeasure, if not outright anger. It signals a combative or defensive mood.

It is probably more acceptable today than in earlier times for people to sit with their legs crossed. During the Victorian era, for instance, a woman would never have crossed her legs except perhaps discreetly at the ankles, nor were men as likely to sit with their legs crossed. Because crossing one's legs is so common today, it has lost, I suspect, much of its negative connotation. Still, it may signal a closed attitude, which might be worth the trouble to avoid. It can also imply a casual demeanor, which may not be appropriate in some situations.

Slouching implies defeat, fatigue, or simply "I don't care." It conveys the impression of an uninterested and uninteresting person, who is not worth the trouble to approach. It signals an individual who is not necessarily unapproachable but one who is bored and tiresome.

Needless to say, a frown is a powerful negative signal. And a neutral facial expression, while not necessarily negative, isn't positive either. Look around in any group of people. Who would you most like to talk to: the frowning person, the person with a neutral expression, or someone smiling?

Other types of behavior can also send out a "No Trespassing" message—staring out a window with your back to the room, looking at the floor, rummaging through your purse or adjusting your clothing—anything that conveys the impression that your attention is elsewhere, and not on making contact.

Come Join Me!

Before you say a word to another person, that person attempts to read your mind through your body language. Fortunately, with a little practice it's easy to convey a positive message. Whether your goal is to make new contacts or to seal friendships with acquaintances, follow what I'll call the "principle of openness."

To appear approachable, keep an open posture. Don't cross your arms or legs. Keep your hands away from your face, so that you don't inadvertently cover part or all of your mouth. Above all, *smile!* Don't wear a fake grin, but keep the corners of your mouth up, not down, and erase those frown lines. A smile is as welcoming to others as a frown is forbidding.

Whether you are sitting or standing, keep your body straight. If you are standing, keep your weight evenly distributed on both feet with one foot perhaps slightly in front of the other—hips straight, shoulders back, chin up. An erect posture conveys confidence and poise, which makes a person seem more interesting and attractive. Of course, this doesn't mean standing at attention, but rather a balanced stance in which, for example, you could recover from a sudden push without falling.

If you can't remember to keep your arms uncrossed, which men seem to have more trouble with than women, keep them behind your back or in your pockets. Neither of these postures is as open as keeping your hands by your sides or up in front ready to gesture, but it's better than keeping them close to your chest. Keep in mind that crossed arms signal combativeness or a judgmental attitude, which throws up a barrier between you and other people.

You may be concerned about giving off unwanted sexual signals. Not to worry—the body language I'm suggesting is not seductive or coquettish. It simply signals that you are an interesting person willing to interact with other people.

The following exercise will help you begin to change body language that may be discouraging people from approaching you.

Exercise
Transforming Your Body Language

In this exercise you will first examine the messages you are unconsciously sending out to people in social situations. Then you will use the self-hypnosis techniques you have learned to substitute more open, friendly body language for your old, guarded bearing.

1. Over the next several days, whenever you are in public, pay attention to your body language: how you sit and stand; what you do with your hands, arms, legs; your facial expression. As soon as possible afterwards, jot down in your notebook what you were doing that could be interpreted as "No Trespassing" signals.

2. When you have identified body language that you need to modify, use self-hypnosis to overwrite those behaviors with friendlier gestures. Relax and induce a trance sufficiently deep for you to visualize yourself at a recent social gathering or with people at work or in some other setting. Visualize the scene appearing on a screen, and watch how the image of yourself on the screen sits, stands, and moves.

3. Watch for the negative signals you identified earlier, and when you see one, change it to a positive signal in the visualization. For example, if you see yourself frowning, change the frown to a smile. If you're crossing your arms, uncross them and put your hands in your lap or in your pockets.

4. Keep visualizing yourself in this way until you feel relaxed and natural while imagining yourself using positive body language in social situations. It may take several sessions to accomplish this goal.

Introductions

Okay, suppose that you're at a party, and your new and improved body language is saying "I'm a warm, interesting person—why not come talk to me?" And somebody does. Now what do you do?

Making Eye Contact

Nothing makes a better first impression than a warm smile combined with meeting someone's gaze eye to eye. Direct eye contact tells other people that they have all of your attention. It says that you are interested in them and that what they have to say is important to you. A case in point: The congressman from my district lost a vote when one of my clients first met him. The politician said the appropriate things, but as he talked he was looking around the room, in effect saying "Well, I'm stuck with you for the moment, but I'm looking for someone more important to talk to."

Of course, you don't want to stare down your new acquaintance. An unwavering, piercing look makes people uncomfortable. You'll want to glance away from time to time, and move your gaze occasionally around the other person's face. But always give the message that you are focused on the person and the conversation by looking him or her in the eye much of the time.

It is not appropriate in every situation to make direct eye contact with another person. You might be asking for trouble by making eye contact with a stranger on the street (depending on where you live) or staring into the eyes of a person in a car beside you at a traffic light. And in some circumstances, direct eye contact can be taken as—can in fact *be*—a sexual invitation.

Shaking Hands

Your first physical contact with a new acquaintance is usually a handshake. Although people in some places hug or kiss at first greeting, a handshake is always acceptable. In our culture, refusal of an extended hand is about as rude as you can get.

Two or three decades ago cultural norms determined which sex extended a hand first in what situations, but no more. Handshaking is now a simple and egalitarian ritual. Either person may extend a hand, and I suggest that you do so any time you are meeting someone. Whether you are female or male, your handshake should be firm, but not clenching, and reasonably brief. It should be accompanied by a smile and a simple greeting, such as "Hello. I'm Jan Jones. It's nice meeting you."

Approaching People

As unappealing as it may seem, introducing yourself to people vastly widens your social horizons. You can't expect to increase your circle of friends appreciably by waiting for people to come to you. Keep in mind that you're not the only person who finds it difficult to make the first move.

When you approach another person for the first time, there is always some risk of rejection and embarrassment—not much, though. People tend to be flattered that you sought them out. Wouldn't you be?

You can reduce whatever small risk there is by following two principles: First, approach people only when their body language suggests they will be receptive. Second, at large gatherings don't approach total strangers. (At a small gathering, you probably won't have to approach anybody, since the host is likely to take care of any introductions.) Look for people you've heard of, say friends of friends or someone who's active in your community. This gives you the double bonus of having a topic of conversation ready made.

Remembering Names

When you meet people, concentrate on remembering their names. If you don't understand a name, ask the person to repeat it or even spell it. Odds are, he or she will be pleased you're trying to get it right. Remembering the name will allow you to approach your new acquaintance much more easily next time.

When you can't remember a name, it's generally because you're distracted. Instead of concentrating on your new acquaintance, you may be busy worrying about whether you left the stove on or more likely about the impression you're making. While you're worrying, you're also missing the opportunity to make a better impression by remembering that name.

You can remember a name easily enough if you make a point to repeat it to yourself three or four times soon after meeting someone. Repeating the name silently to yourself when you first hear it helps fix it in your memory. Then call the person by name during the conversation.

You can also make a mnemonic association with the name. For instance, you might visualize Eva Poarch sitting on a porch in the evening. Frank Browning could be eating a hot dog (frankfurter) with brown mustard, and Tom Grey leading a big gray tomcat on a leash. Not only will this help you remember names, but concentrating on something besides yourself during the encounter will allow you to feel more comfortable and thus to appear more natural.

The next exercise uses visualization to help you consolidate what you've learned, or been reminded of, about making new acquaintances.

Exercise
Practicing Introductions

In this exercise you will use self-hypnosis and visualization to mentally practice meeting people.

1. Use self-hypnosis to relax and induce a trance sufficiently deep for you to visualize yourself at a real or imaginary large social gathering.

2. Use distancing to stand back in your imagination, and look at yourself as objectively as possible as you approach other people for the first time.

3. Visualize using appropriate body language, making direct eye contact, shaking hands, and giving an effective greeting.

4. Practice concentrating on the person's name and using mnemonic strategies to remember the name.

5. Go through steps 1 through 4 until your level of tension remains at a low level when you visualize meeting new people.

The Gentle Art of Conversation

Your task in meeting people is to present yourself as someone it would be nice to know better—pleasant, friendly, warm. In first conversations, it's better to steer clear of arguments and criticism, erudite discourse, and displays of biting wit. You want the person to feel good about talking to you, not put down or put off. Good debates and raucous humor can come later, when you are solid friends. First meetings are times for innocuous questions, compliments, and small talk.

Opening the Conversation

Knowing what to say to get a conversation going is often the hardest part. The following are a few tried-and-true tactics you can use.

Compliments

One way to open a conversation is with a compliment. "What an unusual necklace—it's lovely. Is it Middle Eastern?" This compliment-question combination serves a triple purpose: It opens the conversation, creates good will, and gives the other person an opening to pick up the conversation. I doubt anyone would be adverse to being greeted this way.

Complimenting a person you've just met can be a little tricky. Because you don't know the person, you can usually comment only on his or her appearance, and there may be nothing appropriate to compliment. If the person is well known in your community, you could possibly comment on something he or she has done, such as "I've heard about your fund raising for Hospice. I can't think of another organization more worthy of support."

You don't want a compliment to sound contrived, so don't say it if you don't mean it. Say it if you are sincere, but don't overstate it. You don't want to be gushy or seem to be trying too hard to connect.

If there is nothing immediately apparent about the person to compliment, you can always compliment something about the party. There should be something to remark on—the food, the host, the decorations, some item in the home, the overall atmosphere. When you first enter the room, look around specifically for things to mention later. And keep it positive. Even if the party is a complete bust, don't criticize the host or anything about the party.

Safe Topics

There's always the weather to talk about. "Did you have any trouble getting here through that storm? I was surprised to see so many people here." Talking about the weather may be a cliché, but people at any large party rival the forecasters on the Weather Channel for talk about weather.

With the exception of comments on dismal weather, stay away from negative or pessimistic topics. Avoid politics, religion, personal issues, and controversy of any kind. These are subjects to explore with good friends but not with first-time acquaintances.

Think of several safe topics before you leave home. (The following exercise can help with this.) Perhaps you could comment on the success of the local home team or let a comment about the food lead in to a mention of the new restaurant you recently tried. The idea is to be prepared with a few topics, so that your mind won't go blank after the handshake!

Exercise
Devising Safe Topics

By starting a list of safe conversation-starters now, you'll be well prepared for your next social event.

1. In your notebook, start a page called "Safe Topics." Jot down any you can think of now, and add to the list over the next few days or weeks as you think of them. You might also ask friends how they begin coversations or, if you have the opportunity, listen to how other people handle their first meetings.

2. Then, before you go to your next social event, review the list in your notebook.

3. While you are at the gathering, try out some of your topics. Also listen carefully to other people's openers.

4. After you return home add the new topics you heard to your list.

5. Finally, rate the topics you used and those you heard on a scale of 1 to 10, with 10 being very effective conversation-starters.

6. Continue to add to the list as you encounter effective safe topics, and review the list as you need to, to prepare for future social events. Eventually, opening a conversation will become second nature.

Keeping the Conversation Going

Next to starting a conversation, keeping it going can be the most difficult part of meeting people. You've probably been on one end or the other of a conversation that went something like this when both of you came up blank: "Wasn't it a beautiful ceremony?" "Oh yes, beautiful . . . I love weddings." "Ummm . . . " (pregnant silence) "Oh, there's my husband. 'Bye." Fortunately, it doesn't have to be like that. You can learn ways to keep the ball in play.

Questions and Answers

One tactic for keeping a conversation moving forward is to ask good questions. People usually appreciate an opportunity to talk, especially about themselves. It's simply a matter of lobbing the conversational ball back to them.

There are two basic types of questions. The first type is *closed-ended questions*, which can be answered with a single word or phrase, such as "How long have you lived in the city, Arnold?" or "What kind of work do you do?" Then there are *open-ended questions*, which lead to lengthy replies: "How did your daughter get interested in medicine, Alice?" "Why did you decide to move back East?"

Initially, you will have to ask questions that call for brief replies, so that you'll have a basis for the open-ended questions that keep the conversation going. You would, for example, have to ask about a person's profession before you could ask how he or she got into that profession. The first question calls for a brief response, but the second allows the person to go into as much detail as he or she wishes.

Open-ended questions begin with *how, why,* or an equivalent word or phrase: "How did you come to move here?" "What is it like working at home?" You'll find that one open-ended question soon leads to another. As you begin to know more about someone you've just met, you can ask about a myriad of topics—family, job, interests, history, future plans. One topic will flow smoothly into another, but only if you ask open-ended questions or have the luck to have met a loquacious person who talks without prompting. (Unfortunately, a good many talkative people turn out to be bores, in which case the luck is mostly bad.)

You will want to contribute to the conversation as well—to answer questions as well as to ask them. You should not, however, respond with long-winded replies. Give informative answers to open-ended questions, but don't at this stage go into great detail. Just remember that your goal is to make a new acquaintance who may eventually develop into a friend—not to give your life history, expound upon your views, or monopolize the conversation.

Listening

You won't be able to frame many open-ended questions if you don't listen to what is being said. You need to *concentrate on the conversation*—to think about what is being said, not about your next conversational gambit or what your new acquaintance thinks of you. If you listen carefully, the open-ended questions will come and the conversation will flow.

There's more to listening than just keeping your ears open, however. Even when only one party is doing most of the talking, conversation is still two-way communication. It's simply that the listener's end of the conversation is largely nonverbal. A good, "active" listener uses facial expressions, nods, gestures, and small, appropriate noises or verbal interjections to convey that he or she is listening, understands, and sympathizes.

Perhaps you've had the experience of talking to someone, either in person or on the telephone, who didn't acknowledge what you were saying by responding with "Mm-hmm" or "Okay" at regular intervals. It's disturbing because you don't really know whether or not you're getting your point across. On the other hand, when someone *does* use verbal and behavioral clues to let you know you're being heard, it's reassuring. You find yourself opening up to the person and wanting to say more.

Because of differnces in the way boys and girls are reared, listening often comes more easily for women. Since listening tends to be expected of them at an early age, women are more likely to pick it up naturally. Men usually have to work harder to listen effectively.

Good listening skills are valuable, if not vital, in most areas of life—not just when making new acquaintances. On the job, for example, really listening to what others say creates an impression of thoughtfulness and caring. It improves communication, which leads to more satisfied customers, fewer mistakes, improved efficiency, and happier employees. As a result, many corporations nowadays train their employees in how to listen.

Listening skills are just as valuable elsewhere—in the family, with friends, on committees, you name it. The following exercise will help you determine whether you are a good listener and, if you aren't, will get you started on training yourself to become one.

Exercise
Assessing Your Listening Skills

Instructions: First, photocopy this page. Then, for each of the following statements, rate how often it is true using the five-point Listening Scale below. When you are done, add up your total points.

Listening Scale
1 = Almost never   **2** = Not very often
3 = Occasionally   **4** = Usually   **5** = Almost always

Rating

1. I listen to what's being said instead of planning what I will say next.   _____

2. I listen even though I think I know what the speaker is going to say.   _____

3. I encourage the speaker to continue when he or she hesitates.   _____

4. I let the speaker finish what he or she has to say without interrupting.   _____

5. I listen equally well regardless of the sex or age of the speaker.   _____

6. I maintain eye contact with the speaker.   _____

Rating

7. I ignore distractions around I when I am listening to someone talk. _____

8. I encourage the speaker with smiles, nods, and occasional brief verbal interjections. _____

9. I listen regardless of the speaker's accent, grammar, and choice of words. _____

10. When someone is speaking to me I cease thinking about the problems of the day, what I have to do later, and so forth. _____

Total = _____

Key
35 or higher = Good listener
26 to **34** = Average listener
25 or below = Poor listener

If your total was less than 35, you need to practice your listening skills. Use the questionnaire to pinpoint your particular weak points, and make a conscious effort to work on them. This might mean forcing yourself to listen rather than jumping at the chance to talk, focusing on the conversation and the person who is speaking, or concentraing on making eye contact.

You might also try observing other people in conversation, noticing in particular what the person who *isn't* talking does: nodding, smiling, saying just a word or two, or making a sympathetic noise when the speaker pauses, and so on.

Practice your skills every chance you get. Then in a few weeks rate yourself using the questionnaire again. Keep working on your skills until your score is consistently 35 or more.

Ending the Conversation

You can steer the conversation in a direction you choose through your questions. Most people you meet for the first time will want to keep the conversation light. Occasionally, though, someone will open up and begin to talk about very personal subjects. If you can't find a way to move on to another subject, or don't want to try, it is probably time to end the conversation.

There will probably be occasions when you cannot find a topic of mutual interest. Try as you might, you make no progress. Don't feel defeated. Some people simply don't click—it isn't necessarily a reflection on your social skills. If you find you can't bridge the conversational gap it's time to move on to someone else.

Although there are always exceptions, a first conversation probably shouldn't last more than five or ten minutes. Beyond that, you may find yourself straining to keep things going. Of course, if your new acquaintance is a fascinating conversationalist or the two of you hit upon a topic or two of genuine mutual interest, forget the clock and enjoy yourself.

When you feel it's time to end a conversation, wait for the next lull or pause. If you are standing, extend your hand and tell your acquaintance that you enjoyed meeting and talking with him or her and that you hope the two of you meet again soon. If you are sitting down, say that you enjoyed meeting and talking to him or her and then stand. If your new acquaintance also stands, then extend your hand, smile pleasantly, and say that you hope the two of you meet again soon. If your acquaintance doesn't stand, don't extend your hand but smile and say the same thing or something equivalent.

In the next exercise you will practice your conversational skills using visualization. Once you feel comfortable with imaginary first conversations, it will be time to transfer your skills to reality.

Exercise
Practicing Conversational Skills

As you did in earlier exercises, you will use self-hypnosis and visualization here to "walk through" imaginary conversations, practicing what you have learned so far in this chapter.

1. Use self-hypnosis to relax and induce a trance sufficiently deep for you to visualize yourself at a real or imaginary social event.

2. Imagine that you are meeting someone for the first time, and, using all of the principles discussed in this chapter and prac-

ticed in earlier exercises, visualize introducing yourself, beginning a conversation, keeping it going, and ending it.

3. Repeat these steps with different scenes until your tension level remains low as you visualize talking with new people and conversation starts to seem easy and natural.

Forays into the Real World

If you consistently feel relaxed when you visualize meeting and conversing with new people, you are ready to apply your skills in the real world. The next exercise will help you to make the transition from imagination to reality and put together the work you've done in this chapter. Read it over now and again before you attend your next large social function.

Bear in mind that what you have been learning are just tactics for meeting people. Each tactic has a specific purpose, but they all contribute to one basic strategy: that of shifting your attention away from yourself. By focusing on the interaction and not on yourself, you escape the self-centered anxiety that has held you back for so long. You minimize your nervousness and build your self-confidence, which makes you more appealing and attractive to others.

Exercise
Tracking Your Progress

This is a two-part exercise. It is designed to be done partly before and partly after going to a social gathering. To do the "after" part, you will need to make a copy of the Social Events Progress Log.

1. Before you attend a social event, refer to the list in the Social Events Progress Log to remind yourself of behaviors you want to practice at the gathering. Since you have been practicing them through visualization, they should be quite familiar by now. Then go on to the gathering.

2. When you get home, take a few minutes to rate how well you think you did in each area on a scale of 1 to 10 and record your scores on the log. Repeat the process for each social event you attend until your score in each area is consistently 9 or 10.

Social Events Progress Log

Make a copy of this page before you attend your next social event.

Event Number	1	2	3	4	5	6	7	8	9	10
Appearance										
Clothing	—	—	—	—	—	—	—	—	—	—
Hairstyle	—	—	—	—	—	—	—	—	—	—
Cosmetics	—	—	—	—	—	—	—	—	—	—
Verbal expressions	—	—	—	—	—	—	—	—	—	—
Manners	—	—	—	—	—	—	—	—	—	—
Body Language										
Uncrossed arms	—	—	—	—	—	—	—	—	—	—
Uncrossed legs	—	—	—	—	—	—	—	—	—	—
Balanced standing posture	—	—	—	—	—	—	—	—	—	—
Erect sitting posture	—	—	—	—	—	—	—	—	—	—
Smile	—	—	—	—	—	—	—	—	—	—
Hands away from face	—	—	—	—	—	—	—	—	—	—
First Contact Skills										
Eye contact	—	—	—	—	—	—	—	—	—	—
Handshake	—	—	—	—	—	—	—	—	—	—
Greeting	—	—	—	—	—	—	—	—	—	—
Remembering names	—	—	—	—	—	—	—	—	—	—
Conversational Skills										
Opening conversations	—	—	—	—	—	—	—	—	—	—
Keeping them going	—	—	—	—	—	—	—	—	—	—
Ending conversations	—	—	—	—	—	—	—	—	—	—

Opportunities Abound

We Americans are a restless nation. We move from one geographic location to another, from one job to another, from one social stratum to another, and even from one family to another. Our restlessness contributes to loneliness, but it also presents lonely people with many opportunities.

Perhaps because so large a percentage of the population is on the move, we have an extraordinary number of membership organizations to choose from. They give us a way to fit into any new community, job, or profession quickly and easily. I suspect that we evolved this vast network of organizations partly to accommodate our mobility. Whatever the case, we probably have more types of trade groups, social clubs, interest groups, academic societies— you name it—than any other contemporary nation or any nation in history.

No matter what interests you, there is probably an organization you can join or a class you can take that will further your knowledge, develop your skills, broaden your experience, and introduce you to other people with similar interests. Your job now is simply to find one or more groups that fit you and then put the principles you have learned in this chapter to work. Start looking around. Visit the library, delve into the phone directory, pick up magazines and newletters on your areas of interest, check calendar listings in your local paper. Don't put it off—start today!

9

Becoming Assertive

As you have begun to discover, overcoming loneliness is an active process. It takes effort and energy to belong. People who sit and wait for others to approach them set themselves up for disappointment. Instead of waiting passively for someone else to make a move, you need to take the initiative. One important ingredient for doing so is assertiveness.

Being assertive requires more than simply following a set of rules. To be assertive, you must learn to think assertively. You must understand and *believe* that you deserve to advance, that you are entitled to protect and exercise your rights, and that you have needs and desires that are as important as anyone's.

When I think of a model of assertiveness, I think of Helen, although I'm quite sure she never thought of herself that way. At that time, I hadn't given assertiveness much thought, but I was nonetheless impressed by the way Helen handled unreasonable demands.

Helen was a cleaning woman in the building where I worked. She worked hard and she did a good job. One day I overheard a new staff member asking Helen to do a personal task for him—to clean out his private storage closet. He was loud and demanding, and he talked to her more like a servant than a coworker.

Helen listened to him respectfully, and when he finished speaking, she responded in a calm and steady voice without a trace of anger or resentment. She told him that her duties filled her workday and did not allow her time to do "personal favors."

The man didn't like being refused. Perhaps because he had an audience, he didn't drop it but became more insistent. Once more, Helen listened patiently without interrupting. Then she stated firmly but without rancor, "I understand what you want done, but I'm not the one to do that job. That's a job for a personal servant, and I'm a maintenance worker for the whole department."

When the man sputtered a vulgarity, Helen remained in control of herself but her tone became still firmer. She told him that under no circumstances would she be talked to that way. She would overlook it since he was new on the job. If it happened again, however, she would report the incident immediately to both her supervisor and to his.

With that, Helen went about her duties as if nothing had happened. Her adversary had the good sense to keep quiet and apparently had learned a valuable lesson.

In this chapter, you'll learn and practice Helen's kind of assertiveness. And you'll learn when it's appropriate to be assertive and when it's best to stand aside. The primary goal here is to gain the confidence that comes from knowing how to respond in difficult interpersonal situations. With that kind of confidence, you'll never feel the need to avoid social encounters, which is a major step in overcoming loneliness.

You won't learn how to be rude, pushy, or obnoxious, since those are ingredients of aggression, not assertion. There's nothing self-centered or discourteous about being assertive. Indeed, respect for others is part of the formula for effective assertion.

Recognizing Your Rights

What Are You Entitled To?

In your daily life you play many roles: friend, neighbor, employee, spouse, parent, child. And in each role you have personal rights. Thinking in terms of all of your roles will help you begin to identify your rights. Take a few minutes now to think about your relationships, responsibilities, and activities. Don't confine yourself to the major roles I've mentioned. No doubt you fulfill many more minor roles that are nonetheless important to you, such as club member, hobbyist, volunteer, or pet owner.

In addition to identifying the roles you play in life, you need to clarify the rights that go with each of them. This may be difficult for you if you are accustomed to thinking unassertively (which you will know from having read chapter 4). To get you started, I've listed a few examples below. The examples, of necessity, are not complete, nor will all of them necessarily apply to you. Read the examples, and then settle back in a comfortable chair and use the following exercise to reflect on what you owe other people and what they in turn owe you—how you should be treated by them.

Rights as an Adult Son or Daughter:

- To decide how often I should visit my parents
- To dislike and avoid relatives who are unkind or unfair to me
- To be free from guilt should I decide to spend holidays away from my parents
- To make my own decisions even when they conflict with the desires of my parents
- To rear my children by my rules, rather than my parents'

Rights as a Friend:

- To expect friends to share costs for mutual activities
- To expect items that have been lent to be returned promptly and in good condition
- To expect friends to be on time most of the time
- To expect friends to share in planning time together

- To expect friends to listen as well as talk

Rights as a Consumer:
- To refuse to listen to sales pitches if I so choose
- To expect items I've bought to be replaced or repaired when they don't fit or operate properly
- To be treated courteously and respectfully To be served promptly

Rights as an Employee:
- To be paid fairly for the work I do
- To be treated with dignity and respect
- To have pleasant, safe surroundings
- To have adequate materials, supplies, and space
- To have the support of my supervisor
- To be granted designated time off graciously
- To receive clear instructions about my duties
- To receive feedback about the quality of my work
- To be free from harassment of any kind

Rights as a Spouse:
- To have a share in making decisions that concern me
- To be listened to as well as to listen
- To be treated respectfully and affectionately
- To ask to have sex or to turn it down if I'm not in the mood
- To not be blamed or criticized unfairly

Exercise
Identifying Your Roles and Rights

This exercise will help you begin to recognize the areas in your life where you can begin to use assertiveness to get the things you need and deserve.

1. In your notebook, make a list of all the roles you play in your life. Remember to include minor as well as major roles.

2. Now, taking each of your roles in turn, think about what your rights are in that role. Don't analyze too much; this is a brainstorming exercise. Just list all the rights you can think of without

stopping. When you run out of rights in one role, pick another of your roles and list the rights for that one, and so on until you've exhausted all your roles and rights. You will probably have the same or similar rights listed for several roles.

3. Review the rights you have listed. Place a check mark beside each right that *isn't* currently being honored.

4. Review the *checked* items, and circle the five that are most important to you. Then give each of those items a number from 1 to 5 that indicates its level of importance to you, with 1 being the most important.

5. At the top of a new page in your notebook, write "I have a right to ... " and then the most important of your rights that currently is not being honored.

6. Beneath that line, draw a vertical line down the center of the page. Title one side "Who" and the other "Where." Then, in the Who column, list the people who disregard the right. In the Where column, list the situations in which the right is commonly disregarded.

7. Repeat steps 5 and 6 for each of the five rights you identified as most important.

Here's an example of the list of one woman's most important right. Cameron felt frustrated and bewildered because no one seemed to listen to her.

I have a right to be heard

Who	Where
My boss	*She gives me work but doesn't let me have any input about how it should be done.*
Dad	*When I go to visit he just talks and talks about how I ought to remarry because he thinks I can't make it on my own, even though I can and do.*
Geri	*When we go out she never asks or pays attention to what I want to do. It's always* her *restaurant or* her *movie. She's always got everything planned out ahead of time.*

| Luke's coach | When I try to talk to him about Luke's needing to study more, he just goes on about what a great little pitcher Luke is. |
| Hairdresser | I try to tell her how I want my hair cut, but she always goes ahead and does it her way. |

What's Getting in the Way?

The five rights you listed in the preceding exercise are important to you. Yet they are being disregarded and the quality of your life is being affected. You may have accepted infringement upon these rights without realizing what you were doing.

Just as you will, Cameron used the procedures in the next exercise to help her understand how she might be allowing or even encouraging others to violate her rights. She wasn't happy about what she learned, but she was heartened by it. Although she discovered that she tolerated being ignored, she also saw that she had more control than she had realized.

Cameron detected a strong tendency in herself to be passive in her communication. Instead of describing her wishes clearly, she usually only hinted about them. When she felt strongly about something, she was more outspoken, but she almost never went further if she met resistance.

Even when she disagreed, Cameron usually acquiesced quickly to her supervisor's requests. She discovered that she was inclined to interpret suggestions as orders and requests as demands. Despite an occasional token protest, Cameron never actually challenged her boss with alternative plans or well-thought-out courses of action. She found that she was more likely to hem and haw than to state her point of view.

After careful consideration Cameron concluded that in addition to being passive, she was lazy with regard to communication. It was far easier, for instance, to accept her boss's ideas than to challenge them with well-devised proposals of her own.

Unfortunately the one-sided communication had harmful side effects: Cameron felt increasingly hostile toward her boss and at the same time lost respect for and confidence in herself.

Cameron detected the same passive tendency in her relationship with her father. She might frown, sigh, and say something like "Come on, Dad, drop it, " when he talked about her remarrying. But she never actually told him how disparaging she felt this to be and how it bothered her that he showed so little confidence in her judgment. Her strongest reaction was to pout a bit.

Later, after she learned to be assertive, Cameron told her father that she would like to remarry someday but not for the purpose of gaining a protector and provider. She asked him not to bring the subject up again, but also assured him that she would confide in him when she met someone special. When her father continued to harangue her about remarriage, Cameron told him without a trace of anger that she simply wouldn't respond to him on this subject anymore. And she didn't.

To her chagrin, Cameron saw that she had been unfair to her best friend, Geri. Geri was a well-organized woman who didn't like surprises or ambiguity. She planned things carefully because she was more comfortable when she knew what to expect.

Cameron, on the other hand, preferred to go with the flow. Furthermore, as she had begun to realize, she was more than a little lazy when it came to planning. Geri had merely stepped in with a plan when there was none, and Cameron had been unduly resentful. Cameron found that Geri was glad to go along with any plans she made, provided Cameron didn't wait until the last minute to discuss them with her.

Cameron decided that her son's coach was a pushy, self-centered man who was always going to try to get his way, regardless of what was best for Luke. She made up her mind that a sledgehammer approach was the only one that would work with him. She also concluded that her obligation was to Luke, not to the coach, and it didn't really matter whether the coach agreed with her priorities or not. Once more, she saw how she was unable to get her point across until she stopped dodging and equivocating.

Cameron was rather embarrassed when she realized how she had allowed her hairdresser to badger her into accepting hairstyles she didn't like. But she was also aware that the operative word here was *allow*. The hairdresser may not have been as good a listener as a service provider should be, but Cameron didn't exercise her rights as a customer either. She had never directly said what was acceptable and not acceptable. Nor did she seek out a more receptive hairdresser among the many available to her nearby.

In the following exercise you will analyze how you have allowed your significant rights to be ignored. Be honest with yourself. The objective is to identify how you yourself may be subverting your rights by permitting those rights to be violated.

Exercise
Identifying How You Undermine Your Rights

The six steps in part I of this exercise will take about an hour of undisturbed time. Since you will need to do the exercise for each of the five important rights you identified in the preceding exercise, you will probably want to spread this out over several days.

Part I

1. Go back and read what you wrote in the preceding exercise about the most important of your rights that is not being honored.

2. With this information in mind, use self-hypnosis to relax deeply and induce a trance deep enough for effective visualization.

3. Then visualize as many instances as you can of actual situations in which the right was disregarded. Suggest to yourself that you will recall the situations as vividly and in as much detail as possible, paying particular attention to:

    • What you said just before, during, and immediately after each incident
    • What the tone of your voice was saying.
    • What your body language was saying

4. Concentrate on answering the question "How did my communication influence the other person's response?"

5. Suggest to yourself that you will recall even more about each incident when you are not concentrating on doing so, in the form of dreams, hunches, or recollections. Quite often, the answer to a question asked in trance will not reveal itself at that

time, but will pop into your mind later, when you least expect it. It's similar to suddenly recalling a name that you couldn't remember earlier, when you were trying to remember. The answer also might not be completely straightforward. Instead of a clear memory, it might appear in a dream or just as a feeling or thought that seems correct.

6. In your notebook, record as much as you can remember about your behavior during the incidents both after the hypnosis session and later on, after further recollection.

Repeat these steps for each of your important neglected rights. You will probably find that each repetition of the exercise takes less time than the preceding one.

After you have done this exercise for your five most important neglected rights, it is likely that you will have noticed a common pattern in the way you behave in such situations. If you haven't, do the exercise with other rights you identified earlier but did not mark as being one of your top five priorities.

Keep doing this exercise until the pattern of your behavior begins to emerge.

Part II

1. As you begin identifying the ways you typically permit other people to disregard your rights, record them in your notebook.

2. Be sure to be specific. What exactly is it about what you say (or don't say), your tone or voice, or the way you hold yourself that gives people the message that you won't stand up for yourself or aren't to be taken seriously?

The Role of Emotions

You now know how your actions allow other people to disregard your rights. The next step is to learn why you behave that way. Why do you allow other people to ignore you or to take advantage of you? Why is it easier for you to stand back, to overlook slights, to accept being brushed aside, to play second fiddle?

The answer is that you are responding to your feelings—feelings produced by old messages from your childhood or the kinds of maladaptive thought patterns that we considered in chapter 2.

Before going further, it will be helpful for you do the following exercise, which will enable you to discover which emotions are most associated with your lack of assertiveness. Once you have done the exercise and determined the emotions that are interfering with your ability to assert yourself, read the corresponding sections below. Exercises later in the chapter will then help you in managing these feeling so that they no longer get in the way of becoming assertive.

Exercise
Identifying Problematic Emotions

Read through the steps listed below. Then, when you have sufficient uninterrupted time, do the exercise.

1. Use self-hypnosis to relax deeply and induce a trance deep enough for effective visualization.

2. Visualize a variety of instances in which one of your five important rights was disregarded.

3. Suggest to yourself that you will recall the incidents as vividly and in as much detail as possible, paying particular attention to your feelings and emotions.

4. Concentrate on answering the question "What feelings did I experience in each incident: guilt, fear, anxiety, doubt, anger, or another emotion? Bear in mind that you may feel several emotions simultaneously in any given incident.

5. In your notebook, keep a record for each incident of the feelings you are aware of while doing the visualization.

6. When you have done a number of visualizations, using all five of the rights, tally the number of times you felt each of the emotions.

7. On a new page of your notebook, list the three emotions that you experienced most frequently in order (the first would be

the one you felt the most), leaving several lines of blank space beneath each emotion.

After doing this exercise, it should be clear that the same emotions appear time after time when you behave passively. They emerge when you know your rights aren't being respected, but they can also trigger passive behavior. In particular, the three most common emotions you identified are important determinants of your behavior. Let's consider individually the emotions that often lead to passive behavior.

Guilt

Guilt, in and of itself, is neither all good nor all bad. It is a glue that binds civilization together. It impels people to be more considerate of one another, and it prevents dishonesty and other forms of behavior detrimental to society.

On the other hand, guilt in large doses can be harmful to the individual. While a bit of guilt can be motivating, a liberal quantity can be disabling. A substantial surge of guilt can paralyze, leaving a person as dead in the water as a torpedoed ship. Loren's and Edward's experiences provide telling examples.

When Loren first joined a support group for adult children of alcoholics, she was overwhelmed by guilt. Her guilt kept her bound to an abusive husband who exploited her passivity. There were no children to bind her to the marriage, no pressing economic needs, no undue social pressure—only guilt from within herself.

Her guilt also reinforced her husband's assertion that she was responsible for the severe beatings he administered on a regular basis, and it made Loren unable to refuse her husband's unreasonable demands.

Loren's guilt was not easy to tame. It stemmed from a childhood of observing her mother cater to an alcoholic husband. It was reinforced by strong fundamentalist religious beliefs that a woman's duty is to serve and obey her husband "for better or for worse." Any desires or thoughts she might have that were at odds with that teaching were, according to her beliefs, sinful and shameful. Loren believed deeply that her husband was always right and that she, as a dutiful and subordinate wife, must be at fault when she disagreed. Any behavior at odds with this fervent belief stirred up enough guilt to disable her.

Loren's reaction to abusiveness is an extreme form of unassertive behavior. It vividly illustrates the power of destructive childhood messages. Before she could assert herself, Loren had to identify and discard the old messages that kept her from being assertive. Fortunately, she was eventually able to do so. Today Loren is no longer troubled by guilt. Although she admits to feeling a twinge now and then, in her words, "My guilt now works for me." She says that it signals her when her behavior is off track and needs correcting.

Old messages from childhood don't have to be as blatant as Loren's to affect your behavior as an adult. Most of them are far more subtle. But, even as obtrusive as Loren's childhood messages were, she had trouble detecting them. She only knew that it seemed wrong to stand up to her husband. Before she entered a support group, she had never asked herself why she accepted the abuse.

Very often unassertive behavior results from illogical or irrational thought patterns. Edward, for instance, was in most respects an effective chairman of his company's board of directors. The board's policies were sound, and the company was consistently profitable.

But lately Edward found himself dreading board meetings. He often felt thwarted in his role as chairman, and he was somewhat puzzled by these feelings, since he had always enjoyed maneuvering through the labyrinth of upper management politics before. At first Edward shrugged off his feelings as a symptom of getting older. When he finally faced them head on, however, he realized that, while he was as effective as ever with four of the company's six directors, it was the two new directors, both women, whom he could not "handle."

A product of a fading era, Edward had never before dealt with women as peers. When he had interacted with women previously, they were invariably subordinates, and always compliant, so he had had no reason to be anything but considerate and courtly. Now Edward found himself up against two assertive, talented, knowledgeable women, and he didn't know how to react. His behavior toward women in business had been governed by a pattern of thinking that didn't work with the two new directors.

Even though he was chairman of the board and a master at assertiveness, Edward could not bring himself to be assertive with the two women. In his way of thinking, women were to be protected and, when necessary, politely humored. Open conflict with them was boorish and intolerable for a gentleman. He felt guilty any time he violated a basic edict of his thinking: A man in power must be forceful but always a gentleman.

Despite his ingrained thinking about women, Edward was an intelligent, sensitive man. Once he saw his obtuseness, he was willing to change. He began to educate himself about changing feminine roles, and he modified his thinking to bring it into line with present-day reality. He was able to change his thinking so that he regarded the two women only as directors. He saw them as peers, and he accepted his right to be assertive with any peer and still remain a gentleman. He could now deal with the new directors as he did the old, without guilt.

Although the sources of Loren's and Edward's guilt were entirely different, in both cases their feelings were a response to automatic thoughts. Quite often, guilt feelings are triggered by the kinds of automatic thoughts you learned about in chapter 2. If you have feelings of guilt that prevent you from behaving assertively, you are probably reacting to automatic thoughts as well. Although recognizing the source of your guilt may not be easy, recognizing the thoughts that accompany your guilt feelings will help break the link between guilt and your behavior. The exercise "Managing Your Emotions," later in the chapter, will enable you to discover the automatic thoughts that lead to unassertive behavior and to overwrite those thoughts with positive, affirming statements.

Fear

Like guilt, fear is not necessarily harmful. Without it, we would be blind to risks and constantly in jeopardy. When it is rational, fear helps us to weigh alternatives cautiously so that we stay out of harm's way. Fear can, however, be as powerful as guilt in obstructing assertive behavior. When it is irrational or too strong, it can lead either to unassertiveness or to aggression. Fear can either paralyze or impel to reckless action.

Automatic thoughts stir up the fear that blocks assertiveness. These thoughts are based on childhood messages or on beliefs drawn from unsound conclusions about experiences later in life.

Take Aaron, for example. A 41-year-old account manager in a marketing firm, Aaron slowly realized that he was lonely at work. Up until the past year or so, many of his business associates had also been friends. But lately it seemed that people had been backing away from him. His colleagues didn't seek him out as they had in the past. They rarely asked him to join them for coffee or lunch. They never asked him for advice anymore. Quite often, they responded to his invitations with excuses.

Never one to let a problem simmer, Aaron talked to an associate as soon as he became aware of how isolated he had become. After some prodding, the man reluctantly told Aaron that people had become uncomfortable around him. For months Aaron had been "coming on too strong" about his ideas and projects. He rarely listened to others, constantly interrupting them to interject his opinions. Worse, he put people down when they didn't agree with him. He was unreasonable about budgetary matters and secretarial time, always pushing for more than his fair share.

When he was forced to think about it this way, Aaron agreed that he had become pushy. He hurt people's feelings, and his behavior was obnoxious at times. He could understand why people had been avoiding him. What he had difficulty discerning was why he had become so aggressive at work.

As Aaron eventually learned, his aggression and his loneliness were products of irrational fear. But he wasn't able to recognize the fear until he learned to catch his automatic thoughts. When he did, he discovered that essentially he had been telling himself over and over "I've got to accomplish something now or be thrown out!"

Earlier in his career, Aaron had known two managers in their early forties who were summarily fired. Although he didn't know the facts behind either dismissal, he had concluded that the managers were fired because they were "over the hill and weren't producing." His illogical conclusion was compounded by childhood messages from his depression-era parents, who valued financial security above everything else. When Aaron passed his fortieth birthday, a fear of being fired kicked in. He began to tell himself that he'd better produce quickly or else. The fear became greater and greater until he was frantic to achieve something tangible.

Yet his fear was illogical. He had in fact achieved a great deal, and there was no evidence that he was in any danger of losing his job. Aaron overlooked the good performance reports that he consistently received. He dismissed any compliments from peers or superiors as so much puffery. He discounted his achievements as routine and "nothing special." In short, he fit the facts to his preconceived ideas, rather than changing his ideas to fit the facts.

If, in the preceding exercise "Identifying Emotions," you determined that fear plays a role in preventing you from being assertive, you will need to do further work on controlling that emotion. The exercise "Managing Your Emotions," later in the chapter, will help you pinpoint the automatic thoughts behind the fears and replace them with more adaptive thinking.

Anxiety

Anxiety is a close kin to fear, but it is more amorphous. It is a generalized uneasiness, a dread without a focus. It's the apprehension, the nervousness, you feel in a situation where you know that something is wrong but can't quite put your finger on it.

When it's strong enough, anxiety is accompanied by unpleasant physical reactions. These symptoms vary somewhat from person to person: Some people feel faint because anxiety causes them to hyperventilate. Others hold their breath. Some people blush or stammer or sweat profusely. It's common for an anxious person's voice to quiver or his or her fingers to tremble. The heart beats at a faster pace; the stomach flutters; the body moves restlessly.

People often interpret their anxiety as a sign of weakness and try to conceal it from others. This pattern of thinking leads to avoidance of situations that bring out the physical signs of nervousness. If behaving assertively causes someone to feel anxious, that person is unlikely to be assertive. In time, he or she develops specific fears of the situations that cause anxiety and so avoid them all the more. A common example is the fear of public speaking.

When you think anxious thoughts, your body mobilizes itself for danger. It acts as if you are being threatened by a physical enemy you need to defeat or escape from. This is called the *fight-or-flight* response. The brain signals the adrenal glands to release epinephrine (adrenaline), which in turn stimulates the liver to release stored sugars. This chain of events, among others, energizes the body to deal with a threat.

Because the threat with anxiety is mental and not physical, the body races like an accelerated engine in a car on blocks. And your control over the "engine" is limited until the epinephrine and other hormones metabolize. The loss of control causes more anxious thoughts, which releases more epinephrine. The cycle continues until your body temporarily depletes the hormone supply or you shift the focus of your thoughts.

Eunice experienced some of these unpleasant effects when she was promoted from teacher to principal of her school. From the time she learned of her promotion she felt queasy and apprehensive. She couldn't specify exactly what was bothering her about the change other than "the increase in responsibility."

Eunice learned that she became especially anxious when she had to confront the older, more experienced teachers in the school. Try as she might, she couldn't prevent a quaver from appearing in her voice. She felt that everyone could tell how nervous she was and that they thought she was inept. As a result of her discomfort, Eunice began to avoid dealing directly with this group of subordinates. She didn't recognize this pattern of avoidance, however, until it became so obvious that one of her friends on the faculty questioned her about it. Eunice then realized her anxiety was interfering with the her job performance, and she took steps toward righting the erroneous automatic thoughts that were causing her anxiety.

An exercise later in the chapter, "Managing Your Emotions," will help you uncover the automatic thoughts that produce anxiety for you and keep you from behaving assertively. Another useful technique is that of deep relaxation. You can use it to quell the anxiety that interferes with assertiveness. Your goal is to prevent the fight-or-flight response that dominates your body when you feel highly anxious.

Practice using relaxation in real-life situations as you learned to do in the section in chapter 5 entitled "Fitting Relaxation into Your Daily Life." Apply the principles specifically in situations where anxiety blocks assertiveness (which you identified in the exercise "Identifying Your Emotions," earlier in the chapter).

Doubt

A bit of uncertainty about the right to be assertive is useful; it can motivate you to think through your position carefully. It's a check against unwarranted aggression. Too much doubt, though, leads you to back down when you should stand firm. No matter what words you use, uncertainty reveals itself in your tone of voice and body language, and other people can recognize that doubt and use it to their own benefit.

Andrea, for example, a junior at a small private college, had recently been elected president of a campus service club. Her election was in recognition of her efforts to change the focus of the organization. Although a slim majority of members was in favor of change, an influential minority was against it.

One of the most vocal members of the minority, Scott, made every effort to thwart Andrea's agenda. He detected Andrea's uncertainty about organizational procedures and used this knowledge to his advantage. As Andrea became more comfortable with her new position and set out to learn the rules of order, her doubt faded. Later, in hindsight, she saw how her uncertainty had bequeathed an advantage to her antagonist.

If you are uncertain about your right to be assertive in any given situation, think through your position carefully. Thorough preparation is the first step in overcoming doubt. The next is changing your thinking. The following exercise can help you recognize automatic thoughts that may be undermining your assertiveness and then devise positive affirmations to replace the old, negative thoughts.

Exercise
Managing Your Emotions

This exercise can be applied to almost any emotion that is interfering with your ability to behave assertively. (The exception is anger, which is discussed in the following section.) The three parts of the exercise use techniques you have practiced in earlier chapters. In particular, you may want to review chapter 2 before doing the exercise.

This exercise is designed to be done over a period of time; you will not be able to complete all three parts in one sitting. Parts II and III not only require adequate time for self-hypnosis but repeated sessions as well.

Part I

1. In your notebook, turn to the page where you listed the three emotions that you identified as being most problematic to you in regards to assertiveness.

2. Beneath each emotion, write a statement affirming your right to behave without regard to the emotion. The statement should be brief, positive, true, and to the point. For example, if you felt guilty about disregarding the advice of one of your parents, you might say "I am a thoughtful, careful person who is capable of making decisions for myself."

Part II

1. Use self-hypnosis to relax and induce a trance deep enough for effective visualization.

2. Visualize an instance in which one of your three problematic emotions blocked your ability to behave assertively.

3. When you are aware of the emotion controlling your behavior in the scene, recall the automatic thought or thoughts behind the emotion.

4. Form an image of removing the automatic thought and replacing it with the appropriate affirmation from part I of this exercise.

5. Then visualize the same instance again, but change the scene so that you respond to the affirming statement and are able to be assertive.

6. Visualize several similar instances in which you respond to the affirming statement and behave assertively.

7. Repeat step 6 daily until it seems natural to think in terms of the affirming statement instead of your old automatic thought.

8. Repeat these steps for each of the emotions that prevent you from being assertive.

Part III

1. Use self-hypnosis to relax and induce a trance deep enough for effective visualization.

2. Visualize a variety of instances in which one of your three problematic emotions triggered unassertive behavior.

3. Suggest to yourself that you will recall the instances as vividly and in as much detail as possible, paying particular attention to the automatic thoughts behind the emotion.

4. Keep a ricord of your discoveries in your notebook.

5. Follow steps 1 through 4 for each of your problematic emotions.

Anger

Like all emotions, anger serves a useful function. It can be a red flag that someone is interfering with your rights—a signal for assertiveness. But taken too far, anger becomes rage, the antithesis of a useful signal. An extremely angry person is an emotional creature with poor judgment and little objectivity. If words don't convey the anger, his or her body language will. Either will likely provoke aggression or defensiveness in the other person. Neither will likely lead to useful solutions.

Anger stemming from irrational thinking can also undermine effectiveness. As you learned in chapter 2, thoughts are the seeds of behavior. If thoughts are based on erroneous assumptions, the behavior they breed will also be in error. The following are some ways of thinking that lead to anger.

Labeling

It's human to fit people into neat, discrete categories to explain their behavior. Unfortunately, when the category is negative, you tend to overlook the person's positive traits and concentrate only on the negative ones.

If you classify someone as a dunce, for instance, you'll tend to notice only the stupid behavior, while disregarding anything clever. Then, when he or she does something you consider dumb, you're likely to get more angry than is warranted by the particular situation.

Motivating with Anger

Some people believe that they can change other people through anger. They see anger as motivational, as if they were irate parents scowling at a misbehaving child. The fact is, anger may temporarily suppress behavior, but, once the angry person is out of sight, the behavior is just as likely to come back. Anger may also boomerang, attracting angry, spiteful behavior in return. There are more effective ways to influence people.

Mind Reading

An assumption about what another person is thinking can be the basis for irrational anger. You might, for instance, be annoyed at a neighbor for being rather abrupt at the supermarket. If you think something like "She never has really liked me," you'll probably become angry with her.

In fact, you can't know why the neighbor acted as she did. Maybe she was in pain from a medical procedure and was in a hurry to get home. She could have been worried that the check she was about to write might bounce. Perhaps she was thinking about the woman she saw in her husband's car.

You simply can't know another person's thoughts. No matter how well you know someone, you cannot read his or her mind. Consequently, to be angry about what he or she is "thinking" is absurd.

Fault Finding

Ralph, a top-level supervisor in a factory, was demoted after a year on the job. He was told that he couldn't get along with people. The real reason was that he was ineffective at solving many of the problems that arose during a typical workday.

When something went wrong, Ralph almost always looked for someone to blame. He focused on finding fault, which diverted him from objective problem solving. Ralph, like many people who hunt for blame, ended up frustrated and angry more often than not, since finger-pointing very seldom leads to solutions.

Personalizing

Gina, a 42-year-old stockbroker, was a whiz at investments but a dud socially. She interpreted other people's behavior as if it were directed at her personally. If someone was late for lunch, she believed it was because he didn't respect her enough to be on time. If a friend failed to compliment a new outfit, she must be jealous. Because of self-centered, distorted thinking, Gina was huffy and abrupt with people who had no idea why.

Rule-Bound Thinking

Applying your rules to other people can be a source of anger. Your "shoulds" and "shouldn'ts" may be okay for you but aren't necessarily so for others. Consider Larry, who was always annoyed with someone in his neighborhood for not "doing the right thing." His latest grudge was against his next door neighbor who "shouldn't" have raked leaves from Larry's tree back into Larry's yard. The neighbor "should" have raked them to the street for pickup, as Larry would have done.

Larry was also annoyed with two other neighbors who had been stingy with Halloween treats for Larry's kids. After all, Larry had always felt it important to give generously to children from the neighborhood.

Haunted Thinking

Sometimes we become angry at people, not for what they say or do, but for who they are. This too is an example of distorted thinking.

Julia, for instance, always found Lydia annoying. Almost everything about Lydia got on Julia's nerves. She would have avoided Lydia entirely, if Lydia hadn't been her daughter's mother-in-law.

Julia never thought about why, until her daughter mentioned offhandedly how much Lydia looked like Julia's grandmother. At that moment, Julia realized that she disliked Lydia only because she was reminded of her cold, distant grandmother.

Rob had trouble getting along with his college roommate. He had tried to get another room assignment, but was told that he would have to wait until the end of the term. Actually only one trait bothered Rob—his roommate's bossiness.

Rob was able to accept his roommate once he made an adjustment in his mental attitude: realizing that the roommate was not his bossy older brother and that Rob could ignore any of his demands. Just as Julia had, Rob was responding not to a person in the present but to a ghost from the past.

You too may be responding illogically to some characteristic of a person with whom you are angry. If so, your thinking is haunted by feelings from the past.

The following exercise will help you determine which pattern or patterns of irrational thoughts are causing anger that interferes with your being assertive.

Exercise
Identifying Irrational Thoughts
That Lead to Anger

Since distorted thinking is the major source of inappropriate anger, challenging those thought patterns is the first step in controlling anger.

Inappropriate anger can result from thought patterns other than the seven discussed above, although these seven are probably the most common sources of anger. So before doing this exercise, take a few minutes to review the section entitled "Illogical Thought Patterns," in chapter 2. The patterns discussed there can also lead to self-defeating anger. Keep them in mind as well as you work through the exercise.

1. Use self-hypnosis to relax and induce a trance deep enough for effective visualization.

2. Visualize a variety of instances in which you felt angry with another person.

3. Suggest to yourself that you will recall the instances as vividly and in as much detail as possible, paying particular attention to the thoughts behind your anger.

4. When you become aware of your thoughts, ask yourself "What patterns of distorted thinking does this thought represent?"

5. In your notebook, keep a tally of the types of distorted thinking you uncover and how frequently each of them turn up.

   Here's a list of the common types of distorted thinking:

   - Labeling
   - Mind reading
   - Fault finding
   - Personalizing
   - Rule-bound thinking
   - Haunted thinking
   - Overgeneralizing
   - All-or-none thinking
   - Confusing possibility with probability
   - Filtering
   - Emotional reasoning
   - Catastrophizing

Controlling Your Anger

In the preceding exercise you learned the most common triggers for your anger. Keep these thought patterns in mind and challenge them when you feel anger rising. Look at the situation from the other person's point of view. Be as empathic as you can and look for alternative explanations for their behavior.

Larry, for example, was able to downgrade his anger to irritation when he thought about why his neighbor might have raked leaves from Larry's tree back into Larry's yard. The neighbor had obviously tried to avoid the task of raking leaves, since he had planted only evergreen trees in his yard. He probably meant no harm when he raked the leaves back onto the pile under the tree near the property line. Actually, the neighbor may have been justified in feeling annoyed at Larry for planting a deciduous tree with branches overhanging his yard.

Gina, the stockbroker, found that her social life picked up when she stopped personalizing other people's behavior. It took her some time to break the habit, but she was eventually successful. If a friend forgot her birthday, for instance, Gina no longer felt that the friend was losing interest in her. Instead, she looked for other reasons. Maybe the friend had a poor memory and often overlooked birthdays. Maybe birthdays weren't very important to the friend. It could be that her friend was preoccupied temporarily with personal problems. Whatever the case, Gina stopped seeing troublesome behavior as a dart aimed at her.

Counting to 10 is one way to cope with upsurging anger. A better way is to use the relaxation procedures you've already learned. Keep your body under control, so that you can evaluate the source of your anger. It is up to you to determine whether or not the anger is justified. Stay relaxed while you test yourself for the thought patterns that usually trigger your anger. Keep cool while you look for alternative explanations.

Even if your anger is justified, you will benefit by controlling and releasing anger in measured amounts. I can't think of any situation where a tremendous burst of anger, justified or not, solved a problem. Temper tantrums are self-defeating.

The following exercise will help you practice controlling your anger.

Exercise
Practicing Anger Control

Complete this exercise when you have sufficient undisturbed time for self-hypnosis.

1. Use self-hypnosis to relax and induce a trance deep enough for effective visualization.

2. Visualize a variety of instances in which you felt angry with another person.

3. Suggest to yourself that you will recall the instances as vividly and in as much detail as possible.

4. As you visualize each instance, use the following strategies to prevent or defuse your anger:

- Imagine staying relaxed in the anger-provoking situation.
- Question the thought pattern behind the anger.
- Look for alternative explanations for the other person's anger-provoking behavior.
- Imagine resolving the issue to your satisfaction.

Lights, Camera, Action!

At this point you know your rights and you've learned how your reactions have allowed other people to disregard them. You have examined your thoughts and emotions and seen how they have blocked assertiveness. And you've replaced self-defeating beliefs with beliefs that promote confidence. In short, you have acquired the essential foundation for dealing with people in any social situation. The next chapter will show you how to apply what you have learned in real life.

If you have previously been a minor character, on the sidelines of the social scene, it's now time for you to take a leading role. You are both star and director of your life's movie. Make it a hit!

10

Taking Risks

Assertive people are risk-takers. Rather than staying in the background, waiting for others to make the first move, assertive people put themselves forward, present themselves as they are, and say what they feel. In a sense, this is risky behavior. There's always the possibility of rejection. Keep in mind, though, that there's a greater *probability* of acceptance.

Being assertive is also risky in the sense that not everyone you meet is someone you will want as a friend, or even an acquaintance. It is inevitable that you will encounter uncomfortable situations and troublesome people—whether you set out to meet people or not. Here again, assertiveness is an invaluable tool for dealing with life's routine unpleasantnesses.

The key to any human relationship—from casual to intimate—is communication. The assertiveness skills you have been practicing through self-hypnosis and visualization are a major ingredient in the recipe for overcoming loneliness, because assertive people are good communicators. They are honest and forthright about their interests, their ways of doing things, their feelings, their likes and dislikes.

For a secure relationship to develop, both parties need to understand each other. Assertive people are able to talk about themselves, and they are able to make other people feel comfortable talking about themselves. Honest communication is the adhesive that binds people together. Without it, a relationship will not flourish—acquaintances will remain acquaintances without ever becoming friends.

You are now ready to learn the principles of such communication and how to apply them in social situations. This chapter suggests ways of using assertiveness and the other skills you have learned in earlier chapters in a variety of settings: awkward situations, encounters with difficult people, times when an overture is rejected, and the early stages of friendship, including friendship between members of the opposite sex.

To reach the goal of overcoming loneliness, you must accept the risks inherent in interacting with others. Do so, and you "risk" forming lasting relationships and realizing that you do indeed, at last, belong.

Handling Difficult Situations

You will feel more free to wade into a crowd and speak up if you are prepared to handle a controversial or unsettling situation. The following techniques demonstrate the use of the assertiveness skills you practiced in the last chapter.

Preparing Yourself

Before going into any social situation you dread, it will help to prepare—to clear your mind of any doubts and apprehension. You have all the tools you need for this already. Just apply the techniques you have learned to abolish fear:

- Positive self-talk
- Deep relaxation
- Self-hypnosis
- Imagery

You want to *plan* and *practice* your intended actions. Relax and put yourself into a light trance. Try to anticipate the situation you will be in as accurately as possible. Then visualize yourself using assertiveness techniques successfully.

You might also find it helpful to practice aloud, in private, in front of a mirror. The idea is to implant cues in your unconscious mind, so that your behavior will flow more freely and feel more natural in the actual situation.

Refuse to allow any negative thoughts to intrude as you prepare yourself for a difficult social encounter. Use the power of positive self-talk to affirm your competence and remind yourself that *you have the right to:*

- Be the judge of your own thoughts, opinions, and behavior
- Express your ideas and opinions
- Take a firm position
- Share in conversation
- Offer no excuses or justifications for your behavior
- Make mistakes and correct them as you think best
- Change your mind
- Say "No" or "I don't care"
- Ask for clarification
- Refuse to solve the problems of other people
- Refuse to be monopolized by any person or any group
- Set your own social schedule

Beeline to Assertiveness

Here is a shortcut, a no-frills tactic that goes straight to the heart of the matter in a precarious situation with another person.

Principle 1: Focus on Facts

Don't try to read other people's minds by assuming that you know their feelings or motives. Stick with the facts as you know them, and describe the situation to yourself in a nonblaming way. Otherwise you run the risk of clouding your thinking with anger, resentment, or some other negative emotion.

Let's say that an acquaintance asked you a few days ago to take charge of some charity project, and she is now unexpectedly telling you that someone else will be sharing the project with you. Don't assume at this point that she doesn't think that you can do the job or that you have been too slow getting started.

The only fact you have is that someone will be working on the project with you. Your acquaintance's actions have not been critical. She may be just giving you help to get the job done. It would, of course, have been more considerate for her to have talked with you first.

Principle 2: Describe Your Feelings

You'll want to first determine what you are feeling—describe your feelings to yourself—and prepare to describe them to the other person. Let's say that you feel disappointed and a little hurt about your acquaintance's asking someone else to share the charity project with you. It was important to you to do that project by yourself and you were looking forward to it.

There are three guidelines about feelings that help to defuse anger and hurt:

• *First, use "I" statements instead of "you" statements.* "You" statements come across as blaming and critical. It's better to say "I feel hurt," than "You hurt me." Likewise, "I feel confused," is less likely to cause a defensive reaction than "You really got me confused." In other words, you would want to avoid making your acquaintance feel that she is responsible for your feelings. You may be sad, angry, hurt, disappointed, or confused, but you want to concentrate on solving a problem, not casting blame.

• *Next, be prepared to talk about your feelings, not your opinions.* You could say, for example, "I'm disappointed because I would have liked to have finished what I started." This is preferable to stating an opinion—"I know I could do that project on time by myself"—because your feelings aren't debatable, but your opinions are. It would be a different story, of course, if you had facts to back up your opinion. In that case you could, for example, point out that you did a similar project on time by yourself last year with good results.

- *Finally, connect "I" statements and "feeling" messages with specific behavior.* It would be appropriate to say, "I feel put down when you ask someone else to share the project without talking to me first." This is a combined "I" statement and "feeling" message ("I feel put down") and is connected with specific behaviors of the other person ("when you ask someone else to share the project without talking to me first").

Ratings Principle 3: Decide What You Want

The last of the essential steps of applied assertiveness is making up your mind about what you want out of the situation and then telling the other person clearly what it is. Don't hint or expect him or her to read your mind. It may be too late, for example, to remove the other person from the project, but you should tell your acquaintance directly that you want to know who is in charge of the project and you would like the opportunity to talk over any future changes of any kind. Be open and firm, but don't express irritation or anger.

Using these three principles, along with the three guidelines about expressing feelings, will get your point across without endangering your relationships. It takes practice, but *you can learn to be direct and firm* without expressing anger and irritation. In fact, handling ticklish situations as they arise, instead of ignoring them, will prevent anger from building. This in turn avoids the danger of the explosive outbursts of temper that can be devastating to a relationship.

More Tips and Tactics

Here are some other techniques for handling sensitive situations with other people.

Broken Record

When you are dealing with someone who won't take no for an answer, choose a brief statement to make your point and say it over and over. Rephrase it, but keep repeating the same basic message. You are not obligated to explain further.

Keep coming back to the same point: "I'm sorry I can't volunteer; I have other plans for Saturday ... I know you need help, but I've made other plans ... Thanks for the opportunity, but my plans are firm." The nature of your plans isn't the other person's business. All you need say is that you won't be able to help.

Persistence is a key principle of assertiveness—but persistence without anger, irritation, or loudness. Don't give up easily when you want something that you have a right to. Stick to your guns, returning to and restating the same basic point. "I'm sorry, sir, but you are in our seats ... Here are the ticket stubs for our seats ... The other seats may be as good but we paid for these ... These are *our* seats and we need to take them now."

Assertive Delay

Don't try to deal with a controversial or challenging statement when you are angry or emotional or when you need time to make a decision. Put it off until you can think about your response calmly and clearly. You have a right to delay the discussion if you choose. Operate on your own timetable—not on the other person's.

You could say something like "You may have a point, but I have to think about it first and get back to you," or perhaps "I'll have to reserve judgment on that for a while. Let's talk about it when I have more time."

Agree and Ignore

A useful technique for dealing with criticism is to agree with whatever part of the other person's statement that you honestly can say that you agree with and ignore the rest. By partially agreeing, you take the wind out of your opponent's sails without accepting his or her critical opinions or resorting to argument: "You're right. I am late, and I'm sorry." You don't have to agree that you are an irresponsible person because you are late. Acknowledge the facts, but ignore the opinion.

Assertive Agreement

Another related way to handle criticism is to just say you agree, if you do in fact think it's valid. Unless you want to, you don't have to give an explanation or promise to change. You could say, for instance, "I suppose I did pay too much for it"; you don't have to say anything more.

Back to the Subject

Don't allow discussions, debates, or arguments to get sidetracked onto other issues. Stick with the issue you want to discuss. Say something like "We're getting away from the point" or "That may be, but we're talking about ..." or "That's not what we're talking about; let's stay on the subject." Don't allow the other person to divert you into old conflicts or other arguments.

Defusing Anger

When you are attacked, you can ignore the other person's anger. Defuse the anger by refusing to respond to it. Automatically reacting to anger with anger allows the other person to control your emotions. It would probably be best to put off discussion until the other person has calmed down. You could say "I can see that you are really mad about this. I'm busy now, but I can talk to you about it later today."

Neutralizing Guilt

Acknowledge what's happening when someone tries to manipulate you by making you feel guilty. Then refuse the guilt. Keep irritation out of your voice when you say something like "I don't feel guilty, so there is no reason for me to respond to guilt." Keep in mind that he or she is trying to control you through unfair methods, and use the broken record technique if the person continues to press you.

The following exercise will help you apply assertiveness strategies in real-life situations.

Exercise
Applying Assertiveness Tactics

The two parts of this exercise apply the assertiveness techniques you've read about so far in this chapter to situations that have occurred in your life and those likely to occur in the future:

Beeline to Assertiveness—focus on facts, describe your feelings, decide what you want

- Broken record
- Assertive delay
- Agree and ignore
- Assertive agreement
- Back to the subject
- Defusing anger
- Neutralizing guilt

1. In your notebook, describe a situation from your past in which you could have used each of the assertiveness techniques listed above.

2. Then describe a situation that you expect to occur in the future in which you will use each technique.

Managing Troublesome People

Assertiveness techniques will help you in difficult situations with reasonable, rational people, but they may not be as effective with truly troublesome people. More often than not, it's better to avoid interacting with these people socially. The cost of friendship with a difficult person tends to be greater than the rewards.

Unfortunately circumstances won't always allow you to back away from troublesome people. You might, for example, be trapped for an evening in a foursome with an obnoxious person. You can't avoid a jerk who is seated next to you at a dinner party. And there's always the possibility of being stuck on a committee chaired by an outrageous know-it-all. You'll feel more comfortable venturing out socially if you have some understanding of how to deal with annoying people.

You've no doubt encountered people like these many times. How did you react? You may have acted defensively when there was no need for you to defend yourself. When you encounter difficult people, the first rule of thumb is not to take their comments and behavior personally. Don't blame yourself for the way they behave. Keep in mind that these people are boorish, not you. Chances are, they treat most people much the same way they treat you.

With some troublesome people the basic problem is that they never acquired good manners and consideration for others. More of them, I'm afraid, act the way they do because of some underlying conflict or inner need. Whatever the case, it's not your place to be their teacher or therapist. Your task is to deal with them as effectively, gracefully, and quickly as you can, so that you can expend your time and energy fostering friendships with more rewarding people.

Because troublesome people can be so maddening, it helps to invoke your relaxation response when you must spend time with them. Use positive self-talk to remind yourself that this person—not you—has a serious problem, and you don't intend to be caught up in it.

The following are some specific suggestions for dealing with the kinds of troublesome people that you are likely to encounter socially (hopefully not too often). Remember, *you can't change these people*. These suggestions are intended only to help you manage the situation of the moment:

Aggressive People

Dealing with aggressive people can be an ordeal for anyone, but particularly for those who are reticent and unsure of themselves. To feel comfortable going into any social situation, you must feel prepared to handle another person's aggression. The first step is to recognize aggressive behavior for what it is.

Think about someone you know who makes you feel that you must explain, justify, or apologize for your behavior. The fact that you feel defensive like that is a strong signal that the person is being aggressive. The following exercise will help you recognize your personal reactions to aggressive behavior.

Exercise
Checking Your Reactions to Aggressive Behavior

Instructions: Think of people you know that you feel defensive around. Then answer each of the following questions Yes or No.

	Yes	No
1. Do you avoid those people whenever possible?	___	___
2. Do you feel angry or frustrated when you learn that you must deal with them?	___	___
3. Do you feel agitated during a conversation with them?	___	___
4. Do you have difficulty maintaining eye contact with them?	___	___
5. Do you reply to their direct questions with one- or two-word answers?	___	___
6. Do you find yourself justifying or defending your behavior?	___	___
7. Do you feel tense and uncomfortable listening to them?	___	___
8. Do you feel as if you are being treated unfairly by them, even when you can't identify a specific problem?	___	___
9. Do you leave a conversation with them feeling as if there is unfinished business?	___	___
10. Do you act sullen or withdrawn after meeting with them?	___	___

If you answered yes to four or more questions, the people in question are very likely aggressive types. While it would be nice to avoid them, you may not be able to. You can however, avoid all or most of your unpleasant reactions by using assertive behavior. You will also feel good about yourself when you learn to counter aggressive behavior effectively.

Furthermore, you may be able to affect how the person treats you, even though you can't change him or her. By meeting the aggressive behavior with assertiveness, you'll block the immediate reward that reinforces the aggressive behavior (see chapter 4). If you neutralize the aggression in this way, you will probably weaken it, and in time, the aggressive person will learn that you simply do not respond to aggression. He or she will then be less likely to bother you with it.

A word of warning: You *must* be consistent. You must *always* use assertive responses with aggressive people. Otherwise, you may inadvertently strengthen the aggressive behavior. It is a proven fact that inconsistent reward strengthens, rather than weakens, behavior.

Aggressive people come in a variety of subtypes—bullying, critical, sarcastic—or a single aggressive person may use different aggressive tactics at different times. The following sections describe the most common styles of aggression and how to deal with them.

Bullies

Bullies can be hazardous to your mental health—but only if you allow them to be. They sense your aversion to conflict and reluctance to make a scene and use it to their advantage. They will push relentlessly to get their way. Do you meekly accommodate them or do you stand up to them despite the unpleasantness and embarrassment that might entail?

Bullies do whatever they can to manipulate others. When you must deal with them, the first rule of thumb is to avoid an argument. You can't win, because they have the leverage. They are perfectly willing to fight unfairly, to create a disturbance, to use any kind of pressure necessary to gain control. Your best strategy is to try to find common ground, some way you can compromise toward a fair solution. Let them save face, but don't let them run over you like a bulldozer.

Let a bully have his or her say. Ask questions to convey that you're paying attention, but say outright that you disagree, if you do. Don't use inflammatory language ("You're dead wrong!" "Watch your mouth!" "Who do think you're talking to!"), and don't debate the issue. Give your opinion calmly and courteously but firmly. Unfold your arms, make eye contact, and use such assertiveness tactics as agreeing and ignoring, assertive delay, assertive agreement, broken record, and defusing anger. You won't have fun, but you'll feel good about yourself when it's over.

Know-It-Alls

These people also want compliance from you. They want agreement with their opinions and adherence to their ideas. Convinced that their knowledge and experience are superior to yours, they believe that they deserve to be treated like experts. At best they'll treat your ideas with condescension.

Because know-it-alls are essentially bullies, your best bet is to react to them in the same basic way you would to a bully. Stick with your opinions, but don't debate issues. Instead of arguing, use questions to call attention to dubious points they've made: "I understand that it's much cheaper to fly to Paris in March, but wouldn't I be risking cold, dreary weather?" Often it's effective to put questions in a "what-if" format: "What if it's raining the whole time, as it often does in March, and I can't do what I really want to do, stroll around the city?"

If you know in advance that you will skirmish with a know-it-all at, for example, at a zoning hearing, prepare for the encounter in advance. Know your facts and point out your opponent's weaknesses through questions. Stay cool, knowing that the crowd will be more sympathetic to polite self-assurance than to shrill argument. Use assertiveness tactics and stand by your well-thought-out conclusions. Above all, be courteous if the vote or consensus goes against you. Next to a winner, Americans appreciate a gracious loser.

Putdown Artists

Putdown artists use sarcasm and denigrating comments to pump themselves up at your expense. They often camouflage biting remarks and hurtful innuendoes with humor. Instead of confronting you head on, as bullies and know-it-alls do, they are devious in their attacks. Their aggression is roundabout, which gives you a certain advantage.

Your first impulse might be to ignore putdown artists. Unfortunately, that's not likely to shut them up, because they're playing more to an audience than to you. They get their reward from chipping away at you in front of other people.

As repugnant as it might be to you, your only choice is to tackle the putdown artist head on. You'll be at more of an advantage than you realize, because putdown artists are uncomfortable with direct confrontation.

As always in touchy situations, you will want to be calm and in control of your emotions. Simply ask the putdown artist what he or she meant by the remark that was just made. Say that you found it offensive or hurtful and would like to know why he or she would say or imply such a thing. The trick is to make the putdown artist feel uncomfortable in front of the group without seeming overly aggressive yourself. More than likely, the response will be that you misunderstood or that it was only a joke. Accept the explanation, knowing that he or she will be less likely to put you down in the future.

Other Difficult Types

Exploders

Exploders may appear to be aggressive people; their behavior can certainly look like it. The difference is that, rather than using their outbursts to manipulate, explosive people don't know how to deal effectively with anger. They store up resentment and perceived injustices until they can hold them no longer. Then, suddenly and unexpectedly, all of the accumulated anger bursts out in the behavioral equivalent of an explosion, often at the wrong time and at the wrong person.

If you are the unfortunate target of such an explosion, keep in mind that you don't deserve all that anger. It derives from many sources, few if any of them having much to do with you. Your immediate goal is to calm the person down. It might help to visualize that you are cooling the fire of the furious person with a fire extinguisher.

Avoid saying anything to exacerbate the tantrum. If it isn't appropriate to walk away, listen calmly and patiently. Give assurance that you are aware of his or her concerns through eye contact and gestures, such as nodding your head. Don't challenge a raging person, and don't react with anger, no matter how annoyed you are at being treated so shabbily.

When the angry person has calmed, treat him or her as if nothing out of the ordinary had happened. Unless the person is someone who habitually uses outbursts to control people (see "Aggressive People," above), the exploder usually feels guilty about his or her behavior and apologizes for the outbursts. The person wants to get on with the business at hand as if the tirade had never happened. Let it go.

Falsely Agreeable People

Although not openly aggressive, these people are bullies in their own way, however much they appear on the surface to be accommodating and amiable. Falsely aggreeable (or passive-aggressive) people won't tell you what they want, but try to make you feel guilty or uncomfortable if you don't anticipate their wishes. They'll say, "Oh, it doesn't matter with me. Choose any restaurant you like," then pout and pick at the Mexican food they don't really like. They'll refuse to choose between a movie at home or one in a theater, and then act like a wet blanket if you make the wrong choice.

Don't even think about trying to please falsely agreeable people. You can't read their minds and you shouldn't try. If they won't give you input, make the choice yourself and enjoy it. You don't have to accept the guilt that they try to heap on you. Ignore their put-upon attitude enough times and it may go away. If it doesn't, you don't have to spend time with them. If you continue to try to accommodate people who act as if you've martyred them, you'll be the martyr yourself.

Falsely agreeable people also appear in another guise. They will agree to take on a project or do a favor but then not follow through. Maybe they intend to at the time they make the promise, but you are the one left holding the bag. They can't say no, but have even more trouble doing something they don't want to do.

If you must count on such a person, let him or her know with no waffling that following though is essential. Be clear that the end result is what's important, not simply his or her agreeing to do it. Let the person know that it's okay to say no but not okay to let you down.

Complainers

A certain amount of simply talking about problems—one person venting, the other listening—is a valuable part of friendship and a way of coping with some of life's unavoidable difficulties. But true complainers can be real bores, monopolizing your time with endless whining and griping. The key difference lies in whether both parties are free to vent, or whether one person holds the floor consistently. If it isn't reciprocal, you're dealing with a complainer.

Complainers' complaints may be directed at you, or they may merely want someone to listen to them drone on about other people and situations. As with all troublesome people, debate and argument will get you nowhere. Complainers want someone to listen and agree with them. They generally feel frustrated and unable to cope, but they are not necessarily looking for solutions.

Be that as it may, you must communicate by your actions that you will listen to a complaint, but not passively. After hearing the complaint and thoroughly understanding it, encourage the complainer to look toward some kind of resolution. Encourage him or her to look for solutions, but don't try to supply them yourself unless the complaint is directed specifically at you.

Your goal is to let complainers know that you are not a receptacle for endless complaints, although you are willing to listen and give your input. If they are genuinely looking for solutions, they will be glad for your perspective. If they only want to gripe, they'll seek out more compliant ears in the future.

Deflaters

Deflaters are pessimistic, gloomy people who throw cold water on the plans and ideas of other people. They seem to delight in deflating motivation and enthusiasm, perhaps because it distracts them from their own limitations and failures. These are people who feel powerless and draw comfort from the helplessness of other people.

If it's necessary for you to share your plans with a deflater, listen to his or her comments patiently and without rancor. Argument will only stir up another round of negativity. Once the person has spoken, say that you appreciate his or her concern but you intend to go ahead with your plans even if there is a chance of failure. Then convey that the subject is closed by changing the topic of conversation and sticking with it using the broken record technique, if necessary.

The following exercise will help you plan how you will cope with the various types of troublesome people we all encounter in life. The key to interacting with any of these types is to be objective: See the difficult behavior for what it is. Don't get caught up in the other person's distorted thinking by taking his or her remarks or behavior personally or at face value. Difficult people have problems, but the problems are theirs, not yours.

Exercise
Managing Encounters with Troublesome People

Think about your previous encounters with troublesome people. How did you use to handle difficult situations with each type person listed below? Knowing what you know now, how would you handle them in the future?

- Bullies
- Know-it-alls
- Putdown artists
- Exploders
- Falsely agreeable people
- Complainers
- Deflaters

1. In your notebook, write about how you have reacted in situations with people who fall into each of the above categories.

2. Now plan strategies for dealing with these same people or others like them in the future, using the assertiveness techniques you have learned.

Now that you know how and when to be assertive, all you need is practice. As with any other skill, it will take application and repetition for your new behavior to flow smoothly and naturally. Don't be put off if your new way of relating to people seems false or affected. In time the skills themselves will become ingrained and polished.

Although you may feel awkward and guilty initially, assertiveness will soon become second nature to you. You will find standing up to people and protecting your interests so rewarding that your reservations will fade away. Perhaps to your amazement, you will discover that these skills transfer automatically from one situation to another. Although you are practicing them here in social situations, they will gradually spread to other areas of your life.

Accepting Rejection

Most people are willing or eager to widen their circle of friends, but not everyone you approach will accept you as a friend. Although rejection may hurt, don't assume that you know *why* it occurred, even if the person gives you a reason. The stated reason may be only superficial, because the person may not be aware of the real motivation behind his or her actions or is consciously choosing not to go into it with you.

It could be that the other person is actually drawn to you, but is so fearful of intimacy and commitment that he or she can't take a chance on a close friendship. If so, the person would be more likely to attribute the rejection to defects in you rather than in himself or herself. In actual fact, the reason behind the rejection would be the person's own flaws, but if he or she doesn't recognize this, how could you?

It is also possible to be rejected because your personality or appearance resembles that of someone else—an abusive parent, an irritating coworker, a former lover. Here again, you would never know the truth.

Someone who rejects you could even be doing you a favor. It could be that your personalities or interests were too different for friendship to develop. A subtle rebuff in such an instance is a more typical response than an honest explanation. Nonetheless, cutting off the relationship before you invest time and emotion in it is in your best interests.

You may have approached an individual who makes snap judgments for superficial reasons: the way you dress, what kind of car you drive, where you live, how much money you make. Maybe everybody of your age or sex or religion or ethnic group is disliked by that person. In any case, who needs a friend like that?

When you are rejected, keep in mind that it is an inevitable part of the human condition. It happens to everybody at times, but you don't have to allow anyone except yourself to control your emotions and self-esteem. Don't interpret rejection as a repudiation of your character and integrity, and don't embrace another person's implicit or explicit opinion of you. Counter any negative thoughts with positive self-talk. Then shrug and go on. There are plenty of people out there who would very much like to have you as a friend.

The following exercise offers a framework for reconsidering what happened the last time you offered friendship and were rejected.

Exercise
Coping with Rejection

Take a few minutes to answer the following questions about the last time an offer of friendship you made was apparently rejected. Record your answers in your notebook.

1. Who was the person and what was the situation? How did you go about extending an offer of friendship?

2. Did you communicate your intent clearly to the other person? If so, what makes you think that he or she understood you?

3. What exactly did the other person say or do to reject your overtures toward friendship?

4. Was this actually a rejection or could you have misinterpreted? Could the other person's excuses have been valid?

5. What was your perception of why your overtures were rejected?

6. What were your thoughts and feelings at the time? Did you allow the other person's reaction to control your emotions and self-esteem?

7. How will you react the next time you feel that an offer of friendship is being rejected?

Being a Friend

Although friends may be companions, friends are more than companions. With companions activities are the focus of the relationships. Some companions are people with whom you exchange favors, such as coworkers and close neighbors. They do things for you, and you reciprocate. You chat from time to time and maybe work on an occasional project together. But you probably wouldn't talk about serious problems or reveal intimate details of your life. If these people changed jobs or moved out of the neighborhood, the foundation of your relationship would crumble.

Old friends tend to evolve into companions of a sort when you see them only occasionally, at class reunions or weddings. These are college roommates, "best friends" from high school, army buddies, people you were close to at one time. You enjoy talking of old times and sharing "you had to be there" stories, but you now have little more in common than memories.

You need people to play tennis or walk with, people to invite over for dinner or go to a show with. These kinds of companions are fun and entertaining. You enjoy being with them, and you call them friends. But when the activities are more important than the people, companions aren't really friends. Would they be there for you if you could never engage in a particular activity again? Would you be there for them in time of trouble?

Companions are well worth cultivating. They amuse us and divert us from life's tedious side. They force us out of isolation and keep loneliness at bay. And sometimes they become friends. But casual chums cannot give us what true friends provide.

The Ingredients of Friendship

Of course, the distinction between companion and friend is not black-and-white, either-or; it's more like a spectrum. Companions can be on their way to becoming friends, and vice versa. With some people you may enjoy a kind of limited friendship—more than mere companionship but less than complete intimacy. You can even be very close to someone for a short while, knowing that the relationship is unlikely to last. Friendship is a complex business and not something that should be taken for granted.

Perhaps the one essential factor in being a friend is being involved in your friend's life, not just having fun together but making a difference because you are there for each other. In contrast with companionship, with friendship the person is more important than the activity.

As friends begin to understand and accept each other, they gradually reveal their feelings, ambitions, triumphs, disgraces, and fears. Emotional intimacy cannot develop without self-disclosure, and sharing yourself, not just your time and things, is necessary for trust to build.

Because friends are human and imperfect, understanding and acceptance are hallmarks of friendship. Ideally, you accept friends for who they are, and they do the same for you. Friends don't look at each other in all-or-none terms: "You are either the perfect friend or no friend of mine." They realize that friends have weaknesses as well as strengths.

Friends may not agree with you, but they are there for you when you need support. You can go to them with the bad, as well as the good, and they will offer consolation and cheer. A really good friend will give you the benefit of feedback and honest opinion without being brutal or hurtful. You don't have to play games or try to hide things about yourself.

Friends get annoyed and angry with one another, but they don't gather injustices and harbor resentments. Friends forgive each other's foibles. They try to work out their differences, but if they can't they tolerate them. They realize that friendship is too valuable a commodity to toss aside at the first sign of trouble. True friendship adds luster, enjoyment, and meaning to life.

If you aren't sure whether you've been a friend to others, ask yourself the questions in the following exercise. The questions don't exhaust the characteristics of friendship, but they will help you form objective opinions about yourself as a true friend. If your experience with friendship is limited, use the exercise as a primer, to learn about the attributes of friendship.

Exercise
Evaluating Your Friendships

Instructions: To gauge your contribution to friendships, with a particular person in mind, answer each of the following questions using the scale below. Then, with a different colored pen or pencil, repeat the exercise for each person you consider a good friend.

Scale

1 = Not at all   2 = Somewhat
3 = About halfway or half the time
4 = Mostly   5 = Entirely

Ratings

1. Are you comfortable spending time with your friend if there is nothing special for the two of you to do? _____

2. Are you at ease with your friend when there are lapses in the conversation? _____

3. Can you talk with your friend about disagreements or angry feelings without being indirect or having outbursts of temper? _____

4. Are you sincerely happy for your friend, rather than unduly envious, when something good develops for him or her? _____

5. Do you acknowledge special days and events for your friend, such as birthdays, anniversaries, and promotions? _____

6. Do you worry, rather than feel irritated, if your friend doesn't contact you for a while? _____

7. Are you concerned, instead of annoyed, when your friend is ill or has trouble and you must offer help? _____

8. Do you feel secure and relaxed, as opposed to on guard or on edge, when you are with your friend? _____

9. Are you inclined to forgo judgment about your friend's actions and opinions? _____

Ratings

10. Although you may have differences of opinion and varying tastes, is your basic outlook on life the same as your friend's?   _____

11. Do you know your friend's tastes in music, food, and leisure activities?   _____

12. Are you accepting, rather than resentful, of your friend's relationships with other people?   _____

13. Do you take your friend's wishes into consideration when you are planning activities for the two of you?   _____

14. Do you genuinely like your friend, as opposed to being frequently irritated by him or her?   _____

15. Do you stand by your friend at difficult times even when it is embarrassing for you?   _____

16. Are you willing to share your feelings with your friend?   _____

17. Do you ask for help from your friend when you really need it?   _____

18. Do you listen with compassion when your friend genuinely needs your support?   _____

19. Are you truthful with your friend even when it is awkward or embarrassing?   _____

20. Do you and your friend share common interests and have fun together?   _____

Totals = _____

Key

The higher your score, the better your relationship is with your friend. If any of your scores is 60 or less, go back over the questions and make note of those you answered 1, 2, or 3. These indicate problem areas in the friendship.

It may be that you and your friend are simply not as close or as mutually compatible as you thought; perhaps you are more companions than really friends. Alternatively, your answers may be revealing ways that you can improve your friendship by working to be more caring, open, or tolerant. Spend some time considering how you would like each of your friendships to be, and think about what you could do to bring that about (keeping in mind that this isn't something you can do all by yourself—your friend will have to hold up his or her end).

The following are some pitfalls of friendship. If any of your scores in the above exercise were low, you will want to read this material carefully and consider whether some of it might apply to your relationships. If your scores were acceptable, you might learn how to avoid problems in the future.

Obstacles to Friendship

As with all relationships, it takes a certain amount of effort to make friendships work. They won't blossom without nurturance. If friendships are taken for granted and left to chance, they will slowly disintegrate until nothing much is left.

Their demise can even be hastened by certain actions and attitudes. It won't take long for the following traits to choke off any budding friendship.

Dependency

Dependency is a major obstacle to friendship. Few people want to be embraced by a clinging vine. Although both parties in any relationship—whether it's friendship, marriage, or a business partnership—are dependent upon each other in some respects, excessive dependency will push away even the most supportive friend.

Consider, for example, Adelia, whose chief complaint in therapy was that she was exceedingly lonely. She talked about continual rejection by friends and family despite her efforts to be a good friend. She saw herself as a considerate person who was always available for her friends.

An outgoing, talkative woman, Adelia was also exceptionally generous. She frequently bestowed thoughtful and often expensive gifts on people she liked. To her, gift-giving sealed a friendship and proved that she was accommodating. But she expected a great deal in return for her gifts.

Adelia, who had been engaged two or three times but never married, was phobic about being alone. She worried incessantly about intruders and swindlers. Although she concealed it from herself and others, she also had a low opinion of herself and needed constant reassurance about her worth.

Adelia had difficulty understanding that she could not buy other people's time with her generosity. She had never realized how she imposed upon her friends. Not only did she call them or expect to see them far too often, she was also compelled to keep fishing for praise and tribute, to keep bringing the conversation back to herself. It didn't take very long for Adelia's dependency to push away anyone she had singled out for friendship.

Blame

Blame can be just as destructive as excessive dependency. Adelia tended to shift the blame for her aborted friendships onto the others involved. This served two purposes for her: It kept her from feeling guilty, and it gave her a way to solicit sympathy from her other "friends."

Mort used blame for another purpose. As an adult child of alcoholics, he had always been uneasy with emotional intimacy. He was a good listener but revealed very little about himself. No one really knew Mort because he could not bring himself to trust anyone with his true feelings.

Although he didn't realize it consciously, Mort used blame as a defensive weapon. When anyone got a little too close to him, he found some way to blame them for some injustice or misdeed, although he never discussed the problem with the person. It was a maneuver that kept people at a distance from him, since it allowed him to feel justified in rejecting them.

Tricia depended upon blame to relieve her of the responsibility of self-examination. It was much easier to see fault in others than in herself. That way she could feel righteously indignant with them, rather than anxiously uncomfortable with herself. Shifting blame deflected her attention away from her own faults and preserved her fragile sense of self-worth.

Blaming others for relationship problems worked for Adelia, Mort, and Tricia in that it protected their precarious egos from potential damage. That is, the strategy worked in the short run. In the long run it resulted in the pervasive feelings of inadequacy and worthlessness that emotional isolation begets.

Self-Sacrifice

Self-sacrifice is a weak foundation for friendship. Hunter was the quintessential nice guy who seemed willing to do whatever was necessary to preserve and promote a friendship. He rarely disagreed, expressed his wishes, or displayed his individuality. Indeed, he was a chameleon who tried to be whoever the other person wanted.

The problem was that Hunter was boring—kind and thoughtful, perhaps, but essentially a non-person who added no spice to friendships. Furthermore, Hunter shifted all of the responsibility for decisions and the pace of the relationship onto the other person.

The eventual result was that Hunter was either dropped from a relationship or he was used to the other person's advantage. His exaggerated caring and kindness always eventually backfired, leaving him as alone as ever. Hunter didn't have a clue that his self-sacrificing attitude was the cause of his loneliness, not a solution for it.

Exploitation

Exploitation is a sure way to kill a friendship or to keep it from ever developing. Adelia's extreme dependence was a form of exploitation. Owen's approach was more direct. Instead of using people to prop up his ego, as Adelia did, he swooped down like a proverbial Mongol from the horde to take advantage wherever he could. He borrowed money, abused hospitality, and used friends to make connections. Of course, he rarely reciprocated.

Owen could get away with his exploitation for a while, because he was charming: witty, good looking, and trendy. He could have been a great addition to anybody's repertoire of friends had he not been such a user. In the end, his abusive ways outweighted his entertainment value, and he was inevitably discarded.

Conquest

Conquest is no basis for friendship. Some people attempt to feed their egos by stomping on other people. They instinctively seek out insecure people that they can browbeat. They put down other people to put themselves up. Although bullies like these may be surrounded by lackeys and sycophants, they rarely end up with friends.

A close cousin to the conqueror is the person who only feels comfortable with people who have serious emotional problems. Helene, for example, sought out friends who were self-destructive, confused, and dependent. Although Helene appeared confident and in control, years of chronic illness had left her wracked with doubt about herself. She was not a bully, but she profited from the adulation of people she considered her inferiors. None of her friendships were truly reciprocal and satisfying.

Jealousy

Jealousy is a plague to friendship. It's easy to understand how a person might feel threatened when a close friend begins to spend time with someone else. There is fear that something valuable might be taken away, and that fear takes the guise of jealousy.

Yet, friendship is not weakened from outside the relationship, only from within. True and fast friendship can stand the test of other friendships. The healthier a friendship, the more likely other friendships will complement it, not supplant it.

Marla's friendships, for example, rarely survived her penchant for all-or-none thinking. She always devoted herself to one close friend, but in turn she expected an exclusive relationship. She would do anything for her friend—except share her with others. When anyone else "intruded," Marla reacted with hostility. The result was that Marla usually drove away her friend with her jealousy, as well as the newcomer.

Envy

Envy is an unhealthy emotion lurking about in relationships. It's all too easy to let it come to the forefront when we see that a friend has qualities or things we wish we had. It may be impossible to dispel envy entirely from a friendship, but envy that becomes obsessive and persistent is sure to destroy any relationship.

Pete, a young man I saw briefly in therapy, told me how envy destroyed his closest friendship. He and his friend, Jay, met at work where they were both computer programmers for a large corporation. They hit it off immediately because they had so much in common. They were the same age, both single, and basketball fanatics.

All was well until Jay was promoted to a supervisory position in another department. Pete found himself growing more envious of Jay as he grew more insecure about not having been promoted himself. Instead of talking it over with his friend, Pete grew more distant and constrained. Eventually the friendship faded away completely.

Use the following exercise to help you identify and eliminate obstacles to friendship in your behavior. You have a framework now for detecting and changing traits in yourself that you may not have been aware of before. Be open and objective with yourself as you move further along the path toward belonging.

Exercise
Overcoming Obstacles to Friendship

The pitfalls to friendship discussed above can be caused by either party originally. Both friends, however, participate in perpetuating the problem. Use this exercise to discover and correct obstacles to your enjoying healthy friendships.

1. In your notebook, write about how any of the following obstacles have interfered with your existing or potential friendships:

   • Dependency
   • Blame
   • Self-sacrifice
   • Exploitation
   • Conquest
   • Jealousy
   • Envy

Also note whether it was your behavior or the other person's that created the obstacles.

2. Try to identify obstructive trends in your behavior, such as tendencies toward jealousy and envy that have cropped up over and over. Also look for similarities in the behavior of the various people you have selected as friends or potential friends.

3. Now plan and record strategies for eliminating the obstacles in your behavior and for dealing with people whose behavior is problematic.

Take the Plunge

At this point you have learned everything you need to venture out into the social scene. You know who to steer clear of and how to handle the situation when you can't. You have learned more effective ways of thinking and behaving, how to handle your emotions, and how to talk to people. And you know the important ingredients of true friendship.

The final step is simply to apply this knowledge every chance you get. The next and last chapter will help you create opportunities for doing so, but in the meantime, when a social situation comes along, go ahead and jump right in. The water's fine!

11

Looking Back,
Looking Ahead

At this point in your progress, you may feel like the a neophyte actor waiting to go on stage on opening night: eager, lines and stage directions memorized and rehearsed, but still fighting anxiety. Like the actor, you have all the skills you need to make your way in the world you've always wanted to be a part of. You've done the work, and you're ready for the rewards.

If you still feel uneasy, don't worry; it's natural. Once the actor steps into the spotlight, the sinking feeling of stage fright disappears. The actor is focused on the play—the cast, lines, and action—not on what the audience is thinking. Ultimately the actor experiences a soaring feeling of success in response to the roar of applause. And with each performance, the actor hones skills and gains ease and proficiency.

Similarly, each time you venture out into a social gathering, it will become a little easier and more natural. You will get caught up in the occasion and forget to be nervous. Words and actions will come to you spontaneously. Eventually, you may even begin to wonder why you ever found social occasions so difficult.

In fact, you've already made great progress toward this end. Let's take a minute now to look at your acheivements.

Taking Stock of Your Progress

Remember the Obstacles?

You began your journey by identifying the fears that kept you from venturing out socially over the years. You also examined these fears to discover their underlying themes—the larger fears at the root. Then you took your quest a step further, to destroy their source. You learned how harmful automatic thoughts, distorted self-talk, and erroneous beliefs cause and perpetuate loneliness. Then you proceeded to transform negative emotions into positive ones by discarding old hurtful patterns of thinking and acquiring new helpful patterns.

Illogical self-talk limited your possibilities and made you feel that limitation was what you deserved and were likely to get. You couldn't belong because of old beliefs that made you feel unworthy, unfit, or unwanted. Well, no more! You have abolished negative thinking by deleting these mistaken beliefs and replacing them with realistic beliefs about yourself and other people. You broke out of a mental straitjacket that you had worn for so long that it felt right.

If shame was a barrier between you and other people, your task of learning new beliefs was even more difficult—whether your shame originated in early childhood or developed later in life. In either case, you have learned to push shame aside and replace it with such positive attributes as dignity, self-worth, and admiration for your accomplishments.

Your emotions and behavior are now guided by thought patterns that help you overcome loneliness, because they allow you to feel and act as if you belong. Beware, however, of slipping back into destructive ways of thinking. Your old beliefs were very powerful. They were formed gradually throughout your life, especially during those crucial early years when you were learning how people behave and the world operates.

Consider your original way of thinking as a giant magnet drawing you back into a lonely existence. Accept the fact that you will have to fight the magnet from now on if you wish to belong. It may not always be difficult, however. Each positive social experience will weaken its drawing power. All the same, you must stay vigilant and monitor your thinking, especially for the next couple of years, to keep from falling back into old habits.

You also learned to recognize in yourself common ways of behaving that form a barrier to positive relationships: passivity, aggression, use of alcohol, drugs, or sex as a crutch or shortcut. Recognizing a problem paves the way for overcoming it, which the skills you have learned have enabled you to do.

It might be interesting for you at this point to turn back to the beginning of the notebook you began when you started this book. Review your lists of fears, thoughts, and beliefs. Look at what you wrote about shame. You will probably be amazed at how much you have changed, how far you've come. And, if some of your old ways of thinking and feeling still seem somewhat true, make an effort to continue working on those problem areas.

The Skills You've Built

The first and most basic of the skills you learned to help you in your new life is the ability to relax on command, which enables you to control fear. You are able to release soothing hormones that lull and calm, and you can block the release of epinephrine and other anxiety-producing substances. You have gained control over anxiety by gaining control over your mind and body.

The more you use deep relaxation in real life, the better you get at it and the more automatic it becomes. It's not so different from playing the piano. I had to work very hard to acquire that skill, but now I can read notes on a piece of paper and translate them into music without conscious thought. Although I've been doing it for years, it still amazes me, because I'm not especially talented. I just worked hard.

You've learned to fit relaxation into your daily life, so you are practicing your skills constantly. From time to time, though, you'll need to practice with your basic relaxation and autogenic training tapes. When you do, I suggest that you use the Before-and-After Chart in chapter 5 to check your skill level.

You accomplished something remarkable when you combined your deep relaxation skills with the power of self-hypnosis. If you haven't already, you'll soon notice that the two sets of skills are having a positive impact on virtually every area of your life without further effort on your part. Using them to conquer fear not only subdues self-defeating anxiety, it has the beneficial side effect of enhancing self-confidence. And it comes full circle: Learning that you can control aspects of your fate that you never thought possible before is a sure cure for fear.

If you aren't already, you'll soon be as adept as a world-class athlete at rehearsing skills mentally before applying them in the real world. You know how to induce a trance sufficiently deep to practice and perfect social skills. Each time you think through a skill, it strengthens the mental connections that allow you to perform smoothly and effortlessly in reality. Hypnosis enhances the effect by permitting you to focus your attention—the cognitive equivalent of using a laser beam instead of ordinary light.

You are able to plant hypnotic suggestions that will flourish like flowers in season. There are only two limitations to using them: your imagination in applying the suggestions in your quest to belong and your determination to structure your daily life to allow them to work.

Suggestions aren't magic. You must work with them and not against them. Using hypnotic suggestions is a bit like turning up the volume on a stereo. It won't do a thing unless the power is turned on. And only you can turn on the power by having your daily life moving in the right direction. If you are making efforts to belong, properly phrased hypnotic suggestions will increase the probability that your efforts will pay off.

Along with combating general anxiety, deep relaxation and self-hypnosis have been tools to help you neutralize your specific fears. In effect you chewed away at them bite by bite until they were gone. No doubt you've already realized that you can use this process to help you overcome any kind of specific fear or phobia, from dread of high places to the agony of giving a speech.

You have taken stock of the appearance and behavior of the people you encounter socially and noted changes that you might make to fit in with them. You will be accepted more readily if you look and act like the group you wish to join. Once you have connected, you will be able to express your individuality; then you will be accepted for who you are, not just for how you look and act.

You have also learned and practiced social skills that will serve you well as you ease into the social world. One skill that has probably given you much confidence is initiating and carrying on conversations with strangers. This is a skill that you should practice at every opportunity, since you can function well in any social setting if you can converse. Bear in mind that conversation is at the core of communication, and communication is the essence of social interaction.

You have learned that assertiveness is a major ingredient in the recipe for overcoming loneliness because assertive people are good communicators. They are honest and forthright about their interests, their ways of doing things, their feelings, their likes and dislikes. You changed beliefs, thoughts, and emotions that were interfering with assertiveness, and you learned the principles of assertiveness and how to apply them in social situations.

You also learned how to deal with some of the more difficult situations you may encounter: conflict, troublesome people, and rejection. As a result, you are better able to wade into crowds and speak up, since you are prepared to handle controversial and unsettling situations.

Finally, you learned about friendship. Many lonely people have never had the opportunity to learn what friendship is all about. They don't know what to expect of a friend and what a friend should expect from them. You learned the ingredients of friendship and the obstacles to friendship. You now know that one of the most important principles of friendship is being involved in your friend's life—not just having fun together, but making a difference because you are there.

Many people go their whole lives never learning half of what you now know. So take some time to congratulate yourself. Celebrate—but don't rest on your laurels! To be truly rewarding, knowledge must be applied.

Setting and Pursuing Goals

The world didn't come to a halt while you worked your way through this book. You've been out there leading your daily life, encountering new people in challenging situations. And I expect that you have begun to apply many of the concepts you have learned here.

No doubt, you are finding your new skills paying off as you incorporate them into your daily routine. Keep up the good work, but go a step further to get the maximum benefit. It's time now for you to devise a plan for making your way into whatever social world you choose. Learning to think and act like a social person is the largest part of the journey. Having a systematic plan will help reach your destination faster and more efficiently—think of it as a road map. The following exercise will help you plan your route.

Exercise
Developing a Plan to Belong

Breaking down a goal into attainable steps and setting a timetable for each step is the surest road to success. Although you can apply this approach to any area of your life, in this case your goal is to connect with others by joining an organization or becoming part of a group. Set aside some time to devote to this planning process, and make a commitment to yourself to follow up at intervals, to assess how your plan is working.

1. In your notebook, list below the *interests* you have that you would like your new friends or companions to share, such as outdoor activities, night life, gardening, classic cars.

2. Then list the *places or organizations* where you are likely to encounter people with the interests you listed.

3. Create a *timetable* with deadlines for visiting those places or joining those organizations.

4. After you have followed through on items on your agenda, list the *people* you met and note your *impressions* of them. Place an asterisk by the names of those you'd like to cultivate as friends or companions.

5. Begin immediately to approach these people.

6. After three months and then again after six months review your list of people and note the *status of your relationship* with each of them.

When to See a Professional

Have you made little or no progress toward overcoming your loneliness? If not—provided that you have made a genuine effort to follow the suggestions in this book—it's time to see a mental health professional. You could talk to your physician about a referral, or you could ask someone at your local mental health center for a list of reputable therapists in your area. (Look in the city or county listings of your phone directory under "Health," "Mental Health," or "Public Health.") If you are having financial problems, you might ask for an appointment at the mental health center. The fees there will be assessed on a sliding scale based on income.

Make an appointment for a diagnostic interview, or evaluation. A one-to-one confidential session with a professional will help you decide if you would benefit from individual therapy, group therapy, medication, or some combination of these choices.

Many times group therapy is a good choice for people who have difficulty overcoming loneliness but are not suffering from serious disorders that require individual attention. In fact, the dynamics of the group itself, the interplay among the members, can help you uncover social-interaction problems that might not be so readily apparent in individual counseling. Group members often become substitute parents and siblings, so that you learn a great deal about your early relationships and how they still affect your relationships with other people. Furthermore, group members all have similar problems, so they are sympathetic and understanding. You can learn how to connect with others in a safe and controlled healing environment.

If you do decide to join a group, be sure that it is one that takes a nurturing approach to treatment, not a confrontational one. Ask for a group in which treatment is based on cognitive-behavior therapy, which has been the basis for this book. Cognitive-behavior therapy has been proven to work through extensive research. Don't go into a group following some fad-of-the-moment dreamed up by someone who may be well-meaning but is operating only on hunches.

Now for the Fun Part

I hope you have profited from our time together. It has taken a lot of hard work and self-discipline, but the work was necessary for you to reach your goal of belonging. And now you've made it to the end!

If you've skimmed through the text without really becoming involved or doing the work that's entailed, you may be disappointed at your progress. Don't give up quite yet. Why not go back and give the book a chance to work for you? Take it step by step, little by little. Hang in there! Take as long as you need to work through it, keeping in mind that there are no shortcuts in overcoming habits of a lifetime.

When you've done your best with my suggestions, get out there in the real world and find friends and companions. You may never feel completely ready to take the plunge, but do it anyway. Look at your quest to belong as a game. The hard work is over. It's time now to have the fun that you have been missing out on for so long. Go for it!

References

This book could not have been written without the foundation provided by the work of the following authors.

Andre, Rae. *Positive Solitude: A Practical Program for Mastering Loneliness and Achieving Self-Fulfillment.* New York: Harper Collins, 1991.

Beck, Aaron, and Gary Emery. *Anxiety Disorders and Phobias: A Cognitive Perspective.* New York: Basic Books, 1985.

Bednar, Richard, Gawain Wells, and Scott Peterson. *Self-Esteem: Paradoxes and Innovations in Clinical Theory and Practice.* Washington, D.C.: American Psychological Association, 1989.

Bedrosian, Richard, and George Bozicas. *Treating Family of Origin Problems: A Cognitive Approach.* New York: Guilford Press, 1994.

Beech, H. R., L. E. Burns, and B. F. Sheffield. *A Behavioural Approach to the Management of Stress: A Practical Guide to Techniques.* Chichester, U.K.: John Wiley and Sons, 1982.

Block, Joel. *Friendship: How to Give It, How to Get It.* New York: Macmillan, 1980.

Blume, E. Sue. *Secret Survivors: Uncovering Incest and Its Aftereffects in Women.* New York: John Wiley and Sons, 1990.

Bourne, Edmund. *The Anxiety & Phobia Workbook.* Oakland, Calif.: New Harbinger Publications, 1990.

Borysenko, Joan. *Guilt Is the Teacher, Love Is the Lesson.* New York: Warner Books, 1990.

Bramson, Robert. *Coping with Difficult Bosses.* New York: Fireside, 1992.

Brown, Daniel, and Erika Fromm. *Hypnosis and Behavioral Medicine.* Hillsdale, N.J.: Lawrence Erlbaum Associates, 1987.

Brown, Stephanie. *Treating Adult Children of Alcoholics.* New York: John Wiley and Sons, 1988.

Courtois, Christine. *Healing the Incest Wound.* New York: W. W. Norton, 1988.

Cunningham, Chet. *50 Secrets: How to Meet People and Make Friends.* Leucadia, Calif.: United Research Publishers, 1992.

Davis, Martha, Elizabeth Eshelman, and Matthew McKay. *The Relaxation & Stress Reduction Workbook.* Oakland, Calif.: New Harbinger Publications, 1988.

Desberg, Peter, and George Marsh. *Controlling Stagefright: Presenting Yourself to Audiences from One to One Thousand.* Oakland, Calif.: New Harbinger Publications, 1988.

Gabor, Don. *Speaking Your Mind in 101 Difficult Situations.* New York: Stonesong Press, 1994.

Hammond, D. Corydon. *Handbook of Hypnotic Suggestions and Metaphors.* New York: W. W. Norton, 1990.

Hearn, Janice. *Making Friends, Keeping Friends.* Garden City, N.Y.: Doubleday, 1979.

Jones, Katina Z. *Succeeding with Difficult People.* Stamford, Conn.: Longmeadow Press, 1992.

Krawetz, Michael. *Loneliness Removers.* New York: Henry Holt, 1988.

McKay, Matthew, Martha Davis, and Patrick Fanning. *Thoughts & Feelings: The Art of Cognitive Stress Intervention.* Oakland, Calif.: New Harbinger Publications, 1981.

McKay, Matthew, and Patrick Fanning. *Self-Esteem,* 2d ed. Oakland, Calif.: New Harbinger Publications, 1992.

McMullin, Rian. *Handbook of Cognitive Therapy Techniques.* New York: W. W. Norton, 1986.

Potter-Efron, Ronald, and Patricia Potter-Efron. *Letting Go of Shame.* San Francisco: Harper and Row, 1989.

Powell, Barbara. *Alone, Alive & Well: How to Fight Loneliness and Win.* Emmaus, PA: Rodale Press, 1985.

Pratt, George, Dennis Wood, and Brian Alman. *A Clinical Hypnosis Primer.* New York: John Wiley and Sons, 1988.

Rossi, Ernest, and David Cheek. *Mind-Body Therapy: Methods of Ideodynamic Healing in Hypnosis.* New York: W. W. Norton, 1988.

Scott, Gini. *Resolving Conflict with Others and Within Yourself.* Oakland, Calif.: New Harbinger Publications, 1990.

Spiegel, Herbert, and David Spiegel. *Trance and Treatment.* Washington, D.C.: American Psychiatric Press, 1978.

Williams, Mark. *The Psychological Treatment of Depression.* New York: Free Press, 1984.

Wolpe, Joseph. *The Practice of Behavior Therapy,* 3d ed. New York: Pergamon Press, 1982.

Wolpe, Joseph, and David Wolpe. *Life Without Fear.* Oakland, Calif.: New Harbinger Publications, 1988.

Other New Harbinger Self-Help Titles

Living Without Depression & Manic Depression: A Workbook for Maintaining Mood Stability, $14.95
Belonging: A Guide to Overcoming Loneliness, $13.95
Coping With Schizophrenia: A Guide For Families, $13.95
Visualization for Change, Second Edition, $13.95
Postpartum Survival Guide, $13.95
Angry All The Time: An Emergency Guide to Anger Control, $12.95
Couple Skills: Making Your Relationship Work, $13.95
Handbook of Clinical Psychopharmacology for Therapists, $39.95
The Warrior's Journey Home: Healing Men, Healing the Planet, $12.95
Weight Loss Through Persistence, $13.95
Post-Traumatic Stress Disorder: A Complete Treatment Guide, $39.95
Stepfamily Realities: How to Overcome Difficulties and Have a Happy Family, $11.95
Leaving the Fold: A Guide for Former Fundamentalists and Others Leaving Their Religion, $13.95
Father-Son Healing: An Adult Son's Guide, $12.95
The Chemotherapy Survival Guide, $11.95
Your Family/Your Self: How to Analyze Your Family System, $12.95
Being a Man: A Guide to the New Masculinity, $12.95
The Deadly Diet, Second Edition: Recovering from Anorexia & Bulimia, $11.95
Last Touch: Preparing for a Parent's Death, $11.95
Consuming Passions: Help for Compulsive Shoppers, $11.95
Self-Esteem, Second Edition, $13.95
Depression & Anxiety Mangement: An audio tape for managing emotional problems, $11.95
I Can't Get Over It, A Handbook for Trauma Survivors, $13.95
Concerned Intervention, When Your Loved One Won't Quit Alcohol or Drugs, $11.95
Redefining Mr. Right, $11.95
Dying of Embarrassment: Help for Social Anxiety and Social Phobia, $12.95
The Depression Workbook: Living With Depression and Manic Depression, $14.95
Risk-Taking for Personal Growth: A Step-by-Step Workbook, $14.95
The Marriage Bed: Renewing Love, Friendship, Trust, and Romance, $11.95
Focal Group Psychotherapy: For Mental Health Professionals, $44.95
Hot Water Therapy: Save Your Back, Neck & Shoulders in 10 Minutes a Day $11.95
Older & Wiser: A Workbook for Coping With Aging, $12.95
Prisoners of Belief: Exposing & Changing Beliefs that Control Your Life, $10.95
Be Sick Well: A Healthy Approach to Chronic Illness, $11.95
Men & Grief: A Guide for Men Surviving the Death of a Loved One., $12.95
When the Bough Breaks: A Helping Guide for Parents of Sexually Abused Childern, $11.95
Love Addiction: A Guide to Emotional Independence, $12.95
When Once Is Not Enough: Help for Obsessive Compulsives, $13.95
The New Three Minute Meditator, $12.95
Getting to Sleep, $10.95
The Relaxation & Stress Reduction Workbook, 3rd Edition, $14.95
Leader's Guide to the Relaxation & Stress Reduction Workbook, $19.95
Beyond Grief: A Guide for Recovering from the Death of a Loved One, $13.95
Thoughts & Feelings: The Art of Cognitive Stress Intervention, $13.95
Messages: The Communication Skills Book, $12.95
The Divorce Book, $11.95
Hypnosis for Change: A Manual of Proven Techniques, 2nd Edition, $13.95
The Chronic Pain Control Workbook, $14.95
My Parent's Keeper: Adult Children of the Emotionally Disturbed, $11.95
When Anger Hurts, $13.95
Free of the Shadows: Recovering from Sexual Violence, $12.95
Lifetime Weight Control, $11.95
The Anxiety & Phobia Workbook, $14.95
Love and Renewal: A Couple's Guide to Commitment, $12.95
The Habit Control Workbook, $12.95

Call **toll free, 1-800-748-6273**, to order. Have your Visa or Mastercard number ready. Or send a check for the titles you want to New Harbinger Publications, Inc., 5674 Shattuck Avenue, Oakland, CA 94609. Include $3.80 for the first book and 75¢ for each additional book, to cover shipping and handling. (California residents please include appropriate sales tax.) Allow four to six weeks for delivery.

Prices subject to change without notice.